Lecture Notes in Artificial Intelligence   11866

Subseries of Lecture Notes in Computer Science

Series Editors

Randy Goebel
University of Alberta, Edmonton, Canada
Yuzuru Tanaka
Hokkaido University, Sapporo, Japan
Wolfgang Wahlster
DFKI and Saarland University, Saarbrücken, Germany

Founding Editor

Jörg Siekmann
DFKI and Saarland University, Saarbrücken, Germany

More information about this series at http://www.springer.com/series/1244

Gennady S. Osipov · Aleksandr I. Panov ·
Konstantin S. Yakovlev (Eds.)

Artificial Intelligence

5th RAAI Summer School
Dolgoprudny, Russia, July 4–7, 2019
Tutorial Lectures

 Springer

Editors
Gennady S. Osipov (iD)
Federal Research Center
"Computer Science and Control"
Moscow, Russia

Aleksandr I. Panov (iD)
Federal Research Center
"Computer Science and Control"
Moscow, Russia

Konstantin S. Yakovlev (iD)
Federal Research Center
"Computer Science and Control"
Moscow, Russia

ISSN 0302-9743   ISSN 1611-3349 (electronic)
Lecture Notes in Artificial Intelligence
ISBN 978-3-030-33273-0   ISBN 978-3-030-33274-7 (eBook)
https://doi.org/10.1007/978-3-030-33274-7

LNCS Sublibrary: SL7 – Artificial Intelligence

This Springer imprint is published by the registered company Springer Nature Switzerland AG
The registered company address is: Gewerbestrasse 11, 6330 Cham, Switzerland

Preface

The 5th RAAI Summer School on Artificial Intelligence was held in Dolgoprudy, Russia at the Moscow Institute of Physics and Technology (MIPT) during July 4–7, 2019. MIPT is one of the leading universities in Russia, especially renowned for its achievements in the fields of physics, mathematics, and computer sciences. The school was organized by the Russian Association for Artificial Intelligence which is a major academic non-profit organization in the field of AI in Russia.

More than 100 participants from all over the world (mostly from Russia, but also from Germany, Sweden, China, Turkey, Armenia, Syria, and Iran) took part in a four-day marathon comprised of lectures, workshops, hackathons, industry sessions, etc.

This tutorial book is composed of the selected tutorials by the invited speakers of RAAI Summer School 2019 and of the best students' papers. In total 20 student submissions were received and only 5 of them were chosen by the international Program Committee to be included in the book.

We appreciate the financial support of the school's sponsors (i.e.: MIPT, Yandex, Huawei, AimTech, NLMK, and Tinkoff) without which it would not have been possible to invite top AI experts to deliver the talks and make the participation free for all students.

July 2019

Gennady S. Osipov
Aleksandr I. Panov
Konstantin S. Yakovlev

Organization

Program Committee

Gennady S. Osipov (Co-chair)	President of RAAI, head of Artificial Intelligence Research Institute of Federal Research Center "Computer Science and Control" of the Russian Academy of Sciences, Russia
Ricardo Ribeiro Gudwin (Co-chair)	University of Campinas, Brazil
Alexey Averkin	Federal Research Center "Computer Science and Control" of the Russian Academy of Sciences, Russia
Ildar Batyrshin	Instituto Politecnico Nacional, Mexico
Mikhail Burtsev	Moscow Institute of Physics and Technology, Russia
Vadim Vagin	National Research University MPEI, Russia
Michal Valko	Inria Lille, France
Tamás Gergely	Applied Logic Laboratory, Hungary
Vladimir Golenkov	Belarusian State University of Informatics and Radioelectronics, Belarus
Valeria Gribova	Institute of Automation and Control Processes of the Far Eastern Branch of RAS, Russia
Alexandr Eremeev	National Research Nuclear University MPEI, Russia
Valery Karpov	NRC "Kurchatov Institute", Russia
Namkug Kim	University of Ulsan, South Korea
Sergey Kovalev	Rostov State Transport University, Russia
Vladik Kreinovich	University of Texas at El Paso, USA
Sergey O. Kuznetsov	Higher School of Economics in Moscow, Russia
Oleg Kuznetsov	Trapeznikov Institute of Control Sciences, Russia
Hermann Ney	RWTH Aachen University, Germany
Evgeny Osipov	Luleå University of Technology, Sweden
Vladimir Pavlovsky	Keldysh Institute of Applied Mathematics, Russia
Boris Palyukh	Tver State Technical University, Russia
Witold Pedrycz	University of Alberta, Canada
Andrei Raigorodskii	Moscow Institute of Physics and Technology, Russia
Galina Rybina	National Research Nuclear University MEPhI, Russia
Ruslan Salakhutdinov	Carnegie Mellon University, USA
Vadim Stefanuk	Institute for Information Transmission Problems of RAS, Russia
Valery Tarasov	Bauman University, Russia
Alexander Tulupyev	St. Petersburg Institute for Informatics and Automation of RAS, Russia

Andrey Filchenkov	ITMO University, Russia
Igor Fominykh	National Research University MPEI, Russia
Vladimir Khoroshevsky	Federal Research Center "Computer Science and Control" of the Russian Academy of Sciences, Russia
Roni Stern	Ben Gurion University of the Negev, Israel

Organizing Committee

Aleksandr I. Panov (Co-chair)	Artificial Intelligence Research Institute of Federal Research Center "Computer Science and Control" of the Russian Academy of Sciences, Russia
Andrei Raigorodskii	Moscow Institute of Physics and Technology, Russia
Konstantin Yakovlev	Artificial Intelligence Research Institute of Federal Research Center "Computer Science and Control" of the Russian Academy of Sciences, Russia
Alena Suvorova	Higher School of Economics in Saint-Petersburg, Russia
Nikolay Bazenkov	Trapeznikov Institute of Control Sciences, Russia
Elena Fontalina	National Research Nuclear University MEPhI, Russia
Maria Koroleva	Bauman University, Russia
Margarita Suvorova	Artificial Intelligence Research Institute of Federal Research Center "Computer Science and Control" of the Russian Academy of Sciences, Russia

Contents

Tutorial Papers

Hybrid Intelligent Systems Based on Fuzzy Logic and Deep Learning

Alexey Averkin$^{(\boxtimes)}$

Federal Research Centre of Informatics and Computer Science of RAS, Moscow,
Vavilova, 42, Moscow, Russia
averkin2003@inbox.ru

Abstract. The purpose of this lecture is to establish the fundamental links between two important areas of artificial intelligence - fuzzy logic and deep learning. This approach will allow researchers in the field of fuzzy logic to develop application systems in the field of strong artificial intelligence, which are also of interest to specialists in the field of machine learning. The lecture also examines how neuro-fuzzy networks make it possible to establish a link between symbolic and connectionist schools of artificial intelligence. A lot of methods of rule extraction from neural networks are also investigated.

Keywords: Deep learning · Neural networks · Rule extraction · Convolutional neural network · Machine learning · Artificial intelligence

1 Introduction

This lection introduces the terms and definitions of machine learning that are relevant to the context of extracting rules from classical and deep neural networks. It includes the problem of classification as a whole, as well as rule-based teaching methods and neural networks. Then, we will look at the current state of rule extraction from neural networks. Here we define the problem as well as the main approaches to its solution and present some of the existing rules extraction algorithms. The last part discusses specific problems when working with deep neural networks. At this stage, we also propose some algorithms that can successfully extract rules from these more complex neural networks.

Artificial Neural Networks (ANN) are widely known parallel computing models that exhibit excellent behavior in solving complex problems of artificial intelligence. However, many researchers refuse to use them due to their being a "black box". This means that determining why a neural network makes a specific decision is a difficult task.

This is a significant drawback, since it is difficult to trust the reliability of the network that solves real problems without the ability to make acceptable decisions. For example, this is the case in critical, in terms of safety, applications where hidden failure can lead to life-threatening actions or huge economic losses.

In addition, studying how neural networks extract, store and transform knowledge can be useful for future machine learning methods. For example, increasing the transparency of neural networks can help detect the so-called hidden dependencies that

G. S. Osipov et al. (Eds.): Artificial Intelligence, LNAI 11866, pp. 3–12, 2019.
https://doi.org/10.1007/978-3-030-33274-7_1

are not present in the input data, but appear as a result of their integration into the neural network.

To overcome this lack of neural networks, researchers came up with the idea of extracting rules from neural networks, which can became a bridge between symbolic and connectionist models of knowledge representation in artificial intelligence.

Most authors focus on extracting the most understandable rules, and at the same time they should mimic the behavior of the neural network as precisely as possible, right up to an isomorphic representation of fuzzy rules in the form of a neuro-fuzzy system. Since 1992, since Chang's doctoral thesis on neuro-fuzzy networks, much work has been done in this area, which ended with the creation of the direction of soft computing. Since then, many methods for extracting rules from neural networks have been developed and evaluated, and excellent results have been obtained for many approaches.

However, despite the fact that there are quite a few available algorithms, none of them has ever been explicitly tested in deep neural networks. In addition, most authors focus on networks with only a small number of hidden layers.

Only in the last few years pioneering work has appeared on the analysis of specific methods for extracting rules from deep-seated networks and new algorithms are presented that are capable of performing this task.

2 Methods for Extracting Rules from the Neural Network

In artificial intelligence, neural networks and rule-based learning methods are two approaches to solving classification problems. Both methods are known variants of studying models that predict classes for new data. For many tasks, NN rules-based teaching methods excel in accuracy.

However, neural networks have one major drawback: the ability to understand what a trained concept models, NN is not as strong as for rule based approaches. The concepts learned by neural networks are difficult to understand because they are represented using a large set of parameters [1].

Increasing the transparency of neural networks by extracting rules has two main advantages. First, it gives the user some insight into how the neural network uses input variables to make a decision—and can even reveal hidden functions in NN when the rules are used to explain individual neurons. Identification of particularly important attributes or identification of the causes of neural network errors can be part of the understanding. Trying to make opaque neural networks more understandable, methods for extracting rules eliminate the gap between accuracy and clarity [2–4].

A more comprehensible form is required if, for example, a neural network is to be used in safety-critical applications, such as aircraft and power plants. In these cases, it is extremely important that the system user have the opportunity to check the output of the artificial neural network under all possible input conditions [5].

To formalize the task of extracting rules from a neural network, we give Craven's definition: "Given the trained neural network and the data on which it was trained, create a description of the network hypothesis that is understandable, but comes close to the network prediction behavior" [6].

To distinguish between different approaches for extracting rules from neural networks, Andrews introduced the widely used multidimensional taxonomy [5]. The first dimension they describe is a form (for example, IF-THEN rules or a variant of fuzzy production rules).

The third dimension is the quality of the rules extracted. Since quality is a broad term, it is divided into several criteria, namely, accuracy, fidelity, consistency and comprehensibility. While accuracy measures the ability to "correctly classify previously unseen examples", validity measures the degree to which rules can "imitate" the behavior of a neural network well [2].

The second dimension is called transparency and describes the strategy followed by the algorithm for extracting rules. If the method uses a neural network only as a black box, regardless of the architecture of NN, we call the pedagogical approach. If, instead, the algorithm takes into account the internal structure of the neural network, we call this approach decompositional. If the algorithm uses components of both pedagogical and decomposition methods, then this approach is called eclectic.

The third dimension is the quality of the rules extracted. Since quality is a broad term, it is divided into several criteria, namely, accuracy, fidelity, consistency and comprehensibility. While accuracy measures the ability to correctly classify previously unseen examples, validity measures the degree to which rules can imitate the behavior of a neural network well [2].

Fidelity can be considered as accuracy relative to the output of NN. Consistency can only be measured when the rule extraction algorithm involves learning the neural network instead of processing the already trained NN: The extracted rule set is considered consistent when the neural network generates rule sets that correctly classify test data for different training sessions. Comprehensibility is considered here as a measure of the size of the rules, that is, short and few rules are considered more understandable [5].

In this review we will focus only on the three criteria described. In accordance with [7], we focus on methods that do not impose special requirements on how the neural network was trained before the rules were extracted. In addition, only algorithms that are capable of extracting rules from direct propagation neural networks, despite any other characteristics of the architecture, are analyzed. According to [3] we want the algorithm to offer a high level of generality.

Let us analyze some methods for extracting rules that meet the above characteristics. We start with decomposition approaches. As mentioned earlier, decomposition approaches for extracting rules from neural networks operate at the neuron level. Usually, the decomposition method analyzes each neuron, and forms rules that imitate the behavior of this neuron. For various reasons, we do not take into account all available decomposition approaches in the subsequent review. We consider here the KT algorithm, Tsukimoto's approach and rule extraction through decision tree induction (CRED algorithm).

The KT algorithm was one of the first decomposition approaches for extracting rules from neural networks was presented in [29]. The KT algorithm describes each neuron (layer by layer) with the IF-THEN rules by heuristically searching for combinations of input attributes that exceed the threshold of the neuron. The rewrite module is used to obtain rules that refer to the original input attributes, and not to the outputs of the previous level. To find suitable combinations, the KT method applies a search on the tree, that is, a rule (represented as a node in the tree) at this level generates its child nodes by adding an additional available attribute [8]. In addition, the algorithm uses a number of heuristics to stop the growth of a tree in situations where further improvement is impossible. The algorithm searches for both confirming and non-confirming rules. These are the rules that predict the triggering of a neuron if there is a certain input configuration.

Polinomial Tsukimoto's approach to extracting rules from a neural network is very similar to the KT method. It also uses a layered decomposition algorithm to extract the IF-THEN rules for each neuron, and also monitors the strategy for finding input configurations that exceed the threshold of the neuron. The main advantage of the Tsukimoto method is its computational complexity, which is polynomial, while the KT method is exponential [9]. The algorithm achieves polynomial complexity by searching for relevant terms using the space of multilinear functions. In the second stage, these terms are used to create IF-THEN rules. Subsequently, if any, training data is used to improve the accuracy of the rules. In the last step, the Tsukimoto algorithm attempts to optimize clarity by removing non-essential attributes from the rules.

Another method for extracting rules through decision tree induction was introduced in [10]. Their CRED algorithm converts each output unit of a neural network into a solution, where tree nodes are tested using nodes of a hidden layer, and leaves represent a class. After this, intermediate rules are extracted from this step. Then for each split point used in these rules, another decision tree is created using split points on the input layer of the neural network. In the new trees, the leaves do not directly choose the class. Extracting the rules from the second decision tree leads us to the description of the state of hidden neurons, consisting of input variables. As a final step, intermediate rules that describe the output layer through the hidden layer and those that describe the hidden layer based on the inputs of the neural network are replaced. Then they are combined into construction rules that describe the output of the neural network based on its input data.

The next group of pedagogical approaches of rule extraction based on validity interval analysis, approaches for rule extraction using sampling and rule extraction by reverse engineering the neural network.

Pedagogical approaches, as opposed to decomposition, do not take into account the internal structure of the neural network. The motive in pedagogical approaches is to treat trained NN at the lowest possible level of granularity, that is, as a whole or, alternatively, as a black border [11]. Their idea is to extract the rules by directly matching the input data with the output data [12]. More formally, we can assume that pedagogical approaches have access only to the function of the neural network. This function returns the output of the neural network for random input, but offers no understanding of the internal structure of NN or any weights (except for the number of inputs and outputs in NN). Having NN, this class of algorithms tries to find coherence between possible input variations and outputs created by the neural network, while some of them use specified training data, and some do not. As in the previous section, we will not discuss all possible algorithms, but only briefly go over the main ones.

Rule extraction based on interval analysis approach uses the interval confidence analysis (VIA), a kind of sensitivity analysis, to extract rules that mimic the behavior of a neural network [13]. The main idea of this method is to find the input intervals in which the output signal NN is stable, that is, the predicted class is the same for slightly changing input configurations. As a result, VIA provides the basis for reliably correct rules.

Retrieving rules using sampling represents several methods that follow more or less the same strategy for extracting rules from a neural network using sampling, that is, they create an extensive set of data as a basis for extracting rules. After that, the selected data set is submitted to a standard learning algorithm for generating rules that simulate the behavior of a neural network. In [2] it is proved that the use of sample data exceeds the use of training data in the problems of extracting rules.

One of the first methods that followed this strategy was the Trepan algorithm [14]. Trephine works very much like C4.5 by searching for split points on training data for individual instances of different classes. The main differences from C4.5 are the best strategy for expanding the tree structure, additional split points in the M-of-N style and the ability to choose additional learning examples at deeper points of the tree. As a result, the algorithm also creates a decision tree, which, however, can be transformed into a set of rules, if necessary.

Another of these very general pedagogical approaches that use sampling to extract rules from the neural network is presented in [13]. The algorithm, called Binarized Input-Output Rule Extraction (BIO-RE), is capable of processing only NN with binary or binarized input attributes. BIO-RE creates all possible input combinations and requests them from the neural network. Using the NN output, a truth table is created for each example. From the truth table it is just as easy to go to the rules, if necessary.

ANN-DT is another decision-based sampling method for describing the behavior of a neural network [14]. The overall algorithm is based on CART with some variations in the initial implementation. ANN-DT uses the sampling method to expand the training set so that most of the training sample is still representative. This is "achieved using the nearest neighbor method, in which the distance from the sample point to the nearest point in the training data set is calculated" [14] and compared with the reference value.

The idea of creating a large set of instances at the first stage is also implemented by the STARE algorithm [15]. Like BIO-RE, STARE also forms extensive truth tables for learning. The advantage of STARE is its ability not only to handle binary and discrete attributes, but also to work with continuous input data. For the formation of truth tables, the algorithm rearranges the input data, while for each continuous attribute "it is necessary to sample it over the entire range of values with a high frequency".

The last pedagogical approach using a sample of educational data that we want to briefly present here is KDRuleEx [4]. Like Trepan, the Sethi algorithm also generates additional learning cases where the basis for the following separation points is too small. KDRuleEx uses a genetic algorithm to create new training examples. The technique leads to a decision table that can be converted, for example, into IF-THEN rules, if desired

Eclectic approach are the methods for extracting rules include elements of both pedagogical and decompositional, then such methods are known as eclectic [3]. In particular, eclectic approaches use knowledge of the internal architecture and/or weight vectors in the neural network to complement the symbolic learning algorithm [5].

The fast retrieval of rules from a neural network approach includes the FERNN approach, which first tries to identify the corresponding hidden neurons, as well as the corresponding inputs to the network. For this step, a decision tree is constructed using the well-known algorithm C4.5. The rule extraction process leads to the generation of M-of-N and IF-THEN rules. Having a set of properly classified teaching examples, FERNN analyzes the activation values of each hidden unit. For each hidden unit, activation values are sorted in ascending order. Then use the C4.5 algorithm to find the best split point to form the decision tree. The most interesting from the point of view of this study is the extraction of rules using neuro-fuzzy models On the other hand, systems based on fuzzy rules (FRBS), developed using fuzzy logic, have become a field of active research over the past few years. These algorithms have proven their strengths in tasks such as managing complex systems, creating fuzzy controls. The relationship between both worlds (ANN and FRBS) has been carefully studied. Indeed, this is a close relationship, since equivalence results were obtained [17].

This link gives two immediate and important conclusions. First, we can apply what was discovered for one of the models to the other. Secondly, we can translate the knowledge embedded in the neural network into a more cognitively acceptable language - fuzzy rules. In other words, we get a clear interpretation of neural networks [18–20].

3   Extracting Rules from Deep Neural Networks

Since 2012, the revolution began networks of deep learning. Consider one of the first and probably the most cited works in convolutional NN- Alexnet - it has 7 hidden layers, 650,000 neurons, 60,000,000 parameters. Studied at 2 GPU for 1 week (Picture 1). Where do we get enough images to train her?

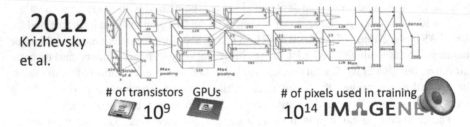

Picture 1. Alexnet - first deep learning champion in image recognition

In 2010 dataset Imagenet has appeared. The emergence of Imagenet brought the learning of neural networks to a whole new level. Parallel rapidly developed computing power, which led computer vision to the kind that we know and love it now. Since 2010, the annual Imagenet competition has also been held, where for the first time in 2012, the Alexnet convolutional neural network won and, since then, the National Assembly has not lost its positions. The last winner, the National Assembly presented by scientists from China, contained 269 layers (Picture 2).

Picture 2. Dataset Imagenet.

To semantic intepretation of the deep learning blackbox neuro-fuzzy networks can be use used instead of full connection layer (Fig. 3). For example, ANFIS (adaptive neuro-fuzzy system) [25] is a multilayer feed forward network. This architecture has five layers such as fuzzy layer, product layer, normalized layer, de - fuzzy layer and total output. The fixed nodes are represented by circle and the node s represented by square are the adapted nodes. ANFIS gives the advantages of the mixture of neural network and fuzzy logic.

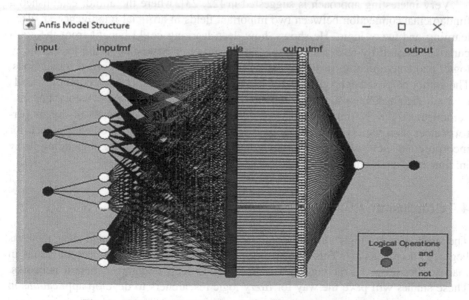

Fig. 3. Structure of ANFIS model for time series forecasting

The aim of mixing fuzzy logic and neural networks is to de-sign an architecture, which uses a fuzzy logic to show knowledge in fantastic way, while the learning nature of neural network to maximize its parameters. ANFIS put forward by Jang in 1993 integrate the advantages of both neural network and fuzzy systems, which not only have good learning capability, but can be interpreted easily also. ANFIS has been used in many applications in many areas, such as function approximation, intelligent control and time series prediction.

A hypothetical system can be created using two components [26]. The first is deep learning feature generation which can be used to create representative features from text directly. The deep learning system would initially be trained on unlabeled data. Once these features are extracted from the deep learning system, they will be integrated into fuzzy-inference systems. These systems can incorporate both the features detected from the deep learning as well as subjective information from an analysts as a method of biasing the system. These two pieces together can be used for classification purposes. The final system would therefore be able to report both classification results and the specific features and rules that were activated for the system to arrive at its conclusion. Additionally, the final system could be further biased by an analyst as a form of feedback.

In previous part has shown that there is a wide variety of algorithms to describe a one-hidden-layer neural network's behavior by rules.. In [21] it was made a first step in investigating the problem of extracting rules from deep neural networks. DNNs have a few characteristics that, compared to one-hidden-layer neural networks, can complicate the rule extraction process. For deep neural networks, the rule extraction problem is very complex. We must not only to explain an output's behaviour, but also to describe the behaviour of a neuron in a hidden layer. In [21] authors give an overview of how decompositional rule extraction algorithms like DeepRED or pedagogical approaches can be used to analyse and explain the behaviour of a DNN.

Very interesting approach is suggested in [22, 23], where the author established a fundamental connection between two important fields in artificial intelligence i.e. deep learning and fuzzy logic. He shows, how deep learning could benefit from the comparative research by re-examining many trail-and-error heuristics in the lens of fuzzy logic, and consequently, distilling the essential ingredients with rigorous foundations. The author proposed deep generalized hamming network (GHN) as such not only lends itself to rigorous analysis and interpretation within the fuzzy logic theory but also demonstrates fast learning speed, well-controlled behaviour and state-of-the-art performances on a variety of learning tasks. In [24] it is presented another approach for incorporating such rule based methodology into neural networks by embedding fuzzy inference systems into deep learning networks.

4   Conclusion

The study of fuzzy logic culminated in the end of the 20th century, and since then has begun to decrease [27]. This decrease can be partly attributed to the lack of results in machine learning. Extracting rules is one way to help understand neural networks. These studies will pave the way for fuzzy logic researchers to develop applications in artificial intelligence and solve complex problems that are also of interest to the machine learning community. Experience and knowledge in the field of fuzzy logic are well suited for modeling ambiguities in big data, modeling uncertainty in the representation of knowledge and providing transmission training with non-inductive inference, etc.

References

1. Craven, M., Shavlik, J.W.: Using sampling and queries to extract rules from trained neural networks. In: ICML, pp. 37–45 (1994)
2. Johansson, U., Lofstrom, T., Konig, R., Sonstrod, C., Niklasson, L.: Rule extraction from opaque models–a slightly different perspective. In: 5th International Conference on Machine Learning and Applications. ICMLA 2006, pp. 22–27 (2006)
3. Craven, M., Shavlik, J.: Rule extraction: where do we go from here. In: University of Wisconsin Machine Learning Research Group Working Paper, pp. 99–108 (1999)
4. Sethi, K.K., Mishra, D.K., Mishra, B.: KDRuleEx: a novel approach for enhancing user comprehensibility using rule extraction. In: 2012 Third International Conference Intelligent Systems, Modelling and Simulation (ISMS), pp. 55–60 (2012)
5. Andrews, R., Diederich, J., Tickle, A.B.: Survey and critique of techniques for extracting rules from trained artificial neural networks. Knowl.-Based Syst. **8**(6), 373–389 (1995)
6. Craven, M.W.: Extracting comprehensible models from trained neural networks. Ph.D. thesis, University of Wisconsin-Madison (1996)
7. Thrun, S.: Extracting provably correct rules from artificial neural networks. Technical report, University of Bonn, Institut für Informatik III (1993)
8. Fu, L.: Rule generation from neural networks. IEEE Trans. Syst. Man Cybern. **24**(8), 1114–1124 (1994)
9. Tsukimoto, H.: Extracting rules from trained neural networks. IEEE Trans. Neural Networks **11**(2), 377–389 (2000)
10. Sato, M., Tsukimoto, H.: Rule extraction from neural networks via decision tree induction. In: International Joint Conference on Neural Networks. Proceedings. IJCNN 2001, vol. 3, pp. 1870–1875 (2001)
11. Tickle, A.B., Andrews, R., Golea, M., Diederich, J.: The truth will come to light: directions and challenges in extracting the knowledge embedded within trained artificial neural networks. IEEE Trans. Neural Networks **9**(6), 1057–1068 (1998)
12. .
13. Thrun, S.: Extracting rules from artificial neural networks with distributed representations. In: Advances in Neural Information Processing Systems, pp. 505–512 (1995)
14. Craven, M.W., Shavlik, J.W.: Extracting tree-structured representations of trained networks. In: Advances in Neural Information Processing Systems, pp. 24–30 (1996)
15. Taha, I.A., Ghosh, J.: Symbolic interpretation of artificial neural networks. IEEE Trans. Knowl. Data Eng. **11**(3), 448–463 (1999)
16. Towell, G.G., Shavlik, J.W.: Extracting refined rules from knowledge-based neural networks. Mach. Learn. **13**(1), 71–101 (1993)
17. Setiono, R., Leow, W.K.: FERNN: an algorithm for fast extraction of rules from neural networks. Appl. Intell. **12**(1–2), 15–25 (2000)
18. Averkin, A., Yarushev, S.: Hybrid neural networks for time series forecasting. In: Kuznetsov, S.O., Osipov, G.S., Stefanuk, V.L. (eds.) RCAI 2018. CCIS, vol. 934, pp. 230–239. Springer, Cham (2018). https://doi.org/10.1007/978-3-030-00617-4_21

19. Pilato, G., Yarushev, S.A., Averkin, A.N.: Prediction and detection of user emotions based on neuro-fuzzy neural networks in social networks. In: Abraham, A., Kovalev, S., Tarassov, V., Snasel, V., Sukhanov, A. (eds.) IITI'18 2018. AISC, vol. 875, pp. 118–125. Springer, Cham (2019). https://doi.org/10.1007/978-3-030-01821-4_13
20. Averkin, G.P., Yarushev, S.A.: An approach for prediction of user emotions based on ANFIS in social networks. In: Second International Scientific and Practical Conference Fuzzy Technologies in the Industry, FTI 2018–CEUR Workshop Proceedings, pp. 126–134 (2018)
21. Zilke, J.R., Loza Mencía, E., Janssen, F.: DeepRED – rule extraction from deep neural networks. In: Calders, T., Ceci, M., Malerba, D. (eds.) DS 2016. LNCS (LNAI), vol. 9956, pp. 457–473. Springer, Cham (2016). https://doi.org/10.1007/978-3-319-46307-0_29
22. Fan, L.: Revisit fuzzy neural network: demystifying batch normalization and ReLU with generalized hamming network. In: NIPS 2017 (2017)
23. Fan, L.: Revisit Fuzzy Neural Network: Bridging the Gap between Fuzzy Ljgic and Deep Learning. Technical Report (2017)
24. Bonanno, D., Nock, K., Smith, L., Elmore, P., Petry, F.: An approach to explainable deep learning using fuzzy inference. In: Proceedings of the SPIE 10207, Next-Generation Analyst V, 102070D (2017)
25. Jang, S.R.: ANFIS: adaptive-network-based fuzzy inference systems. IEEE Trans. Syst. Man Cybernet. **23**, 665–685 (1992)
26. Bonanno, D., Nock, K., Smith, L., Elmore, P., Petry, F.: An approach to explainable deep learning using fuzzy inference. In: Hanratty, T.P., Llinas, J. (eds.) Next-Generation Analyst V. Proceedings of the SPIE, vol. 10207 (2017)
27. Goodfellow, I., et al.: Generative ad- versarial nets. In: Ghahramani, Z., Welling, M., Cortes, C., Lawrence,N. D., Weinberger, K.Q., éditeurs: Advances in Neural Information Processing Systems 27, pp. 2672–2680. Curran Associates, Inc. (2014)

Data Science: Similarity, Dissimilarity and Correlation Functions

Ildar Z. Batyrshin[(✉)] [iD]

Instituto Politécnico Nacional, Centro de Investigación en Computación,
Av. Juan de Dios Bátiz S/N, Nueva Industrial Vallejo,
07738 Ciudad de México, CDMX, Mexico
batyr1@gmail.com

Abstract. The lecture presents a new, non-statistical approach to the analysis and construction of similarity, dissimilarity and correlation measures. The measures are considered as functions defined on an underlying set and satisfying the given properties. Different functional structures, relationships between them and methods of their construction are discussed. Particular attention is paid to functions defined on sets with an involution operation, where the class of (strong) correlation functions is introduced. The general methods constructing new correlation functions from similarity and dissimilarity functions are considered. It is shown that the classical correlation and association coefficients (Pearson's, Spearman's, Kendall's, Yule's Q, Hamann) can be obtained as particular cases.

Keywords: Similarity measure · Pearson's product-moment correlation · Spearman's rank correlation · Kendall's rank correlation · Yule's Q

1 Introduction

Data Science is the buzzword of the last decade. One of the goals of Data Science is to extract knowledge, insights and usable information from various types of data. Data Science courses typically include the topics on statistical data analysis, machine learning methods and data mining. Correlation, association, similarity, relationship and interestingness coefficients or measures play an important role in data analysis, classification tasks and data mining. Dozens of such measures have been created for various types of data, and articles on these indicators are cited in hundreds and thousands of papers [3, 13, 14, 20, 23–25, 27]. Such measures are defined for dichotomous or real valued variables measured for sampling units, for rankings, binary or real valued vectors of attributes, time series, fuzzy sets of different types, probabilistic distributions, images, rating profiles etc. These measures used in information retrieval, data classification, machine learning, analysis of relationships and decision making in ecology, computational linguistics, image and signal processing, financial data analysis, bioinformatics and social sciences. Often, measures introduced for one type of data give misleading results when they are used for analysis of relationships between data of another type [8]. There is a need in construction of a general theory of similarity, correlation and association measures, which will be able to analyze general

© Springer Nature Switzerland AG 2019
G. S. Osipov et al. (Eds.): Artificial Intelligence, LNAI 11866, pp. 13–28, 2019.
https://doi.org/10.1007/978-3-030-33274-7_2

properties of these measures independent on domain or for large class of data types. Such a theory will make it possible to transfer the methods of constructing association measures from one domain to another and propose such measures for new data types.

The first steps in construction of the general theory of similarity, dissimilarity and correlation measures have been done in [7, 9, 10] where the fundamental results on definition and construction of association measures (correlation coefficients) on sets with involution operations have been proposed. It was shown that many known correlation coefficients can be considered as functions defined on an underlying set with involution operation and satisfying a simple set of properties. The general methods of construction of these functions from suitable similarity or dissimilarity functions have been proposed. These results can be considered as an alternative solution of the Kendall's problem of construction of general correlation coefficient [22]. Kendall proposed a formula that gives as particular cases Pearson's product-moment correlation, Spearman's and Kendall's rank correlation coefficients but it was not clear how to obtain from this formula other known association and correlation coefficients and how to build correlation coefficients for other domains. The approach proposed in [7, 9, 10] gives possibility to construct the classical correlation coefficients that can be obtained from Kendall's formula, the Yule's Q and Hamann coefficients together with some other association coefficients for binary data and gives a tool for constructing new correlation coefficients on new domains.

Similarity, dissimilarity and correlation measures or coefficients are considered in this lecture as functions defined on an underlying set Ω and satisfying some reasonable sets of properties. Generally, these functions can be considered as *association functions*, measuring (may be non-statistical) associations or relationships between objects. The methods of construction of such functions, the transformations of them and relationships between them studied in [7, 9, 10]. This paper presents a short and updated description of some part of author's Lecture on RAAI Summer School 2019. Due to the limit on the size of the paper it was not possible to include all topics discussed in [9] and in this lecture. The presented paper can be considered as complementary to the [9]. It includes new methods of construction of correlation functions presented recently on INES 2019 [10] and contains more examples of (dis)similarity and correlation functions illustrating these methods. The list of references includes only several works. Hundreds or thousands papers have been published on related topics during more than one hundred years. Of course it was not possible to include most of them. Some useful references can be found in the papers cited in the list of references.

2 Examples of Similarity Measures and Correlation Coefficients for Different Domains

2.1 Binary n-Tuples

Consider n-tuple $x = (x_1, \ldots, x_n)$, $x_i \in \{0, 1\}, i = 1, \ldots, n$. It can represent an object x described by n binary features, attributes or properties such that $x_i = 1$ if the object x possesses the i-th attribute and $x_i = 0$ in the opposite case. Denote X the set of attributes possessed by x. In statistics, a binary n-tuple can denote n measurements of a dichotomous variable or property x for n sampling units. $x_i = 1$ denotes that the property x fulfilled for the unit i, and $x_i = 0$ otherwise. We use here the first interpretation of binary n-tuples. For two binary n-tuples $x = (x_1, \ldots, x_n)$, $y = (y_1, \ldots, y_n)$ denote:

- a the number of attributes possessed by both objects x and y, when $x_i = y_i = 1$;
- b the number of attributes possessed by x and not by y, when $x_i = 1, y_i = 0$;
- c the number of attributes possessed by y and not by x, when $x_i = 0, y_i = 1$;
- d the number of attributes not possessed by both objects x and y, when $x_i = y_i = 0$.

The numbers a and d usually referred to as the numbers of *positive and negative matches*, respectively. Below are examples of similarity and association measures for binary n-tuples [13]:

Jaccard similarity measure:

$$S_J = \frac{a}{a+b+c} = \frac{|X \cap Y|}{|X \cup Y|},$$

Simple Matching similarity measure:

$$S_{SM} = \frac{a+d}{a+b+c+d} = \frac{|X \cap Y| + |\bar{X} \cap \bar{Y}|}{n},$$

Hamann coefficient:

$$A_H = \frac{(a+d) - (b+c)}{a+b+c+d} = \frac{|X \cap Y| + |\bar{X} \cap \bar{Y}| - |X \cap \bar{Y}| - |\bar{X} \cap Y|}{n},$$

Yule's Q association coefficient:

$$A_{Y-Q} = \frac{ad - bc}{ad + bc} = \frac{|X \cap Y| \cdot |\bar{X} \cap \bar{Y}| - |X \cap \bar{Y}| \cdot |\bar{X} \cap Y|}{|X \cap Y| \cdot |\bar{X} \cap \bar{Y}| + |X \cap \bar{Y}| \cdot |\bar{X} \cap Y|}.$$

2.2 Real Valued n-Tuples

Consider n-tuples $x = (x_1, \ldots, x_n)$, $y = (y_1, \ldots, y_n)$ with real valued components.

Cosine similarity measure:

$$cos(x, y) = \frac{\sum_{i=1}^{n} x_i y_i}{\sqrt{\sum_{i=1}^{n} x_i^2} \sqrt{\sum_{i=1}^{n} y_i^2}},$$

where $x_i, y_i \geq 0$, $i = 1, \ldots, n$.

Pearson's product-moment correlation coefficient:

$$r = \frac{\sum_{i=1}^{n}(x_i - \bar{x})(y_i - \bar{y})}{\sqrt{\sum_{i=1}^{n}(x_i - \bar{x})^2}\sqrt{\sum_{i=1}^{n}(y_i - \bar{y})^2}},$$

where $\bar{x} = \frac{1}{n}\sum_{i=1}^{n} x_i$, $\bar{y} = \frac{1}{n}\sum_{i=1}^{n} y_i$.

For both measures, it is supposed that denominators do not equal to zero.

2.3   Rankings

Consider two rankings of n objects $x = (x_1, \ldots, x_n)$, $y = (y_1, \ldots, y_n)$ containing n different integer ranks, $1 \leq x_i, y_i \leq n$, i.e. "without ties".

Spearman's rank correlation coefficient [12, 18, 22]:

$$\rho = 1 - \frac{6\sum_{i=1}^{n} d_i^2}{n(n^2 - 1)},$$

where $d_i = x_i - y_i, i = 1, \ldots, n$.

Kendall's rank correlation coefficient [12, 18, 22] for real valued n-tuples $x = (x_1, \ldots, x_n)$, $y = (y_1, \ldots, y_n)$ without ties, i.e. $x_i \neq x_j$, $y_i \neq y_j$ for all i, j:

$$\tau = \frac{NC - ND}{n(n-1)/2},$$

where NC is the *number of concordant pairs* (i, j) calculated as follows:

$$NC = \sum_{i=1}^{n-1}\sum_{j=i+1}^{n} s_{ij}, \quad \text{and} \quad s_{ij} = \begin{cases} 1, & if\ (x_i - x_j)(y_i - y_j) > 0 \\ 0, & otherwise \end{cases},$$

and ND is the *number of disconcordant pairs* calculated as follows:

$$ND = \sum_{i=1}^{n-1}\sum_{j=i+1}^{n} d_{ij}, \quad \text{and} \quad d_{ij} = \begin{cases} 1, & if\ (x_i - x_j)(y_i - y_j) < 0 \\ 0, & otherwise \end{cases}.$$

Note that only the ordering of the component values of n-tuples is used.

2.4   Finite Probabilistic Distributions

Suppose $x = (x_1, \ldots, x_n)$ is a finite probabilistic distribution, i.e. $x_i \geq 0$, for all $i = 1, \ldots, n$, and $\sum_{i=1}^{n} x_i = 1$.

Bhattacharyya coefficient is defined as follows [1]:

$$S(x, y) = \sum_{i=1}^{n} \sqrt{x_i y_i}.$$

2.5 Kendall's General Correlation Coefficient

Kendall [22] considered the problem of constructing *general correlation coefficient*. For two *n*-tuples $x = (x_1, \ldots, x_n)$ and $y = (y_1, \ldots, y_n)$ he defined it as:

$$r = \frac{\sum_{i,j=1}^{n} a_{ij} b_{ij}}{\sqrt{\sum_{i,j=1}^{n} a_{ij}^2 \sum_{i,j=1}^{n} b_{ij}^2}},$$

where the values a_{ij} calculated from the values x_i and x_j, similarly b_{ij} calculated from y_i and y_j, such that the following conditions are fulfilled: $a_{ij} = -a_{ji}$, $b_{ij} = -b_{ji}$, $a_{ii} = b_{ii} = 0$ for all $i, j = 1, \ldots, n$. As particular cases of this formula he obtained Spearman's and Kendall's rank correlation coefficients, and Pearson's product-moment correlation coefficient. How to obtain other correlation coefficients from this formula does not clear.

3 Similarity and Dissimilarity Functions

The examples of similarity measures and correlation coefficients considered in the previous section show that there is a variety of such indicators for different types of data. Generally, there are introduced tens of such measures and coefficients [13, 14, 27]. To analyze the general properties of these measures, possible relationships between them and to study the methods of their construction in [9] it was proposed to consider these measures as functions defined on a universal domain Ω and satisfying some simple sets of properties. Three main types of such functions have been considered: similarity, dissimilarity and correlation functions, which can be used as models of similarity, dissimilarity and correlation measures and coefficients, respectively. Below we introduce these functions and consider some of their properties. More results can be found in [9].

Further, for brevity, similarity and dissimilarity functions will be referred to as *(dis) similarity functions* or as *resemblance functions*.

3.1 Definition of Similarity, Dissimilarity and Correlation Functions

Let Ω be a nonempty set that will be referred to as a *universal domain* or an *underlying set* in definition of similarity and correlation functions. As Ω we can consider domain specific for a considered data type: the set of all binary *n*-tuples, the set of all real valued vectors of the length *n*, the set of all fuzzy sets defined on some domain *X*, the set of some images or objects considered in some problem, etc.

A function $S : \Omega \times \Omega \to [0, 1]$ is called a *similarity function* on Ω if for all x, y in Ω it is *symmetric*:

$$S(x, y) = S(y, x),$$

and *reflexive*:

$$S(x, x) = 1.$$

A function $D : \Omega \times \Omega \to [0, 1]$ is a *dissimilarity function* on Ω if for all x, y in Ω it is *symmetric*:

$$D(x, y) = D(y, x),$$

and *irreflexive*:

$$D(x, x) = 0.$$

These functions are called *complementary* if for all x, y in Ω it is fulfilled:

$$S(x, y) + D(x, y) = 1.$$

For complementary (dis)similarity functions we have:

$$S(x, y) = 1 - D(x, y), D(x, y) = 1 - S(x, y). \tag{1}$$

A function $A : \Omega \times \Omega \to [-1, 1]$ is a *correlation function* (association measure) on Ω if for all x, y in Ω it is *symmetric*:

$$A(x, y) = A(y, x),$$

reflexive:

$$A(x, x) = 1,$$

and *negative*: $A(x, y) < 0$ for some x, y in Ω.

Such correlation functions will be referred to as *weak* correlation functions if they will not satisfy inverse relationship property considered in Sect. 4. In Sect. 4 we define a strong (invertible) correlation function on a set Ω with involution operation.

It is easy to see that the indicators considered in the previous section belong to the following classes of functions:

- **Similarity functions:** Jaccard, Simple Matching, Cosine (if all x_i and y_i have non-negative values) similarity measures and Bhattacharyya coefficient;
- **Correlation functions:** Hamann and Yule's Q coefficients, Pearson's product-moment correlation coefficient, Spearman's and Kendall's rank correlation coefficients, Cosine (if x_i and y_i can have positive and negative values).

3.2 Examples of Complementary (Dis)Similarity Functions

Jaccard (see Sect. 2.1):

$$S_J(x,y) = \frac{a}{a+b+c} = \frac{|X \cap Y|}{|X \cup Y|},$$

$$D_J(x,y) = \frac{b+c}{a+b+c} = \frac{|X \oplus Y|}{|X \cup Y|}.$$

Simple Matching (Sect. 2.1):

$$S_{SM}(x,y) = \frac{a+d}{a+b+c+d} = \frac{|X \cap Y| + |\bar{X} \cap \bar{Y}|}{n},$$

$$D_{SM}(x,y) = \frac{b+c}{a+b+c+d} = \frac{|X \oplus Y|}{n} = \frac{1}{n}\sum_{1}^{n}|x_i - y_i|.$$

Cosine (Sect. 2.2):

$$cos(x,y) = \frac{\sum_{i=1}^{n} x_i y_i}{\sqrt{\sum_{i=1}^{n} x_i^2}\sqrt{\sum_{i=1}^{n} y_i^2}}, x_i, y_i \geq 0, i = 1, \ldots, n.$$

$$D(x,y) = \frac{1}{2}\sum_{i=1}^{n}\left(\frac{x_i}{\sqrt{\sum_{i=1}^{n} x_i^2}} - \frac{y_i}{\sqrt{\sum_{i=1}^{n} y_i^2}}\right)^2.$$

Bhattacharyya (Sect. 2.4):

$$S(x,y) = \sum_{i=1}^{n}\sqrt{x_i y_i}.$$

$$D(x,y) = \frac{1}{2}\sum_{i=1}^{n}\left(\sqrt{x_i} - \sqrt{y_i}\right)^2.$$

The last dissimilarity function is called Hellinger discrimination, Matusita measure or Squared-Chord distance.

3.3 Fuzzy Relations and Kleene Algebra of Resemblance Functions

Here, similarity and dissimilarity functions will be also referred to as *resemblance functions*. A resemblance function is a symmetric function $R : \Omega \times \Omega \rightarrow [0,1]$, which is reflexive or irreflexive. We will say that two resemblance functions *have the same type* if both are reflexive or both are irreflexive.

Resemblance function R can be considered as a *fuzzy relation* [2, 17, 28, 29], given by membership function: $\mu_R : \Omega \times \Omega \rightarrow [0,1]$, where $\mu_R(x,y)$ is the strength of the relation R between x and y. The properties of fuzzy relations can be extended on resemblance functions.

Denote $\mathcal{P}(S), \mathcal{P}(D)$ and $\mathcal{P}(R)$ the sets of all similarity, dissimilarity and resemblance functions, respectively, defined on the set Ω. We have $\mathcal{P}(S), \mathcal{P}(D) \subset \mathcal{P}(R)$ and $\mathcal{P}(S) \cup \mathcal{P}(D) = \mathcal{P}(R)$. Define the operations *intersection* $\cap$ and *union* $\cup$ of resemblance functions R_1 and R_2 on the set Ω for all x, y in Ω as follows:

$$(R_1 \cap R_2)(x, y) = min\{R_1(x, y), R_2(x, y)\},$$

$$(R_1 \cup R_2)(x, y) = max\{R_1(x, y), R_2(x, y)\}.$$

The set $\mathcal{P}(R)$ will be a distributive lattice [11], partially ordered by the relation:

$$R_1 \subseteq R_2 \text{ if } R_1(x, y) \leq R_2(x, y) \text{ for all } x, y \text{ in } \Omega.$$

The sets $\mathcal{P}(S)$ and $\mathcal{P}(D)$ are distributive sublattices of $\mathcal{P}(R)$. For all similarity functions $S_1, S_2 \in \mathcal{P}(S)$ and dissimilarity functions $D_1, D_2 \in \mathcal{P}(D)$ it is fulfilled:

$$S_1 \cap S_2, S_1 \cup S_2 \in \mathcal{P}(S), \quad D_1 \cap D_2, D_1 \cup D_2 \in \mathcal{P}(D),$$

$$S_1 \cap D_1 \in \mathcal{P}(D), \quad S_1 \cup D_1 \in \mathcal{P}(S).$$

Consider similarity and dissimilarity functions defined for all x, y in Ω by:

$$D_0(x, y) = 0, \quad D_1(x, y) = \begin{cases} 0, & if \ x = y \\ 1, & otherwise \end{cases}.$$

$$S_0(x, y) = \begin{cases} 1, & if \ x = y \\ 0, & otherwise \end{cases}, \quad S_1(x, y) = 1,$$

D_0 is the least element of $\mathcal{P}(D)$ and $\mathcal{P}(R)$, S_1 is the greatest element of $\mathcal{P}(S)$ and $\mathcal{P}(R)$, S_0 is the least element of $\mathcal{P}(S)$ and D_1 is the greatest elements of $\mathcal{P}(D)$.

The complement $N(R)$ of a resemblance function R is defined for all x, y in Ω by: $N(R)(x, y) = 1 - R(x, y)$. This operation is *involutive*, i.e. for all R in $\mathcal{P}(R)$ we have: $N(N(R)) = R$. The complement of the similarity and dissimilarity functions will be equal to their complementary dissimilarity and similarity functions (1), respectively:

$$N(D) = S, \quad N(S) = D.$$

The lattice $\mathcal{P}(R)$ with the complement N will be a normal De Morgan (Kleene) algebra [5] where for any resemblance functions R_1 and R_2 *De Morgan laws*:

$$N(R_1 \cap R_2) = N(R_1) \cup N(R_2), \quad N(R_1 \cup R_2) = N(R_1) \cap N(R_2),$$

and *normality*:

$$R_1 \cap N(R_1) \subseteq R_2 \cup N(R_2),$$

are fulfilled.

Entropy of Resemblance Functions. On the Kleene algebra of resemblance functions one can introduce a *measure of non-probabilistic entropy* of these functions [5, 9, 15]. Similarity and dissimilarity functions such that $S(x, y) = D(x, y) = 0.5$ for all $x \neq y$ in Ω, have the maximal entropy and the uncertainty of making decision "x and y are similar" is maximal for such functions [9].

3.4 Min-Transitivity and Hierarchical Clustering

A symmetric and reflexive fuzzy relation $S : \Omega \times \Omega \to [0, 1]$ is called a *fuzzy similarity (fuzzy equivalence) relation* [29] if for all x, y, z in Ω it satisfies *min-transitivity*:

$$S(x, z) \geq min\{S(x, y), S(y, z)\}.$$

A dissimilarity function D complementary to min-transitive similarity function is called an *ultrametric* and satisfies for all x, y, z in Ω the *ultrametric inequality*:

$$D(x, z) \leq max\{D(x, y), D(y, z)\}.$$

For any $\alpha \in [0, 1]$ the α-cut of fuzzy relation S defines a crisp relation $S_\alpha \subseteq \Omega \times \Omega$ as follows: $S_\alpha = \{(x, y) \in \Omega \times \Omega | S(x, y) \geq \alpha\}$. α-cuts are nested such that from $\alpha > \beta$ it follows $S_\alpha \subseteq S_\beta$.

Optimal and Invariant Hierarchical Clustering. All α-cuts of the min-transitive similarity function (fuzzy equivalence relation) $E : \Omega \times \Omega \to [0, 1]$ are non-fuzzy equivalence relations; hence they define nested partitions of the set Ω on equivalence classes of these relations. These properties of fuzzy equivalence relations give rise to consider *hierarchical clustering* [21] of the set Ω with similarity function S as a *min-transitive transformation* of this similarity function S into a fuzzy equivalence relation E. Tamura et al. [26] proposed to transform S into its transitive closure $\hat{S}$ that will be fuzzy equivalence relation. It was shown [16, 19], that this method coincides with a spanning tree clustering and with a version of the single linkage hierarchical clustering algorithm.

Batyrshin [4, 6] showed that the solution of the problem of *optimal approximation* of similarity function by fuzzy equivalence relation has the form $E = \widehat{F(S)}$, i.e. it can be presented as the min-transitive closure of similarity function $F(S)$, where F is a "correction" of S such that $F(S) \subseteq S$. In addition, it was studied the problem of construction of *invariant hierarchical clustering algorithms* which are *invariant under monotone transformations of similarity values* and *under initial numbering (indexing) of objects*. The solution of this problem also have been presented in the form $E = \widehat{F(S)}$, where $F(S) \subseteq S$. The parametric family of invariant corrections F has been proposed [4, 6].

3.5 Equivalent Resemblance Functions

Two resemblance functions R_1 and R_2 of the same type defined on the set Ω called *equivalent (by ordering)* [3, 24] if for all x, y, u, v in Ω it is fulfilled:

$$R_1(x, y) \leq R_1(u, v) \quad \text{if and only if} \quad R_2(x, y) \leq R_2(u, v).$$

It is clear that two equivalent resemblance functions should have the same type.

A continuous, strictly increasing function $\varphi : [0, 1] \rightarrow [0, 1]$ such that $\varphi(0) = 0$ and $\varphi(1) = 1$ is called an *automorphism* of the interval $[0, 1]$.

Proposition 1. If R is a resemblance function on Ω and φ is an automorphism of the interval $[0,1]$ then the function R_1 defined for all x, y in Ω by:

$$R_1(x, y) = \varphi(R(x, y)),$$

will be a resemblance function equivalent to R.

Below there are examples of simplest equivalent transformations of resemblance functions:

$$R_1(x, y) = R^2(x, y), \quad R_1(x, y) = \sqrt{R(x, y)}.$$

For example, instead of dissimilarity function

$$D(x, y) = \frac{1}{2} \sqrt{\sum_{i=1}^{n} \left(\frac{x_i - \bar{x}}{\sqrt{\sum_{i=1}^{n}(x_i - \bar{x})^2}} - \frac{y_i - \bar{y}}{\sqrt{\sum_{i=1}^{n}(y_i - \bar{y})^2}} \right)^2 },$$

one can use the equivalent dissimilarity function

$$D(x, y) = \frac{1}{4} \sum_{i=1}^{n} \left(\frac{x_i - \bar{x}}{\sqrt{\sum_{i=1}^{n}(x_i - \bar{x})^2}} - \frac{y_i - \bar{y}}{\sqrt{\sum_{i=1}^{n}(y_i - \bar{y})^2}} \right)^2 .$$

Equivalent Resemblance Functions and Invariant Clustering. Equivalence of (dis) similarity functions supposes that the use of such functions in some classification algorithm will give equivalent results. As such clustering algorithms one can use hierarchical clustering algorithms invariant under monotone transformations of similarity values discussed in previous section.

4   Correlation Functions

4.1   Correlation Functions and Correlation Triplets

In Sect. 3 we introduced the definition of correlation function as follows.

A function $A : \Omega \times \Omega \rightarrow [-1, 1]$ is a *correlation function* (association measure) on Ω if for all x, y in Ω it is *symmetric*:

$$A(x, y) = A(y, x),$$

reflexive:

$$A(x, x) = 1,$$

and negative: $A(x, y) < 0$, for some x, y in Ω.

Correlation function will be called a *weak* correlation function if it does not satisfy the inverse relationship property considered below. Here we consider and extend some results introduced in [10].

Proposition 2. Suppose S and D are similarity and dissimilarity functions on Ω such that for some x, y in Ω it is fulfilled: $S(x, y) < D(x, y)$, then the function defined for all x, y in Ω by:

$$A(x, y) = S(x, y) - D(x, y), \tag{2}$$

is a correlation function. If S and D are complementary then the function A will be a correlation function if for some x, y in Ω it is fulfilled: $S(x, y) < 0.5$.

The obtained formula for A has the reasonable interpretation: *the correlation between x and y is positive if the similarity between them is greater than the dissimilarity, and the correlation is negative in opposite case.*

If the similarity S and dissimilarity D functions are complementary then the correlation function A defined by (2) is called *complementary* to S and D. Complementary functions S, D and A will be denoted as (S, D, A) and called a *correlation triplet*. From the definition of the complementary (dis)similarity functions and from (2) it follows that the similarity, dissimilarity and correlation functions from the correlation triplet (S, D, A) can be obtained one from another for all x, y in Ω as follows:

$$S(x, y) = 1 - D(x, y), \quad D(x, y) = 1 - S(x, y), \tag{3}$$

$$A(x, y) = 2S(x, y) - 1, \quad S(x, y) = \tfrac{1}{2}(A(x, y) + 1). \tag{4}$$

$$A(x, y) = 1 - 2D(x, y), \quad D(x, y) = \tfrac{1}{2}(1 - A(x, y)). \tag{5}$$

4.2 Examples of Constructing Correlation Functions from (Dis)Similarity Functions

Hamann coefficient A_H (see Sect. 2.1). The Simple Matching similarity measure $S_{SM}(x, y) = \frac{a+d}{a+b+c+d}$ has the complementary dissimilarity function $D_{SM}(x, y) = \frac{b+c}{a+b+c+d}$. From (2) we obtain:

$$A(x, y) = S(x, y) - D(x, y) = \frac{a+d}{a+b+c+d} - \frac{b+c}{a+b+c+d} = \frac{(a+d) - (b+c)}{a+b+c+d} = A_H.$$

Yule's Q association coefficient A_{Y-Q} (Sect. 2.1). The function $S_Y(x,y) = \frac{ad}{ad+bc}$ is the similarity function and the function $D_Y(x,y) = \frac{bc}{ad+bc}$ is it's complementary dissimilarity function. From (2) we obtain:

$$A(x,y) = S(x,y) - D(x,y) = \frac{ad}{ad+bc} - \frac{bc}{ad+bc} = \frac{ad-bc}{ad+bc} = A_{Y-Q}.$$

Note that similarly to Yule's Q association and Hamann coefficients it is easy to construct the most of correlation functions considered for binary data [13].

Pearson's product-moment correlation coefficient r (Sect. 2.2). The function

$$D(x,y) = \frac{1}{4}\sum_{i=1}^{n}\left(\frac{x_i - \bar{x}}{\sqrt{\sum_{i=1}^{n}(x_i - \bar{x})^2}} - \frac{y_i - \bar{y}}{\sqrt{\sum_{i=1}^{n}(y_i - \bar{y})^2}}\right)^2,$$

is the dissimilarity function. From (5) obtain Pearson's product-moment correlation coefficient:

$$A(x,y) = 1 - 2D(x,y) = 1 - \frac{1}{2}\sum_{i=1}^{n}\left(\frac{x_i - \bar{x}}{\sqrt{\sum_{i=1}^{n}(x_i - \bar{x})^2}} - \frac{y_i - \bar{y}}{\sqrt{\sum_{i=1}^{n}(y_i - \bar{y})^2}}\right)^2$$

$$= \frac{\sum_{i=1}^{n}(x_i - \bar{x})(y_i - \bar{y})}{\sqrt{\sum_{i=1}^{n}(x_i - \bar{x})^2}\sqrt{\sum_{i=1}^{n}(y_i - \bar{y})^2}} = r.$$

Spearman's rank correlation coefficient ρ (see Sect. 2.3). Consider the function:

$$D(x,y) = \frac{3\sum_{i=1}^{n}(x_i - y_i)^2}{n(n^2 - 1)}.$$

It satisfies the properties of dissimilarity functions and from (5) we obtain the Spearman's rank correlation coefficient: $A(x,y) = 1 - 2D(x,y) = 1 - \frac{6\sum_{i=1}^{n}d_i^2}{n(n^2-1)} = \rho$.

Kendall's rank correlation coefficient τ (Sect. 2.3). Consider the functions:

$$S(x,y) = \frac{\sum_{i=1}^{n-1}\sum_{j=i+1}^{n}s_{ij}}{n(n-1)/2} = \frac{NC}{n(n-1)/2},$$

$$D(x,y) = \frac{\sum_{i=1}^{n-1}\sum_{j=i+1}^{n}d_{ij}}{n(n-1)/2} = \frac{ND}{n(n-1)/2}.$$

They are the complementary similarity and dissimilarity functions, respectively, such that $S(x,y) + D(x,y) = 1$, and from (2) we obtain $A(x,y) = \frac{NC-ND}{n(n-1)/2} = \tau$.

4.3   Strong (Invertible) Correlation Functions on the Sets with Involution Operation

Initially the correlation function (association measure) was defined on the set with involution operation [7] as function satisfying inverse relationship property considered below. Such correlation functions will be called here *strong* or *invertible correlation functions*. It is surprising that all correlation functions considered above are invertible. For this reason, the correlation function which is not invertible will be called a *weak correlation function*.

A function $N : \Omega \to \Omega$ is called a *reflection* or a *negation* on Ω if it satisfies for all x in Ω the *involutivity* property:

$$N(N(x)) = x,$$

and if it is not an identity function, i.e. for some x in Ω it is fulfilled: $N(x) \neq x$.

An element x in Ω such that $N(x) = x$ is called a *fixed point* and the set of all fixed points of the reflection N on Ω is denoted as $FP(N, \Omega)$ or $FP(\Omega)$.

Definition 1. [7] Let N be a reflection on Ω and V be a subset of $\Omega \backslash FP(\Omega)$ closed under N. A *strong correlation function* (association measure) on V is a function $A : V \times V \to [-1, 1]$ satisfying for all x, y in V the properties:

$$A(x, y) = A(y, x), \qquad \text{(symmetry)}$$
$$A(x, x) = 1, \qquad \text{(reflexivity)}$$
$$A(x, N(y)) = -A(x, y). \quad \text{(inverse relationship)}$$

The strong correlation function also will be referred to as an *invertible correlation function*.

Theorem 1. The correlation function A from a correlation triplet (S, D, A) is invertible if and only if the complementary similarity and dissimilarity functions satisfy the following properties:

$$S(x, y) + S(x, N(y)) = 1, \quad D(x, y) + D(x, N(y)) = 1.$$

These properties will be called *bipolarity* properties and corresponding functions S and D will be called *bipolar*, see [8, 10]. The value 1 equals to the sum of the pole values 0 and 1 of the interval $[0, 1]$ of similarity and dissimilarity values. It is clear that S is bipolar if and only if its complementary dissimilarity function D is bipolar.

Similarly, the property of inverse relationship of correlation function can be written in the form of *bipolarity*:

$$A(x, y) + A(x, N(y)) = 0,$$

taking into account that $0 = -1 + 1$, i.e. zero equals to the sum of the pole values of the interval $[-1, 1]$ of correlation values. With this terminology the Theorem 1 can be formulated as follows: *The correlation function A from a correlation triplet (S, D, A) is bipolar if and only if the similarity and dissimilarity functions S and D are bipolar.*

The   proof   follows,   for   example,   from   (4):
$A(x, y) + A(x, N(y)) = 2S(x, y) - 1 + 2S(x, N(y)) - 1 = 2(S(x, y) + S(x, N(y)) - 1)$,
and the first sum equals to zero if and only the last sum equals to zero.

For complementary (dis)similarity functions we have: $S(x, y) + D(x, y) = 1$ and
bipolarity of these functions is equivalent to the properties:

$$D(x, y) = S(x, N(y)), \quad S(x, y) = D(x, N(y)). \tag{6}$$

Hence to prove the inverse relationship property of the correlation function A it is
sufficient to show the fulfillment of the bipolarity or (6) properties for the (dis)similarity
functions S or D used in construction of A by means of (2), (4) or (5).

One can show that all correlation functions considered in Sect. 4.2 are invertible
with respect to suitable involutions. See some results in [10].

4.4 Constructing Strong Correlation Functions from Co-symmetric (Dis) Similarity Functions

Similarity S and dissimilarity D functions are *consistent* on the set Ω with involution
N if for all x in Ω it is, respectively, fulfilled [9]:

$$S(x, N(x)) = 0, \quad D(x, N(x)) = 1.$$

Resemblance function R is *co-symmetric* on the set Ω with involution N if for all
x, y in Ω it is fulfilled [9]:

$$R(N(x), N(y)) = R(x, y).$$

It was shown [7, 9] that a resemblance function R is co-symmetric if and only if for
all x, y in Ω it is fulfilled the following property:

$$R(x, N(y)) = R(N(x), y).$$

Proposition 3 [7]. Invertible correlation function is co-symmetric.

Proposition 4 [10]. Bipolar resemblance function is consistent and co-symmetric.

Theorem 1 says that for construction of invertible correlation function from its
complementary (dis)similarity functions by (2), (4) or (5) we need to have bipolar (dis)
similarity functions. To construct such functions for specific domain is not always easy.
From Proposition 4, one can conclude that consistent and co-symmetric (dis)similarity
functions may be not so restrictive than bipolar functions, and it is easier to construct
such (dis)similarity functions than bipolar functions. The following theorem shows
how to use them for constructing invertible correlation functions.

Theorem 2 [7]. Let N be a reflection on Ω and V be a nonempty subset of $\Omega \backslash FP(\Omega)$
closed under reflection N. Let $S : V \times V \to [0, 1]$ be a co-symmetric and consistent
similarity function, then the function $A : V \times V \to [-1, 1]$ defined for all x, y in V by:

$$A(x, y) = S(x, y) - S(x, N(y)), \tag{7}$$

is a strong correlation function on V.

The formula (7) has the simple interpretation: *the correlation between x and y is positive if x is more similar to y than to its negation and the correlation is negative in the opposite case.*

More general methods of constructing invertible correlation functions (association measures) have been proposed in [7, 9, 10]. These methods instead of difference operation in (7) use pseudo-difference operations and instead of consistent similarity functions in (7) they can use similarity functions satisfying weaker conditions.

5 Conclusion and Future Directions of Research

This work presents a short and updated version of a part of author's Lecture on RAAI Summer School 2019. The presented paper can be considered as complementary to the [9]. It includes new methods of construction of correlation functions presented recently on INES 2019 [10] and contains more examples of (dis)similarity and correlation functions illustrating these methods. As a future work, it is supposed to extend the developed approach on other types of association and relationships measures and on other domains.

Acknowledgements. This works partially supported by the project SIP 20196374 IPN and by Organizing Committee of RAAI Summer School. The author thanks all organizers of RAAI Summer School and editors of this book. Special thanks to doctors Gennady Osipov, Alexander Panov and Maria Koroleva.

References

1. Aherne, F.J., Thacker, N.A., Rockett, P.I.: The Bhattacharyya metric as an absolute similarity measure for frequency coded data. Kybernetika **34**, 363–368 (1998)
2. Averkin, A.N., Batyrshin, I.Z., Blishun, A.F., Silov, V.B., Tarasov, V.B.: Fuzzy sets in models of control and artificial intelligence. Pospelov, D.A. (ed.) Nauka, Moscow (1986). (in Russian)
3. Batagelj, V., Bren, M.: Comparing resemblance measures. J. Classif. **12**, 73–90 (1995)
4. Batyrshin, I.Z.: Methods of system analysis based on weighted relations, Ph.D. dissertation. Moscow Power Engineering Institute, Moscow (1982). (in Russian)
5. Batyrshin, I.Z.: On fuzzinesstic measures of entropy on Kleene algebras. Fuzzy Sets Syst. **34**, 47–60 (1990)
6. Batyrshin, I., Rudas, T.: Invariant hierarchical clustering schemes. In: Batyrshin, I., Kacprzyk, J., Sheremetov, I., Zadeh, L.A. (eds.) Perception-Based Data Mining and Decision Making in Economics and Finance, pp. 181–206. Springer, Heidelberg (2007). https://doi.org/10.1007/978-3-540-36247-0_7
7. Batyrshin, I.Z.: On definition and construction of association measures. J. Intell. Fuzzy Syst. **29**, 2319–2326 (2015)

8. Batyrshin, I., Monroy-Tenorio, F., Gelbukh, A., Villa-Vargas, L.A., Solovyev, V., Kubysheva, N.: Bipolar rating scales: a survey and novel correlation measures based on non-linear bipolar scoring functions. Acta Polytechnica Hungarica **14**, 33–57 (2017)
9. Batyrshin, I.: Towards a general theory of similarity and association measures: similarity, dissimilarity and correlation functions. J. Intell. Fuzzy Syst. **36**(4), 2977–3004 (2019)
10. Batyrshin, I.Z.: Constructing correlation coefficients from similarity and dissimilarity functions. In: INES 2019, IEEE 23rd IEEE International Conference on Intelligent Engineering Systems, Hungary, 25–27 April. IEEE, Gödöllő (2019)
11. Birkhoff, G.: Lattice Theory, 3rd edn. American Mathematical Society, Providence (1967)
12. Chen, P.Y., Popovich, P.M.: Correlation: Parametric and Nonparametric Measures. Sage, Thousand Oaks (2002)
13. Choi, S.S., Cha, S.H., Charles, C.T.: A survey of binary similarity and distance measures. J. Syst. Cybern. Inform. **8**, 43–48 (2010)
14. Clifford, H.T., Stephenson, W.: An Introduction to Numerical Classification. Academic Press, New York (1975)
15. De Luca, A., Termini, S.: A definition of a nonprobabilistic entropy in the setting of fuzzy sets. Inform. Control **20**, 301–312 (1972)
16. Dunn, J.C.: A graph theoretic analysis of pattern classification via Tamura's fuzzy relation. IEEE Trans. Syst. Man Cybern. **3**, 310–313 (1974)
17. Fodor, J.C., Roubens, M.R.: Fuzzy Preference Modelling and Multicriteria Decision Support, vol. 14. Springer, Dordrecht (1994). https://doi.org/10.1007/978-94-017-1648-2
18. Gibbons, J.D., Chakraborti, S.: Nonparametric Statistical Inference, 4th edn. Dekker, New York (2003)
19. Gower, J.C., Ross, G.J.S.: Minimum spanning trees and single linkage cluster analysis. Appl. Stat. **18**, 54–64 (1969)
20. Janson, S., Vegelius, J.: Measures of ecological association. Oecologia **49**, 371–376 (1981)
21. Johnson, S.C.: Hierarchical clustering schemes. Psychometrika **32**, 241–254 (1967)
22. Kendall, M.G.: Rank Correlation Methods, 4th edn. Griffin, London (1970)
23. Legendre, P., Legendre, L.F.: Numerical Ecology, 2nd edn. Elsevier, Amsterdam (1998). English edn.
24. Lesot, M-J., Rifqi, M., Benhadda, H.: Similarity measures for binary and numerical data: a survey. Int. J. Knowl. Eng. Soft Data Paradigms **1**, 63–84 (2009)
25. Rauschenbach, G.V.: Proximity and similarity measures. In: Analysis of Non-Numerical Information in Sociological Research, Nauka, Moscow, pp. 169–202 (1985). (in Russian)
26. Tamura, S., Higuchi, S., Tanaka, K.: Pattern classification based on fuzzy relations. IEEE Trans. Syst. Man Cybern. **1**, 61–66 (1971)
27. Tan, P.N., Kumar, V., Srivastava, J.: Selecting the right interestingness measure for association patterns. In: 8th Proceedings of Eighth ACM SIGKDD International Conference on Knowledge Discovery and Data Mining, pp. 32–41 (2002)
28. Zadeh, L.A.: Fuzzy sets. Inf. Control **8**, 338–353 (1965)
29. Zadeh, L.A.: Similarity relations and fuzzy orderings. Inf. Sci. **3**, 177–200 (1971)

Mathematical Foundation of Cognitive Computing Based Artificial Intelligence

Tamás Gergely$^{(\boxtimes)}$ and László Ury

Applied Logic Laboratory, Budapest, Hungary
gergely@all.hu, uss@t-online.hu

Abstract. Today Cognitive computing and Artificial Intelligence (AI) face the same challenges namely, simulate human thought processes and mimic the way human brain works. The main difference between Cognitive computing and AI is: (i) AI models various functions of human intelligence, where computer is one of the modelling means though often the most important one, i.e. intelligence is in the focus while (ii) Cognitive computing models human thought processes and simulates the hypothetical way human brain works as computation.

Our aim is to develop a theoretically and methodologically well-founded theory of AI together with a unified computational theory, which will provide specific tools and methods for Cognitive computing.

To achieve our goal we follow a methodology triangle, consisting of a conceptual-philosophical, a system theoretical and a logical-mathematical component. Computing will play a fundamental role in both system-theoretical and logical-mathematical methodological components.

Hereby we concentrate on the development of the logical-mathematical foundation in detail by the use of category theory, which provides an excellent frame for defining all notions necessary for developing a universal theory for computing, specification, cognitive reasoning, information, knowledge and their various combinations. Foundation theory is by the use of the so-called constitutions, the mathematical basis for the cognitive computation. Logical foundation will be developed as a special constitution and cognitive computing processes are defined by using situations, infons and information. The main properties are discussed with some examples.

Keywords: Categorical theoretical foundation · Cognitive computing · Specification theory · Cognitive reasoning · Computing theory · Logic programming

1 Introduction

1.1 Artificial Intelligence Today

What is meant by artificial intelligence? So far not a single conceptual apparatus has been formed, nor there is a single conceptual justification and a single scientifically based methodology. Besides, there has not yet been developed a

G. S. Osipov et al. (Eds.): Artificial Intelligence, LNAI 11866, pp. 29–64, 2019.
https://doi.org/10.1007/978-3-030-33274-7_3

generally accepted philosophical foundation in the form of such epistemology and ontology, which would consider and respond to the challenges that arise during the development of the field of artificial intelligence (AI).

The High-Level Expert Group on AI of the European Commission dealing with the definition of AI provides the following definition for AI [1] as a scientific discipline: *AI includes several approaches and techniques, such as machine learning (of which deep learning and reinforcement learning are specific examples), machine reasoning (which includes planning, scheduling, knowledge representation and reasoning, search, and optimization), and robotics (which includes control, perception, sensors and actuators, as well as the integration of all other techniques into cyber-physical systems).*

Today, modern dictionary definitions focus on AI since it is a field that applies computer science and how machines can imitate human intelligence (human-like rather than becoming human). The English Oxford Living Dictionary [31] gives this definition: The theory and development of computer systems able to perform tasks normally requiring human intelligence, such as visual perception, speech recognition, decision-making, and translation between languages.

At the same time The Encyclopedia Britannica defines artificial intelligence as it the ability of a digital computer or computer-controlled robot to perform tasks commonly associated with intelligent beings. The term is frequently applied to the project of developing systems endowed with the intellectual processes characteristic of humans, such as the ability to reason, discover meaning, generalize, or learn from past experience [32].

The term *artificial intelligence* is frequently applied to systems endowed with the intellectual processes characteristic of humans, such as the ability to make decisions, to solve problems, to understand texts, to recognize pictures, to learn from an actual activity and a past experience, etc. There are different technologies that get ranked as artificial intelligence and there are different types of AI.

The current wave of AI innovation focuses on several real-life applications of artificial intelligence that often start with words such as *smart, intelligent, predictive* and, indeed, *cognitive*, depending on the exact application and vendor. One major issue is that artificial intelligence is indeed a broad concept and reality, covering many technologies and realities that lead to misunderstandings about what it exactly means. Some people are actually speaking about machine learning when they talk about AI. The most advertised AI tools by Google, Facebook etc. are mainly or only machine learning and, mostly, deep learning related. This is why the wide public thinks that all new AI applications are carried out only with this type of machine learning. However, neither machine learning, nor deep learning are synonyms for AI. They are only one of the many areas of AI research. Moreover, deep learning is a technology of the 1980's while trained with more data, 1970's *neural networks with hidden layers* gave better results; and then it was renamed as deep learning and was hyped as such.

Today, AI is a conglomerate of techniques, technologies and of various research and development directions. Machine learning and especially deep learning are the most common methods. However, deep learning technology, from the application point of view has been close to its limit. Artificial intelligence urgently needs to be promoted to a new stage, and to achieve breakthroughs in the development of an appropriate underlying theory.

1.2 Cognitive Computing

As AI applications became more and more widespread, a new name, Cognitive computers appeared. This actually is a renaming that has not brought much new to the content of AI. Cognitive computing is a term really, that has been popularized by IBM mainly to describe the current wave of artificial intelligence with a twist of purpose, adaptiveness, self-learning, contextuality and human interaction. The latter, the human one is the key here and without a doubt, also easier to digest than all those AI-related science fiction scenarios.

Note that thanks to science fiction, many people think of artificial intelligence as a computer or robot thinking like a person, including self-awareness and independent will. Instead, what we call cognitive computing uses the ideas behind neuroscience and psychology to **augment** human reasoning with better pattern matching while determining the optimal information a person needs to make decisions.

However, if we peel off the marketing catches from the notion of Cognitive computing used by IBM then we get back AI with one important difference. Namely, Cognitive computing emphasizes the augmentation of human intelligence instead of mimicking it. This is why it is claimed that IBM's Watson is armed with perception and understanding that is refined and expanded with every interaction. Moreover, it should be appropriate for supporting the solution of problems that encompass enormous amounts of information and discernment.

Cognitive computing is primarily a marketing term indicating a computing service that is able to understand, reason and learn from the data it is supplied with. In essence, it is the application of machine learning and artificial intelligence to data processing. IBM is the flag bearer for cognitive computing. Presumably, it wanted a term that differentiated its Watson cloud based service from the ocean of other such services. IBM has its own definition of cognitive computing, cited below [8]:

Cognitive computing refers to next-generation information systems that understand, reason, learn, and interact. These systems do this by continually building knowledge and learning, understanding natural language, and reasoning and interacting more naturally with human beings than traditional programmable systems.

IBM's volatile, often science-fiction-like allegations have provoked serious criticism (see e.g. Schank [23]) . Independently from IBM's way Cognitive computing has its history, see for a brief state of the art Gutierrez-Garcia and López-Neri [15]. The notion of Cognitive computing appeared in Schank [22], where natural language understanding and knowledge structures were in the focus. e structures were in the focus.

Valiant [25] defined cognitive computing as *a discipline that links together neurobiology, cognitive psychology and artificial intelligence.* Brasil et al. [6] state that cognitive computing is *a collection of emerging technologies inspired by the biological processing of information in the nervous system, human reasoning, decision making, and natural selection.*

Today, Cognitive computing refers to the ability of automated systems to handle conscious, critical, logical, attentive, reasoning modes of thought. Semantic computing facilitates and automates the cognitive processes involved in defining, modelling, translating, transforming, and querying the deep meanings of words, phrases, and concepts. This claim is very similar to that of AI.

Therefore, Cognitive computing faces the same challenges that AI does. Cognitive computing aims to simulate human thought processes and mimic the way human brain works, addressing complex situations are characterized by ambiguity and uncertainty. AI aims to perform operations analogous to learning and decision making in humans. Intelligent personal assistants can recognize voice commands and queries, respond with information, or take desired actions quickly, efficiently, and effectively.

Today the main difference between Cognitive computing and AI is the following:

1. AI aims to model various functions of human intelligence with different levels of detail and abstraction, where computer is one of the modelling means but very often the most important one, i.e. intelligence is in the focus while,
2. Cognitive computing aims to model human thought processes and simulate the hypothetical way the human brain works, i.e. computing is in the focus.

The fundamental shortcoming of the two areas is that neither has a uniform system of concepts, theoretical and methodological foundations. Instead, both consist of a conglomerate of technologies and methods. For example, Cognitive computing would also need a unified computational theory that should be developed with specific tools and methods that support the modelling of the main features of cognizing and thinking processes. However, such theory does not exist as yet, though there had been some attempts, see e.g. Amir [3].

At the same time there is a complex approach to provide a theoretical framework for cognitive computing together with some advances in the study of cognitive computing theories and methodologies in cognitive informatics, soft computing, and computational intelligence, see Wang [27] and [28]. This approach provides conceptual and behavioural models of cognitive computing. It also introduces mathematical tools such as inference algebra and denotational mathematics to deal with the design and implementation of cognitive computing systems.

Note Wang [27] defines Cognitive computing as the conglomerate of *more intelligent technologies beyond imperative and autonomic computing, which embodies major natural intelligence behaviours of the brain such as thinking, inference, learning, and perceptions.*

However, it is important to emphasize that the formal modelling of the cognitive processes aims to mimic the fundamental mechanisms of the brain. This approach develops a model for the brain architecture called Layered Reference Model of the Brain (LRMB), see Wang [26]. This model formally and rigorously explains the functional mechanisms and cognitive processes of the natural intelligence. A comprehensive and coherent set of mental processes and their relationships is identified in LRMB, that encompasses 37 cognitive processes at six layers known as the sensation, memory, perception, action, meta cognitive, and higher cognitive layers from the bottom-up. The modelling tools are computers. Therefore this approach leads to the area where the processes of human intelligence are to be modelled by the use of computers. This is the area of computational mind. Computationalism is the main way of seeing the cognitive processes. Computationalism is a family of theories about the mechanisms of cognition. The main relevant evidence for testing computational theories comes from neuroscience, though psychology and AI are relevant, too. Computationalism comes in many versions, which continue to guide competing research programs in philosophy of mind as well as psychology and neuroscience. Computation theoretic approach is grounded in the idea that the mind, in many ways works like a digital computer; the mind is parsing internal representations (symbols) in algorithmic ways.

In order to appropriately use the notion of computing it is important to clarify its nature. Computation is an ambiguous concept and computer scientists, philosophers and cognitive scientists who use the concept can contest some claim using it and do not realise they are not actually in disagreement with each other, even though it looks as if they were. For a deep and detailed analysis of the notion of computing we refer to Fresco [10].

Moreover, instead of going into detail review of the main approaches to the computation theory of mind we refer to some good works that represent the current state of the art in this area, such as Ivancevic [17], Milkowski [20] and Piccinini [21].

1.3 What We Offer

Our aim is to develop a theoretically and methodologically well founded theory of AI, where this abbreviation means Amplifier for Intelligence. This AI will be able to act as genuine problem-solving companion understanding and responding to complex problem situations. This AI system will be able to act either as a partner system for cooperative functioning with a human agent or as an autonomous cognitive system for a well-defined problem area. As to become a cooperative partner for human agents, the system has to function very similarly to humans. e.g., it should be able to communicate and understand natural language, reason in a compatible way, learn from its experience, etc. AI will be able to cognize the environment and itself including the co-operative partner. Namely, this AI will be able to self-reflection.

The cognizing activity may run on a wide scale from learning objects, events till discovering various tendencies and regularities. This expected activity would realise the data $\rightarrow$ information $\rightarrow$ knowledge transformation and processing at different computation levels. Special attention will be devoted to the knowledge change and management that results during the data $\rightarrow$ information $\rightarrow$ knowledge transformation and processing.

The long-term vision is to develop a theoretically well-founded, coherent, integrated theory, technology and design methodology for a new computation paradigm – the so-called **CO**gnitive **I**ntelligence co-**O**perating **S**ystem (*COIOS*). *COIOS* supports Collaborative Intelligence, where humans and AI systems are joining their abilities. Therefore, in our case AI will be a symbiosis rather, instead of a replacement.

Unlike traditional computers within the von Neumann paradigm, COIOS-systems will be able to interpret and gain novel insights from data, solve problems and make decisions without explicit algorithmic instructions from humans. Instead of being programmed to perform pre-defined tasks, they will act as genuine problem-solving companions able to understand and respond to complex problem situations. Unlike data-centric processing of the traditional computers COIOS analyses data and processes information in a cognitive way and deals with knowledge in a goal-oriented way. Essentially this processing targets the reduction of the uncertainty of a problem situation of ignorance.

According to the proposed vision COIOS-systems take problem situations with various uncertainties as their input, and they resolve or decrease these uncertainties via cognitive reasoning, without relying on predefined problem-solving algorithms known in advance. Bearing this in mind COIOS will realise a reasoning-based, uncertainty-driven, upper-level computation.

To achieve our goal we follow a methodology triangle which consists of a conceptual-philosophical, a system theoretical and a logical-mathematical component. In the proposed approach computing will also play a fundamental role in both system-theoretic and logical-mathematical methodological components. The conceptual-philosophical component provides a formal epistemology with cognizing agents and ontology characterising the world to be cognized. Formal epistemology deals with data analysis, information extraction and knowledge acquisition with respect to an actual problem situation and the active cognizing agent. System-theoretic component provides the main principles for the organisation of cognizing processes, which are controlled by directed thinking. Directed thinking is goal-oriented and connected with a cognizing agent's problem solving activity.

It will be developed by the use of category theory, which provides an excellent frame for defining all notions necessary for elaborating a universal theory for computing, specification, cognitive reasoning, information, knowledge and there various combinations. The foundation theory is provided by the use of so-called constitutions, which form the mathematical basis for cognitive computation. The logical foundation will be developed as a special constitution.

Two constructive versions of set theory will be provided:

1. *clFSA* theory of finite sets with atoms and classes,
2. *cclFSA* theory of finite sets with atoms, classes and co-classes.

It is shortly described how *clFSA* permits to describe the entire traditional computation theory including e.g. program semantics, computation power of various programming languages, various programming paradigms like instructional, declarative programming and program specification. It is shown how *cclFSA* can support the description of the programs that use metadata called information and knowledge in a strong mathematical frame.

It is shown how various specific approaches such as granular programming or probabilistic programming can be represented in the proposed approach.

In a general setting, the mathematical theory provides an important method to extend a given theory according to specific needs. This method is the inductive and co-inductive extension in constitutions.

By the use of the proposed mathematical tools it is shown how cognitive reasoning can be handled in the proposed logical-mathematical framework. The main specificities of cognitive reasoning for cognitive computing are connected with the possibility to handle

1. The dynamic nature of the reasoning-based cognitive computation processes. The dynamic characterisation of the cognitive computation processes will be based on the representation of a cognitive reasoning process as a motion from ignorance to knowledge.
2. Spatial strategies, which permit to combine data driven statistical and cognitive data processing with the logic based modification calculi.
3. The *semantic* or *contentual* aspects of reasoning, whereas traditional instructional and declarative programming articulate statements inferentially, according only to their shape, without regard to reference. A referential reasoning is proposed, which is based on a special dual (semantic-syntactic) approach, which uses a set of axioms, which entirely and uniquely describes the semantic structure. The latter is considered as a model of our initial knowledge about the subject domain.
4. Indeterminacy and temporal contradictions of the cognitive computation processes in contrast to correctness of traditional instructional and declarative programs. A special formal approach can be provided to deal with the logical contradictions.
5. It provides a scientifically well-founded general approach that possesses methods and tools for modelling, designing and generating information processing responsible for the formation of cognitive processes of artificial cognitive systems. The proposed approach, at the same time, provides an innovative logical foundation for the entire area of cognitive reasoning and it provides support for cognitive system development at the following three levels of abstraction: conceptual, formal, and realisational levels.

Cognitive computing processes will be defined using situations, infons and information. However, the well-known constructions of situations, infons and information (see e.g. Barwise [5] or Devlin [9]) are used in a modified way, which will be formalised by the use of the proposed methods of extension. Here Cognition Kernel will be one of the main constructs, which generalises (i) the information theory and the corresponding data analysis together with a referential reasoning system, and (ii) the multilevel organisation of situation related information and knowledge management processes. Thus Cognitive Kernel will provide an adequate framework to handle the data → information → knowledge transformation and processing. Cognitive computing is defined by the use of Cognition Kernel.

2   The Mathematical Foundation

Considering the formalism used in the present paper we first of all assume that the reader is familiar with the basics of set theory and with a basic course on mathematical logic. Moreover, reading Sect. 2 also requires familiarity with a basic course in category theory. However, the reader not familiar with the latter can avoid Sect. 2 and can read the paper as a constructive specification theory based on the theory of finite sets which uses a special first order language as a specification language.

2.1   Constitution Theory

The basic foundational construct is the so-called constitution theory, which provides a logical and category theoretical frame for the development of the cognitive computation theory within the framework of the proposed approach. The first order logic provides the operative tool-set for the constitution theory. Compact constitutions form an important class, which provides the foundation for (i) descriptive theory to describe and investigate various aspects of costructivity necessary for any type of computations, (ii) specification theory to provide a framework for specifying computational objects.

Definition 1. *A **pre-constitution** $\mathbb{P}$ is a pair (Uni, Cons) where*

1. Uni is a category.
2. Cons is a subcategory of Uni such that $Ob\,Cons = Ob\,Uni$.
3. For any diagram

where $c \in Mor\,Cons$ there exists its colimit

*such that c' also belongs to Mor Cons. This property is called **hierarchy persistence** property of the pre-constitution $\mathbb{P}$.*

Example 1. Let *First* denote the category of all first order theories and theory morphisms between them. A morphism $Th_1 \rightarrow Th_2$ is called conservative iff it is a composition of a renaming map and of a conservative extension in the original sense. Let *FCons* denote the subcategory of *First* generated by the class of all conservative theory morphisms. It is an easy exercise using Craig interpolation theorem to prove that the pair (*First, FCons*) is a pre-constitution, further on be denoted as $\mathbb{FOL}$.

Example 2. The following logical systems satisfy the Craig interpolation property and hence their theories with the conservative extensions form a pre-constitution:

- classical first order logic;
- classical higher-order logic;
- ω-logic;
- intuitionist first order logic;
- intuitionist type theory;
- classical temporal logic;
- intuitionist temporal logic.

Example 3. In Burstall, Goguen [7] introduced the notion of institution to give a categorical-theoretical approach to model theory. For an institution can be defined the interpolation property as well. It can easily prove that institutions with interpolation property form a pre-constitution.

Example 4. (For details see Gergely, Ury [12]) It is well-know that a Cartesian-closed category having a subobject classifier is called topos. A topos form a pre-constitution. Moreover if *Uni* is an arbitrary finitely cocomplete category within which partial maps are representable then (*Uni, Mon(Uni)*) is a pre-constitution. Accordingly a famous theorem partial maps in topoi are representable. For details see Gergely, Ury [12]

Definition 2. *A* **constitution** $\mathfrak{L}$ *on a pre-constitution* $\mathbb{P} = (Uni, Cons)$ *is a function* $\mathfrak{L}$ *from Uni to the category Mor(Uni) such that:*

1. *if Th is an object of Uni then* $\mathfrak{L}(Th)$ *is a conservative morphism over Th called the* **superstructure** *of Th;*
2. *if f is a morphism then* $\pi_1(\mathfrak{L}(f)) = f$*;*
3. *for all* $Th \in Obj(Uni)$ *the following diagram is a colimit with respect to* $(\mathfrak{L}(Th), f)$ *where:*

$$
\begin{array}{ccc}
\bullet & \xrightarrow{\;\pi_2(\mathfrak{L}(f))\;} & \bullet \\
{\scriptstyle \mathfrak{L}(Th)}\Big\uparrow & & \Big\uparrow{\scriptstyle \mathfrak{L}(Th')} \\
Th & \xrightarrow{\;f\;} & Th'
\end{array}
$$

Definition 3. *Let* (*Uni, Cons*) *be a pre-constitution. A constitution* $\mathfrak{L}$ *on it is said to be* **perfect for an object** $Th \in Ob\ Uni$ *iff there is a morphism* red_{Th} *such that*

$$(\mathfrak{L}(cod(\mathfrak{L}(Th))), red_{Th})$$

is a projection system, i.e. the diagram below commute:

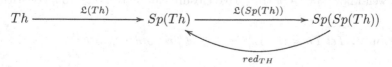

$$
Th \xrightarrow{\;\;\mathfrak{L}(Th)\;\;} Sp(Th) \xrightarrow{\;\;\mathfrak{L}(Sp(Th))\;\;} Sp(Sp(Th))
$$
$$
red_{TH}
$$

where $Sp(Th)$ and $Sp(Sp(Th))$ is the codomain of $\mathfrak{L}(Th)$ and $\mathfrak{L}(\mathfrak{L}(Th))$, respectively. $Sp(Th)$ is called the **superstructure** *of Th.*

Definition 4. *A constitution $\mathfrak{L}$ on a pre-constitution $\mathbb{P} = (Uni, Cons)$ is compact iff for all object of $Th \in Ob\ Uni$ $\mathfrak{L}$ is perfect for Th.*

Definition 5. *Fix a pre-constitution $\mathbb{P} = (Uni, Cons)$. Let $C(\mathbb{P})$ be the following category:*

$ObC(\mathbb{P}) \rightleftharpoons \{\mathfrak{L} \mid \mathfrak{L}\ is\ a\ constitution\ on\ \mathbb{P}\}$
$Mor(C(\mathbb{P})) \rightleftharpoons \{F : \mathfrak{L}_1 \to \mathfrak{L}_2 \mid F : Obj(Uni) \to Mor(Uni)\ such\ that\ \mathfrak{L}_1(Th) \circ F(Th) = \mathfrak{L}_2(Th)\}$.

The last condition in the definition of $Mor(C(\mathbb{P}))$ means that the following diagram commutes:

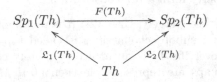

$$Sp_1(Th) \xrightarrow{\ F(Th)\ } Sp_2(Th)$$
$$\mathfrak{L}_1(Th) \qquad \mathfrak{L}_2(Th)$$
$$Th$$

Theorem 1. *Let $\mathbb{P} = (Uni, Cons)$ be a pre-constitution and let $\mathfrak{L}$ be a constitution on it. Let us suppose that Uni has countable coproducts. There is a unique (up to natural isomorphism) constitution $\mathfrak{L}'$ and a morphism $F : \mathfrak{L} \to \mathfrak{L}'$ such that*

1. *$\mathfrak{L}'$ is compact;*
2. *for any $G : \mathfrak{L} \to \mathfrak{L}''$ with closed $\mathfrak{L}''$ there is a factorization through F; i.e. there is a (unique) H such that* $L \xrightarrow{\ F\ } L'$ *commutes in $C(\mathbb{P})$.*

$$L \xrightarrow{\ F\ } L'$$
$$G \searrow \qquad \swarrow H$$
$$L''$$

3. *This $\mathfrak{L}'$ is denoted as $\mathfrak{L}^*$*

2.2   *FOL*-Based Constitutions

In this subsection we define a compact constitution $\mathbb{Y}$ called **fixed-point constitution**. The superstructures of this constitution add least and greatest fixed-point to each monotone operators. From now we will work in the first-order pre-constitution $\mathbb{FOL}$. A constitution called *FOL*-based if it is a constitution on a full subcategory of $\mathbb{FOL}$. In the sequel we give some examples for such constitution usable in computing, AI and cognitive computing.

The well-know notion of transitive closure can be turned into a constitution.

Definition 6. *Let $Th = (\sigma, Ax)$ be a fixed first-order theory.*

1. *A first-order operator in Th is a triple (Φ, R, X) written as $\Phi(R, X)$ where R is an X-type new relation symbol, Φ is a $\sigma \cup \{R\}$-type formula free variables of which belongs to X. The set of variables X is called the type of $\Phi(R, X)$*
2. *$\Phi(R, X)$ is called monotone iff for any new X-type relation symbols S*

$$Ax \vdash (\forall X \; R(X) \rightarrow S(X)) \rightarrow \forall X \; (\Phi(R, X) \rightarrow \Phi(S, X))$$

3. *For any $\psi(X)$ let*

$$\tilde{\Phi}(\psi)(X) \text{ be the formula } \Phi(R, X)[\psi/R].$$

It is clear that $\tilde{\Phi}$ is a function of type $Form_\sigma(X) \rightarrow Form_\sigma(X)$
4. *Let us denote Δ_{Th} be denote the set of all **monotone first-order operator** in Th.*

Let $\top_X$ and $\perp_X$ be denote the X-type truth and falsity, respectively. If a first-order operator $\Phi(R, X)$ is monotone in Th then we got an infinite chain

$$\perp_X \rightarrow \tilde{\Phi}(\perp_X) \rightarrow \tilde{\Phi}(\tilde{\Phi}(\perp_X)) \ldots \ldots \tilde{\Phi}(\tilde{\Phi}(\top_X)) \rightarrow \tilde{\Phi}(\top_X) \rightarrow \top_X$$

where each individual implication is provable in Th.

Definition 7. *$Th = (\sigma, Ax)$ be a fixed first-order theory and fix a set $\mathcal{F}$ of monotone first-order operators.*

1. *Let $\tilde{\Phi} \in \mathcal{F}$ be an X-type monotone first-order operation. A formula $\psi(X)$ is called a left fixed-point of $\tilde{\Phi}$ iff $Ax \vdash \tilde{\Phi}(\psi) \rightarrow \psi$ and called a right fixed-point of $\tilde{\Phi}$ iff $Ax \vdash \psi \rightarrow \tilde{\Phi}(\psi)$.*
2. *For any $\tilde{\Phi} \in \mathcal{F}$ let add two new X-type relation symbols Φ^μ and Φ^ν together the following axioms:*
   (a) $\tilde{\Phi}(\Phi^\mu) \rightarrow \Phi$ and $\Phi \rightarrow \tilde{\Phi}(\Phi^\mu)$
   (b) for an arbitrary σ-type formula $\psi(X) : (\psi \rightarrow \tilde{\Phi}(\psi)) \rightarrow (\Phi^\nu \rightarrow \psi)$
   (c) for an arbitrary σ-type formula $\psi(X) : (\tilde{\Phi}(\psi) \rightarrow \psi) \rightarrow (\psi \rightarrow \Phi^\mu)$
   (d) Let $Ind(\mathcal{F})$ denote this new set of axioms.

Theorem 2. *Let $Th = (\sigma, Ax)$ be a fixed first-order theory. For an arbitrary $\mathcal{F} \subset \Delta_{Th}$ the axiom system $Ax \cup Ind(\mathcal{F})$ is conservative over Ax. It means that there is a constitution Ind on the pre-constitution $\mathbb{FOL}$ which renders each Th the conservative extension $Ax \cup Ind(\Delta_{Th})$*

Let us suppose that the restriction of first-order operations are categorical. It means that for all Th there is a $Th_{\mathcal{F}} \subset \Delta_{Th}$ given in such a way that a theory morphism $Th^1 \rightarrow Th^2$ transfer $Th^1_{\mathcal{F}}$ into a subset of $Th^2_{\mathcal{F}}$. If so then there is a constitution $Ind_{\mathcal{F}}$ on the pre-constitution $\mathbb{FOL}$ which renders each Th the conservative extension $Th_{Ax} \cup Ind(Th_{\mathcal{F}})$. One of the most well-known example of such a restriction is as follows. For any σ let us consider the positive existential formulas of the form $\psi(X, X')$ where ψ free variables as stated and X is a copy of X'. Any such formulas generate a monotone first-order operators as $\exists U R(U) \wedge \psi(U, X)$. For any Th let $T\mathcal{R}$ let denote the set of all monotone first-order operator defined in such a way. Let $Tran$ be denote this constitution on the pre-constitution $\mathbb{FOL}$.

Theorem 3. *$Tran$ is a compact constitution on the pre-constitution $\mathbb{FOL}$.*

2.3 Inductive and Coinductive Extensions in Constitutions

It is obvious that it is not enough to just add fixed-points to underlying theory. Let $Th = (\sigma, Ax)$ be a first order theory. There are many situations when we need to add new types, functions and relations to the original similarity type σ. All these additional symbols we can collect into a new similarity type θ. Of course the similarity type has not, but the axiom system Ax has to improve new axioms and axiom schemas. If these axioms are short to inductive and coinductive ones then we can formulate a theorem similar to Theorem 1.

In details. Let us fix a similarity type η. Let $\mathbb{FOL}(\eta)$ denote the pre-constitution containing only those theories (σ, Ax) where $\eta \subset \sigma$. Let ζ be a new similarity type and let Eq and Eq^c be a set of quasi-equations and quasi-coequations, respectively based on the similarity type $\zeta + \eta$.

Theorem 4. *Let η, ζ and Eq, Eq^c as in above. There is a least (up to natural isomorphism) constitution denoted by $\mathbb{Y}(\eta, \zeta, Eq, Eq^c)$*

1. *$\mathbb{Y}(\eta, \zeta, Eq, Eq^c)$ is compact,*
2. *All superstructures satisfy $Eq + Eq^c$,*
3. *All monotone operators in each superstructures have least and greatest fixed points,*
4. *If $\mathfrak{L}$ is such a constitution on $\mathbb{FOL}(\eta)$ that satisfies the previous assumptions then there is a unique (up to natural isomorphism) morphism (up to natural isomorphism) $\mathbb{Y}(\eta, \zeta, Eq, Eq^c) \to \mathfrak{L}$.*

For any $Th \in Obj\mathbb{FOL}(\eta)$ the superstructure of Th, i.e. the codomain of the morphism $\mathbb{Y}(\eta, \zeta, Eq, Eq^c)(Th)$ is called **canonical d-inductive extension of** Th (d for double because extension was constructed by using both equations and coequations. If Eq^c is empty we simply say inductive extension or if we want to emphasize that Eq^c is empty we say **simple inductive extension**. If $\mathfrak{L}$ is such a constitution that satisfies the first three assumption of the theorem then $\mathfrak{L}$ is also called d-inductive extension of the extension system (η, ζ, Eq, Eq^c).

In Subsect. 3.2 we demonstrate that for a large part of computing theory the simple inductive extensions are sufficient. Coequations need to speak about cognitive aspects of computation.

Remark 1. There is a clear definition of quasi-equations. Let σ be an arbitrary similarity type. A σ-type formulas in the form $\tau_1 = \tau_2$ where $\tau_i (i = 1, 2)$ are σ terms are called **equation**. A formula in the form

$$\bigwedge_{j=1..n} e_j \to e$$

where $e_j (j = 1..n), e$ are σ-type equations is called a **quasi-equation**. If n = 0 then we get back the notion of equation. See Grätzer [14]. Unfortunately there is no such an elegant and easily usable definition for *quasi-coequations*.

One of the main advantages of the d-inductive extensions is, that there are universal ones. Let η, ζ be fixed and let $\mathbb{EQ}(\eta, \zeta)$ denote the set of all $(\eta + \zeta)$-type equations. Let $d\nabla(\eta, \zeta)$ be the category of all d-inductive extensions on (η, ζ, Eq, Eq^c)

where $Eq, Eq^c \subset \mathbb{EQ}_{(\eta, \zeta)}$. The morphisms are the natural transformations between the functors. Also let $\nabla(\eta, \zeta)$ be the category of all simple inductive extensions on $(\eta, \zeta, Eq, \emptyset)$

Theorem 5. *Let η, ζ be arbitrary but fixed similarity types.*

- *Both $d\nabla(\eta, \zeta)$ and $\nabla(\eta, \zeta)$ are really categories;*
- *$d\nabla(\eta, \zeta)$ has terminal objects. Any terminal object of $d\nabla(\eta, \zeta)$ is called* **d-universal extension** *on (η, ζ).*
- *$\nabla(\eta, \zeta)$ has terminal objects. Any terminal object of $\nabla(\eta, \zeta)$ is called* **simple universal extension** *or just* **universal extension** *on (η, ζ).*

2.4 Constitutional Set Theories

Two versions of set theory are provided by the modification of the von Neumann-Bernays-Gödel set theory. The modification augments the set theoretic operations with fixed points of monotone operators. Namely, the so obtained set theories are as follows:

- *cHF* is a compact constitution where superstructures are the finite sets with atoms and classes augmented with least fixed points of positive existential operators (*cl* stands for classes),
- *clFSA* is a compact constitution where superstructures are the finite sets with atoms and classes augmented with least fixed points of monotone operators (*cl* stands for classes),
- *cclFSA* (*ccl* stands for classes and coclasses) a compact constitution where superstructures are the finite sets with atoms, classes and co-classes augmented with least and greatest fixed points of monotone operators.

It is shortly explained how *clFSA* permits to describe the entire traditional computation theory including e.g. program semantics, computation power of various programming languages, various programming paradigms like instructional, declarative programming and program specification, see e.g. Ury, Gergely [24]. For a short description of how *clFSA* looks like see 7.1. It is clear that for a fixed similarity type σ and the axiom system Ax the new axioms of $clFSA(\sigma, Ax)$ depends only on σ. Let $cFSA_\sigma$ denote this set of axioms.

The unifying theories developed in [16] can build using *cHF* instead of ZFC.

Note that the use of the above two set theories is useful because they are universal as can be seen in the following theorem.

Theorem 6. *Let η, ζ be arbitrary but fixed similarity types.*

- *$clFSA(\eta)$ is a simple universal extension on (η, ζ)*
- *$cclFSA(\eta)$ is a d-universal extension on (η, ζ).*

Remark 2. We emphasize that there was not any assumption "how large" is ζ or the set of equations. However we suppose that both of them are recursively enumerable then $clFSA(\eta)$ and $cclFSA(\eta)$ are also recursively enumerable.

3   Examples

3.1   Specifications as Constitutions

Given a pre-constitution $\mathbb{P} = (Uni, Cons)$ we can think that a specification itself defines the object perfectly. Later on we shall see that the elements of $Ob(Uni)$ are generally a set of algebraic equations or formulas. However, in our definition the notion of a specification is in an abstract form without any fixed meaning. Whatever we can say about the specifications it is identical with the properties of the category Uni.

One of the most important properties of the specifications is that they can be interpreted by each other. In the case of algebraic and logical specification theories these interpretations turn out to be homomorphisms or theory presentations. However, in our definition the notion of interpretation is as abstract as those of the specifications. See in Maibaum [19].

Definition 8. *Let $\mathbb{P} = (Uni, Cons)$ be a pre-constitution and let $\mathfrak{L}$ be a constitution on it. An L-refinement is a pair of morphisms (f, c) as shown below iff there are two morphisms c', d' such that if*

$$Th_1 \xrightarrow{\ f\ } Th_2^c$$
$$\uparrow c$$
$$Th_2$$

then c splits such that

1. the diagram below commutes:

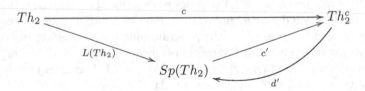

2. and (c', d') is a projection pair.

Theorem 7. *Let $\mathbb{P} = (Uni, Cons)$ be a pre-constitution and let $\mathfrak{L}$ be a constitution on it. $\mathfrak{L}$-refinements are closed under composition iff $\mathfrak{L}$ is a compact constitution.*

An abstract specification theory is developed by the use of category theory, which allows the characterization of specification languages and the provision of the necessary conditions to operate with specifications, e.g. to put them together or to refine or to modularize them. Here only shown the condition necessary for stepwise refinement of specifications is shown. A specification classical first order language which can be used as a specification one. As it can be seen this theory is appropriate to support formal specifications with a "constructive" definition theory. It is shown how the specification language Z can be developed in this set theoretical framework so that it becomes more transparent from semantical point of view and more useable due to the "constructive" fixed point theory. Moreover, we develop the constructive version of the specification theory by using logic programming ideas. First, logic programming is defined for the abstract specification theory and then logic programming is developed in the proposed set theoretic framework.

One of the desired properties of a specification theory is the correct handling of the hierarchical specification. In our frame any interpretation $c : P \to S$ can be considered as a hierarchical specification. Specification P contains the so called primitive specification part and by using c and S we add some extra to this primitive specification part. It is a natural assumption with respect to the hierarchical specifications that any interpretation of the primitive part can be extended to an interpretation of the entire hierarchical specification. It means that any $f : P \to P'$ can be extended to a commutative diagram below:

$$
\begin{array}{ccc}
S & \xrightarrow{\ f'\ } & S' \\
\uparrow{\scriptstyle c} & & \uparrow{\scriptstyle c'} \\
P & \xrightarrow[\ f\ ]{} & P'
\end{array}
$$

However, in most cases initial and terminal specifications do not exist at all. This is the reason why we restrict the hierarchical specifications to conservative ones. Definition 8 (1) axiomatizes the existence of the initial specification for conservative hierarchical specifications.

3.2   Computing Theory

3.2.1   Instructional Programs

Intuitively it is evident that the main problem in defining the IO-relation of a program is connected with the definition of program iteration. Since e.g. denotational semantics renders a relation to a program, the reflexive and transitive closure of this relation corresponds to iteration. We are interested in internalizing, thus we deal with the formulas defining the relations. Therefore the main question is whether the reflexive and transitive closure of an arbitrary formula is definable. It is an easy exercise to prove that using least fixed-points the denotation of the **while** programs can be defined. However, Hoare, Jifeng [16] shows that the correct definition of the denotation of recursive procedure calls requires the greatest fixed-points.

Programs operate on their data environments. If we are interested in the change caused by the execution of a program in its environment then the input-output semantics defined as a binary relation on data sequences, is suitable. A great variety of program properties are connected with the relational semantics, e.g. partial correctness, quasi-total correctness, pseudo-total correctness, etc. See e.g. Gergely, Ury [13].

3.2.2   Logic Programs

The traditional way of programming according to Wirth can be represented as programs = algorithms + data structures (see Wirth [29]). An important combination of traditional programming with the declarative one can take place in the case of data declaration. The latter means that data structure component of the Wirth's characterization of programs should be given by declarative tools, i.e. by the use of logic. In this case programs = algorithm + logic + realisation, where logic may consists of functional and relational parts. The logic component allows to define abstract data types which by the use of realization define the constructive model over which the execution of algorithms, i.e. the computation takes place.

Logic programming takes place in models constructed according to the logic programs. We suppose that a similarity type δ given. Any logic program contains definitions of new relation symbols. The goal of a logic program, i.e. the question which one should be answered reflects these new relations, see e.g. Gergely, Szőts [11]. Let us fix a rich enough similarity type η and a constructive interpretation $\mu : \delta \to cTerm_\eta$. We consider how we can define relations new with respect to μ by the use of logical program's approach.

Since we aim to develop logic programming in *cclFSA*, so the constructivity should be defined with respect to this system axioms. Intuitive meaning of a *constructive* model is that any component of that is computable in *cclFSA*. To define the required notion of constructive model first we have to define an appropriate notion of model, and the notion of computability over this model.

If η a given similarity type and Ax is an η-type set of formulas let $cFSA_\eta(Ax)$ denote the axioms of the superstructure $cclFSA(\eta, Ax)$. If Ax is empty we simply write $cFSA_\eta$.

Definition 9. *Let σ be a fixed similarity type. A function $\mu : \sigma \to cTerm_\eta$ is called an* **interpretation** *of σ in $cFSA_\eta$. An interpretation η* **generates a σ-type model** *in a model $\mathbf{V} \in Mod(cFSA_\eta)$ iff the followings hold in $\mathbf{V}$:*

(a) for all $s \in sort(\sigma)$, $\eta(s)$ is a non-empty class in $\mathbf{V}$;
(b) for all $\rho \in rel(\sigma)$, $\mu(\rho)$ is a subclass of $\top\{\mu(s_i)|i = 1, \ldots, n\}$, where $\rho : s_1, \ldots, s_n$ is the arity of ρ;
(c) for all $f \in fun(\sigma)$, $\mu(f)$ is a functional class of the form $\top\{\mu(s_i)|i = 1, \ldots, n\} \to \mu(s)$, where $f : s_1, \ldots, s_n \to s$ is the arity of f.

We say that μ generates a σ-type model in $cFSA_\eta$ iff for all $\mathbf{V} \in Mod(cFSA_\eta)$ μ generates a σ-type model in $\mathbf{V}$. The σ-type model $\mathbf{A}$ generated by μ in $\mathbf{V}$ is denoted by $\mathbf{V}(\mu)$.

Proposition 1. *Let μ be an interpretation. There is a class formula $IM?(\mu)$ which is valid in a model iff μ generates a model in that set-theory, i.e.*

$$\mathbf{V} \models IM?(\mu) \text{ iff } \mathbf{V}(\mu) \text{ exists.}$$

An interpretation $\mu : \sigma \to cTerm_\eta$ is said to be **correct** *in $\mathbf{V}$ iff the model $\mathbf{V}(\mu)$ exists.*

Let us see how to restrict the investigation of formulas to a given interpretation only.

Definition 10. *Let $\mu : \sigma \to cTerm_\eta$ be fixed and let $\varphi \in cForm_\sigma$. Let us define the **relativization** φ^μ of φ along μ by induction on the complexity of φ in the following way.*

(A) First for any term $\tau \in Term_\sigma$ let us define a relation $R_\tau(x, y^\tau)$ (where $x = var(\tau)$ and y^τ is a new variable) which expresses the fact that $\tau(x) = y$:

- *if $\tau = x$ is an s-sorted variable then $R_\tau(x, y^\tau) \leftrightharpoons x = y^\tau \wedge x \in \mu(s)$;*
- *if $\tau = f(x_1, \ldots, x_n)$ and $f : s_1, \ldots, s_n \to s$ then $R_\tau(x, y^\tau) \leftrightharpoons \bigwedge\{R_{\tau i}(x, y^{\tau i}) | i \in n\} \wedge (y^{\tau 1}, \ldots, y^{\tau n}, u^\tau) \in \mu(f) \wedge y^\tau \in \mu(s)$.*

We remark that $R_\tau(x, y)$ implies that $y \in \mu()s$ where $s = sort(\tau)$.

(B)

- *if $\varphi = \rho(\tau_1, \ldots, \tau_n)$ then*
  $\rho^\mu \leftrightharpoons \exists y^{\tau 1} \ldots \exists y^{\tau n} \bigwedge\{R_{\tau i}(x, y^{\tau i}) | i \in n\} \wedge (y^{\tau 1}, \ldots, y^{\tau n}) \in \mu(\rho)$
- *if $\varphi = \neg \psi$ then $\varphi^\mu \leftrightharpoons \neg(\psi^\mu)$*
- *if $\varphi = \psi_1 \vee \psi_2$ then $\varphi^\mu \leftrightharpoons (\psi_1{}^\mu) \vee (\psi_2{}^\mu)$*
- *is $\varphi = \exists x \psi$ then $\varphi^\mu \leftrightharpoons \exists x(x \in \mu(s) \wedge (\psi^\mu))$, where $s = sort(x)$*

The following statement shows that relativization restricts the investigation of validity of formulas to the given interpretation.

Theorem 8. *Let $\mu : \sigma \to cTerm_\eta$ be an interpretation and let $\mathbf{V}(\mu)$ be the model generated by μ in $\mathbf{V}$. Let $\varphi \in cForm_\sigma$ and let $k \in Val(\mathbf{V}(\mu))$*

$$\mathbf{V}(\mu) \models \varphi[k] \text{ iff } \mathbf{V} \models \varphi^\mu[k]$$

Definition 11. *Let $\mu_\sigma : \sigma \to cV$ be a fixed injection. μ_σ is called the **canonical interpretation** of σ in $\mathbf{cFSA}_\eta$. Let φ^σ denote the relativization of φ along μ_σ.*

Definition 12. *Let $\mathbf{V} \models^\sigma \varphi$ denote the fact that a closed formula is true in every interpretation of σ in $\mathbf{V}$. If so we say that φ is **valid** in $\mathbf{V}$. Take $cFSA_\eta \models^\sigma \varphi$ iff for all $\mathbf{V} \in Mod(cFSA_\eta)$, $\mathbf{V} \models^\sigma \varphi$. If so we say that φ is **valid** in $\mathbf{cFSA}_\sigma$.*

Let us consider the main properties of this notion of validity. Let $\mu : \sigma \to cTerm_\eta$ be an arbitrary interpretation. Let $\mu = \mu_\sigma$ be a shorthand for the formula $\bigwedge\{\mu(l) = \mu_\sigma(l) | l \in \sigma\}$.

Theorem 9. *Let us suppose that φ is a closed σ-type formula. Let $\mathbf{V}$ be an arbitrary model of $cFSA_\eta$. Let $\mu : \sigma \to cTerm_\eta$ be an interpetation.*

(A) Let us suppose that u generates a model in $\mathbf{V}$. The followings are equivalent:

- *$\mathbf{V}(\mu) \models \varphi$;*
- *$\mathbf{V} \models \varphi^\mu$;*

$- Th(\mathbf{V}) + IM?(\mu_\sigma) + (\mu = \mu_\sigma) \models \varphi^\sigma.$

(B) $\mathbf{V} \models^\sigma \varphi$ iff $Th(\mathbf{V}) + IM?(\mu_\sigma) \models \varphi^\sigma$

(C) $cFSA_\eta \models^\sigma \varphi$ iff $cFSA_\eta + IM?(\mu_\sigma) \models \varphi^\sigma.$

Now we define the computability in $cFSA_\eta$ by the use of the theory of programs developed for the programming language P_η. The necessary notions used bellow can be found in Appendix 1.

Definition 13. *(A) Let C be a class in a model $\mathbf{V}$ of $cFSA_\eta$. C is called **computable in** $\mathbf{V}$ iff there is a program $p \in P_\eta$ such that*

$$C = dom\ Den_{\mathbf{V}}[\![p]\!]$$

*(B) A class C is called **enumerable in** $\mathbf{V}$ iff there is a computable surjection $\omega \to C$.*

*(C) The class C is called **p∃-definable in** $\mathbf{V}$ iff there is a term*

$$t \in cTerm\Sigma^+(\eta; \{D\})$$

such that $C = Yt$, i.e. C is the least fixed point of the equation $D = t(D)$.

Theorem 10. *Let $\mathbf{V}$ be a model of $cFSA_\eta$, and suppose that the class Atom $\leftrightharpoons \{x|\underline{atom}(x)\}$ is enumerable in $\mathbf{V}$. The p∃-definable, the enumerable and the computable classes are the same in $\mathbf{V}$.*

We remark that the assumption of Theorem 5.9 in most cases is true, e.g. if Atom is finite or equivalent with ω.

Theorem 11. *If Atom is enumerable in $\mathbf{V}$ then AC holds in $\mathbf{V}$.*

Definition 14. *An interpretation $\mu :\to cTerm_\eta$ is called **constructive in** $\mathbf{V}$ iff for all $l \in \sigma$, $\mu(l)$ is computable in $\mathbf{V}$.*

Example 5. Let σ contain the following symbols:

$0, 1 :\to d$
$+, \times : d, d \to d$

Let interpret these symbols in the 'usual' way:

$\mu(d) \leftrightharpoons \omega$
$\mu(0) \leftrightharpoons 0$
$\mu(1) \leftrightharpoons \{0\}$
$\mu(+) \leftrightharpoons \lambda x, y.\ x + y$
$\mu(\times) \leftrightharpoons \lambda x, y.\ x * y$

where $+$ and $*$ is the sum and product of natural numbers. It is clear that μ generates a model in $cFSA_\sigma$ and in any $\mathbf{V}$ it is constructive.

Example 6. From the point of view of functional programming it is a very interesting question whether a factor of a constructive model is constructive again. Consider the following simple example. Again let σ be as in 5.12. Take the following interpretation:

$\xi(d) \leftrightharpoons \omega \times \omega$

$\xi(0) \leftrightharpoons (0,0)$

$\xi(1) \leftrightharpoons (\{0\},0)$

$\xi(+) \leftrightharpoons \lambda(a,b),(c,d)\,.\,(a+c,b+d)$

$\xi(*) \leftrightharpoons \lambda(a,b),(c,d)\,.\,(ac+bd,ad+bc)$

Clearly ξ is a correct interpretation in any model of $cFSA_\sigma$. Moreover, ξ is clearly constructive.

Let us define the following equivalence on $\xi(d)$:

$$(a,b) \equiv (c,d) \text{ iff } a+d = b+c$$

One can check that *equiv* is a congruence relation on $\mathbf{V}(\xi)$. Clearly $\mathbf{V}(\xi)/\equiv$ is a model for integer numbers $(\underline{Z},0,1,+,*)$. It is a question whether $\mathbf{V}(\xi)/\equiv$ is constructive.

The following theorem gives an answer to this question.

Theorem 12. *Let $\mu : \sigma \to cTerm_\eta$ be a constructive and correct interpretation of σ in a model $\mathbf{V}$. Let us suppose that $\equiv$ is a decidable congruence relation on $\mathbf{V}(\eta)$, i.e. both $\equiv$ and its complement are computable in $\mathbf{V}$. Moreover, let us suppose that all the classes $\mu(s) \in sort\ \sigma$ are enumerable in $\mathbf{V}$. If so then $\mathbf{V}(\mu)/\equiv$ is constructive in $\mathbf{V}$.*

Now we can turn to prove the existence of $\mu/\equiv$. Take

$$\mu/\equiv (s) \leftrightharpoons \{x | x \in \mu(s) \wedge \forall y (\ulcorner y \urcorner < \ulcorner x \urcorner \to \neg y \equiv x)\}$$

By using the computability of $\ulcorner\ \urcorner$ and the decidability of $\equiv$ the right hand side of this equation is a $p\exists$ term in $cFSA_\eta$. Hence $\mu/\equiv$ is well defined on $sort(\sigma)$. Take

$$\mu/\equiv (\rho) \leftrightharpoons \{(x_1,\ldots,x_n) | \exists y_1,\ldots,\exists y_n \bigwedge x_i \equiv y_i \wedge \rho(y_1,\ldots,y_n)\}$$

$$\mu/\equiv (f) \leftrightharpoons$$

$$\{(x_1,\ldots,x_n,x) | \exists y_1,\ldots,\exists y_n, \exists y \bigwedge x_i \equiv y_i \wedge x \equiv y \wedge f(y_1,\ldots,y_n) = y\} \quad (1)$$

It is clear that $\mu/\equiv : \sigma \to cTerm_\eta$ is an interpretation. Since $\equiv$ is a congruence relation $\mu/\equiv$ is correct in $\mathbf{V}$. By using the enumerability of classes one can check that $\mu/\equiv$ is a computable relation.

Returning to the example it is easily provable that $\omega \times \omega$ is enumerable in $cFSA_\eta$ and of course $\equiv$ is decidable. It means that $\xi/\equiv$ exists and it is computable in any model of $cFSA_\eta$.

Definition 15. *Let σ be a similarity type. Let*

$$\Gamma_\sigma \leftrightharpoons \{P_s | s \in sort\ \sigma\} \cup \{P_f | f \in func\ \sigma\} \cup \{P_\rho | \rho \in rel\ \sigma\}$$

*be a fixed set of class variables. Any function $\Phi : \Gamma_\sigma \to cTerm\Sigma^+(\eta; \Gamma_\sigma)$ is called a **presentation of** σ in $\mathbf{cFSA}_\sigma$. A **presentation is correct** in a model $\mathbf{V}$ of $cFSA_\sigma$ if the interpretation $Y\Phi : \sigma \to cTerm_\eta$ is correct, i.e. if $\mathbf{V}(Y\Phi)$ exists.*

Theorem 13. *Let us suppose that Atom is enumerable in $\mathbf{V}$. Let Φ be a correct presentation of σ in $\mathbf{V}$. $V(Y\Phi)$ is a constructive model of σ in $\mathbf{V}$.*

It is clear that the models of $cFSA_\sigma$, within which Atom is enumerable, have significant properties. So we give the following definition:

Definition 16. *A model $\mathbf{V}$ of $cFSA_\sigma$ is called textbiconstructive iff Atom is enumerable in $\mathbf{V}$.*

Proposition 2. *'Atom is enumerable' is definable in $cFSA_\eta$.*

Proof. Let $U(x, y)$ be a universal computable relation with respect to the computable classes. 'Atom is enumerable' is expressible with the following class formula:

$$\exists x(\{y | U(x, y)\} = Atom)$$

$\square$

Theorem 14. *'Atom is enumerable' is independent from $cFSA_\eta$.*

Proof. Clearly $cFSA_\eta$ + 'Atom is enumerable' is a conservative extension of $cFSA_\eta$. Let A be an uncountable set and fix a standard model $\mathbf{V}$ in such a way that Atom in $\mathbf{V}$ is just A. One can check that

$$\mathbf{V} \models \neg \text{'Atom is enumerable'}.$$

We note, that by the downward Lövenheim-Skolem theorem there is also a computable $\mathbf{V}$ within which Atom is not enumerable. $\square$

Theorem 15 *(on the existence on constructive models). Let $\mathbf{V}$ be a constructive model of $cFSA_\eta$. In $\mathbf{V}$ the $p\exists$-definable and computable classes are the same and therefore any correct presentation $\Phi : \sigma \to cTerm_\eta$ generates a constructive model $\mathbf{V}(Y\Phi)$ of σ in $\mathbf{V}$.*

This theorem plays an important role in the forthcoming chapters.

Definition 17. *Let $\eta_1 \supset \eta$ and let $\mu : \eta_1 \to cTerm_\eta$ be such a correct interpretation of η_1 in $cFSA_\eta$ that for all $\mathbf{V} \in Mod(cFSA_\sigma)$ $\mathbf{V}(\mu) \restriction_\eta = \mathbf{V}$. Moreover let μ be constructive. In this case μ is called a **constructive extension of** $cFSA_\eta$.*

Theorem 16. *Let $\eta_2 \supset \eta_1 \supset \eta_0$ and μ_{i+1} be a constructive extension of $cFSA_{\eta i}$ $(i = 0, l)$. μ_2 is a constructive extension of $cFSA_{\eta 0}$.*

Definition 18. *Let R be a set of new relation symbols. A rule is of the form*

$$\rho(\tau_1, \ldots, \tau_2) \Leftarrow \varphi$$

where $\tau_i \in Term_{\eta 1}$, $\varphi \in p \exists (0, \delta \cup R)$.

*A logic program is a finite set of rules. A logic program u is called **well-formed** iff whenever u contains two rules of the form*

$$\rho(\tau_1{}^i, \ldots, \tau_{ni}{}^i) \Leftarrow \varphi_i \ (i = 1, 2)$$

then $\rho_1 = \rho_2 (\in R)$ implies $n_1 = n_2$ and $sort(\tau_j{}^1) = sort(\tau_j{}^2)$ $(j = 1, \ldots, n_1)$. Let $LP_\delta(R)$ denote the set of all well-formed logic programs.

Let $S = sort\ \delta$. Let S' be a copy of S with bijection ι. Define an S'-sorted similarity type σ_u for any $u \in LP_\eta(R)$. Take sort $\sigma_u \leftrightharpoons S'$. Define

$$rel\ \sigma_u \leftrightharpoons \{\rho \in R | \text{ there is a rule } \rho(\ldots) \Leftarrow \varphi \text{ in} u\} \cup rel\ \delta.$$

The arity of ρ is $\rho : \iota(s_1), \ldots, \iota(s_n)$ and u contains a rule of the form

$$\rho(\tau_1, \ldots, \tau_n) \Leftarrow \varphi$$

and for all $i = 1, \ldots, n$ $\iota_i = sort(\tau_i)$. Since u is well-formed, this definition of arity is correct. Let

$$func\ \sigma_u \leftrightharpoons func\ \delta.$$

Let $X \leftrightharpoons (x_1, \ldots, x_n)$. Let $X \in \Gamma$ be a shorthand for $\bigwedge \{x_i \in \Gamma_{si} | i \in n\}$, where s_i is the sort of x_i. Let $\varphi[\Gamma]$ denote the relativization of σ along $\mu_{\sigma u}$.

Definition 19. *Let $u \in LP(R)$ be a well-formed logic program. By using u we define a presentation $u^\wedge$ in the following way:*

(a) Let $\rho \in rel\ \sigma_u$. Take
  $u^\wedge(\rho) \leftrightharpoons$
   $\cup \{\{x | \exists y_1, \ldots, \exists y_n \bigwedge \{y_i = \tau_i | i \in n\} \wedge \varphi[\Gamma]\} | \rho(\tau_1, \ldots, \tau_n) \Leftarrow \varphi' \in u\}$
(b) $u^\wedge(s) \leftrightharpoons$
   $\cup \{\{x | \exists x_1, \ldots, \exists x_n\ x = x_i \bigwedge (x_1, \ldots, x_n) \in \Gamma_\rho\} | \rho \in rel_{\sigma n} sort\ x_i = s\}$
   $\cup \{\{f(x_1, \ldots, x_n) | X \in \Gamma\} | y \in func\ \sigma\ f : s'_1, \ldots, s'_n \to s\}$
(c) $u^\wedge(s) \leftrightharpoons$
   $\{(x_1, \ldots, x_n, y) | y = f(x_1, \ldots, x_n) \wedge X \in \Gamma\}$

where $f : s'_1, \ldots, s'_n \to s'$.

Proposition 3. *Let u be a well-formed logic program. Then $u^\wedge$ is a correct presentation with respect to μ.*

Definition 20. *Any logic program u generates a set of axioms Ax(u) which is called the* **logic generated by the logic program u** *in the following way:*

$$Ax(u) \leftrightharpoons \{\varphi \to \rho(\tau_1, \ldots, \tau_n) | \rho(\tau_1, \ldots, \tau_n) \Leftarrow \varphi' \in u\}.$$

Similarly, you can give another set of axioms which describes how u˄ was generated from the original sorts and functions. Let Gen(u˄) denote this fact. Namely if σ ⇋ σ_u then take:

$$Gen(u\hat{\ }) \leftrightharpoons \{\mu_\sigma(s) \subset \mu(s) | s \in sort\ \delta\}$$
$$\cup \{\mu_\sigma(f) \subset \mu(f) | f \in func\ \delta\}$$
$$\cup \{\mu_\sigma(\rho) = \mu(\rho) \upharpoonright \mu_\sigma(s_1) \times \ldots \times \mu_\sigma(s_n) | \rho : s_1, \ldots, s_n \in rel\ \delta\}$$

Theorem 17. *Let u be a well-formed logic program and* $\mathbf{V} \in Mod(cFSA_\eta)$ *be a model.* $\mathbf{V}(Yu\hat{\ })$ *is called* **the denotation of u** *and it is denoted by* $Den_\mathbf{V}[\![u]\!]$. *Clearly* $Den_\mathbf{V}[\![u]\!] \in Mod_\sigma$. *If* $\mathbf{V}$ *and* $\mu : \delta \to cTerm_\eta$ *are constructive then so is* $Den_\mathbf{V}[\![u]\!]$.

Theorem 18. *Let u be a well-formed logic program and fix a* $\mathbf{V} \in Mod(cFSA_\eta)$. *Take* $\sigma \leftrightharpoons \sigma_u$. *Let* $\rho(\tau_1, \ldots, \tau_k)$ *be a positive ground atomic formula from* $Form_\sigma$. *Then*

$$Den_\mathbf{V}[\![u]\!] \models \rho(\tau_1, \ldots, \tau_k)\ \textit{iff}$$
$$Th(\mathbf{V}) + IM?(\mu_\sigma) + Gen(u) \vdash Ax(u)^\sigma \to \rho(\tau_1, \ldots, \tau_n)^\sigma$$

To formalize the initial property of $Den_\mathbf{V}[\![u]\!]$ let us consider the following category **C**. Let us fix a model $\mathbf{V} \in Mod(cFSA_\sigma)$. The objects of **C** are pairs (ξ, ι) where $\xi : \sigma_u \to cTerm_\sigma$ and $\iota : \xi \upharpoonright func\ \sigma \to \mu$ is a morphism between two interpretations in **V**. Moreover, we suppose that ι is an embedding.

The morphisms of **C** are the morphisms $\kappa : \xi_1 \to \xi_2$ which commute with ι's:

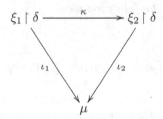

This category is called **the model category generated by u** and denoted by **C**(u).

Theorem 19. $Den_\mathbf{V}[\![u]\!]$ *with the natural injection is the initial object in* **C**(u).

We show that logic programming based on Horn-formulas is only a particular case of our definition. Indeed let δ be a similarity type such that $rel\ \delta$ is empty. Let $\underline{Herb}(0, \delta)$ be the minimal Herbrand model generated from δ in $cFSA_\eta$. Clearly, there is an interpretation $\Theta : \delta \to cTerm_\eta$ which defines this model. Clearly Θ is constructive in $cFSA_\eta$.

Definition 21. *A well-formed logic program $u \in LP_\delta(R)$ is called a* **Horn-type logic program** *iff each rule $\rho(\tau_1, \ldots, \tau_n) \Leftarrow \varphi$ belonging to u is Horn-type, i.e. $\varphi \to \rho(\tau_1, \ldots, \tau_n)$ is a Horn-formula.*

It is clear that the mathematical tools defined in Chaps. 5.1–5.3 fits well for Horn-type logic programs. By using Theorem 5.29 and the construction of Θ we can give another version of initiality. Let $u \in LP_\Theta(R)$ be a fixed Horn-type logic program. Take $\sigma \leftrightharpoons \sigma_u$. Let $\mathbf{V}$ be a fixed constructive model of $cFSA_\eta$.

Theorem 20. *Let $\mathbf{C}$ be the category the objects of which are σ-type correct interpretations in a constructive model $\mathbf{V}$, and the morphisms of which are the interpretations between them. Then $\mathbf{V}(Yu\,\hat{}\,)$ is the initial object of $\mathbf{C}$.*

Corollary 1. *Let u be a well-formed Horn-type logic program. Let $\rho(\tau_1, \ldots, \tau_n)$ be a positive ground atomic formula from $Form_\sigma$.*

$$cFSA_\eta \models \rho(\tau_1, \ldots, \tau_n) \text{ iff}$$
$$cFSA_\eta + IM?(\mu_\sigma) \vdash Ax(u)^\mu \to \rho(\tau_1, \ldots, \tau_n)^\mu$$

Moreover, let $\mathbf{V}$ be a fixed model of $cFSA_\sigma$. Then

$$\mathbf{V}(Yu\,\hat{}\,) \models \rho(\tau_1, \ldots, \tau_n) \text{ iff}$$
$$Th(\mathbf{V}) + IM?(\mu_\sigma) \vdash Ax(u)^\mu \to \rho(\tau_1, \ldots, \tau_n)^\mu$$

By the use of a fixed point theory, which allows us to have solutions definable in $cFSA_\sigma$ we will be able to work with definable least fixed points. To achieve this we use the positive existential (or constructive) functionals over which the fixed point theory with the usual properties may be developed. Note that this functional class consists of only the functions considered as computable. By the use of this fixed point theory we get the traditional logic programming case. Let us suppose that η' contains finitely many new constant symbols: $A_1, \ldots, A_n$. Let us denote the formula

$$\bigwedge \{\underline{atom}(A_i)|i = 1, \ldots, n\} \wedge \forall x \underline{atom}(x) \to \bigvee \{x = A_i|i = 1, \ldots, n\}$$

by $\underline{Const}$.

Theorem 21. $cFSA_\eta\,' + \underline{Const}$ *has an initial term model $\mathbf{V}_i$.*

Let μ be the same as in the previous example.

Theorem 22. *Let u be a well-formed logic program. Let $\rho(\tau_1, \ldots, \tau_n)$ be a positive ground atomic formula from $Form_\sigma$. Then*

$$\mathbf{V}_i(u) \models \rho(\tau_1, \ldots, \tau_n) \text{ iff}$$
$$cFSA_\eta + IM?(\mu_\sigma) + \underline{Const} \vdash Ax(u)^\mu \to \rho(\tau_1, \ldots, \tau_n)^\mu$$

3.2.3 Other Programming Paradigm

The proposed theoretic frame is appropriate to describe and analyse various other approaches in programming. We mention here only the rough set theory, which was proposed as an approach to support intelligent data analysis and data mining. Approximation is the basic concept of rough set theory. Let us suppose that a set X should be described with the terms of attribute values from a given set A. Then according to the rough set theory two operations are defined assigning to every X two sets $A^*(X)$ and $A^*(X)$ called the A-lower and the A-upper approximation of X, respectively. Note that the A-lower approximation of a set is the union of all A-granules that are included in the set, whereas the A-upper approximation of a set is the union of all A-granules that have a nonempty intersection with the set. Rough set theory gives us one of the important backgrounds for that type of computing when the aim is to deal with inexact solutions of computational problems. Rough set theory plays an important role in granular computing. The basic ingredients of granular computing are granules such as subsets, classes, objects, clusters, and elements of a universe. These granules are composed of finer granules that are drawn together by distinguishability, similarity and functionality. Based on complexity, abstraction level and size, granules can be measured in different levels. A problem domain may exist at the highest and coarsest granule. Granules at the lowest level are composed of elements of the particular model that is used. Granulation is one of the key issues in granular computing for problem solving. See e.g. Akama et al. [2], Kumar et al. [18] and Yao [30]. Note that the two-sided approximation of the sets used by rough set theory can be provided by the fixed point equations. The approximation itself is realized by the smallest and largest fixed points. At the same time the granules to be used in the approximation will be given in the universe that will correspond to the actual problem domain.

4   Cognitive Computing

4.1 Motivations

Computing is the basic method for representing, model and investigate processes of human intelligence in the fields of Artificial Intelligence, Cognitive computing and Computational theory of mind. Thus, our goal is to develop a general computation theory that considers all the important aspects of this modelling. It is essential to handle the various levels of computation, from computation that uses purely syntactic digits to computation at the content level that among others interprets data, information and knowledge. Our further aim is to provide a theoretical framework, which will able to consider all the processes of the data → information → knowledge transformation and processing.

The theoretical framework - developed above - will permit to represent, model and investigate the main processes of cognizing under the control of direct thinking by the use of appropriately defined and constructed computing, which we call cognitive computing.

4.2   Basic Definitions

Let $Th = (\sigma, Ax)$ be a fixed theory. Cognitive processes are defined by the use of situations, infons and information. The proposed extension will formalise the well-known constructions of situations and information. See Devlin [9] or Barwise [5]. Let ι be a new similarity type containing the followings.

1. A sort s for **situations**,
2. A sort b, i for **basic infons** and **infons** respectively,
3. A sort tv for **truth values**,
4. A functional symbol $\kappa : s, i \rightarrow tv$. κ gives the truth value to an infon in a situation
5. A sort k for **knowledge**.
6. A function $\tau_i : k, s \rightarrow i$. τ is the **query function** which in a given situation produces an infon by the use of the actual knowledge.

Let us add an axiom stating that **infons** form the greatest set containing all the basic infons and if A is an infon and S is a situation then the triple κ, S, A is also an infon. Let $\mathcal{I}$ be the fixed-point equation describing this. According to Barwise [5] well-founded infons are the elements of the least fixed-points of the equation $\mathcal{I}$. Let BC_ι denote this set of axioms.

It is clear that $Th \rightarrow Th + BC_\iota$ form a constitution on $\mathbb{FOL}$. According to Theorem 1 there is a least compact constitution containing this constitution. Let $\mathbb{CB}$ denote this constitution. $\mathbb{CB}$ is the so-called **cognitive base constitution** (compact by definition).

4.3   Cognitive Processes

We recall the **modification calculi** from Anshakov, Gergely [4] see Chapters 10 and 18. To treat non-monotonity of reasoning process we need to

1. differentiate external and internal truth values
2. add a new type r for **reasoning** to clarify why we think that about the truth value of an infon in a given situation
3. have inference rules for handling records which can contain infons, information and/or knowledge (see Anshakov, Gergely [4] pp. 145–149).

Now we are ready to give a short description of what we mean by **cognitive process**. Again, fix a theory $Th = (\sigma, Ax)$. Using the superstructure $SP_{\mathbb{CB}}(Th)$ a cognitive process

1. is a logic program in the sense of 3.2.2, its inner logic is the above stated modification calculus. This is able to extract infons, to generate new information and knowledge.
2. is also a process that can generate new processes, start, terminate and eliminate processes and can communicate with other processes.
3. can have a lot of query functions to interact with its environment.
4. can have a predefined goal.

Let PC_ι denote the axioms describing the aboves. Again we can define a closed constitution $\mathbb{CK}$ over $\mathbb{FOL}$ being the least compact-one containing the axiom systems BC_ι and PC_ι.

Note that only those processes are called cognitive processes, which can generate, store and use new elements of the sort k, i.e. new information and knowledge elements.

Now we define the important notion Cognition Kernel as follows.

Definition 22. Cognitive Kernel *is a compact constitution C on $\mathbb{FOL}$ together with an embedding (in functor category) of $\mathbb{CK}$ into itself.*

5 Cognitive Computing

A goal-oriented organisation of cognitive processes form cognitive computing. The goal is usually related to the solution of a given problem situation, i.e. to the reduction of the uncertainty level of a problem situation.

The Cognitive computing theory will provide a mathematically well-defined classification of the possible types of computing and it will consider a special theory of realisation. The Cognitive computing theory allows the investigation and the determination of the theoretical limitations of the computing based modelling of intelligent processes. Thus in addition to the computational capabilities and limitations of different programming paradigms, the multi-layer cognitive computing can be explored and a framework can be developed that support the realization of the data $\rightarrow$ information $\rightarrow$ knowledge transition processes that use thought-driven cognitive processes. At the beginning generic and/or specific data analytical methods will provide infons from the data and then from the generated set of infons the corresponding information will be built. This information is used to decrease the uncertainty of the actual problem situation. The methods and information successfully used in the solution of the problem situation will form knowledge candidates. The latters will become knowledge only after a successful checking done by the use of the existing knowledge repository.

In this context, generalizations of the concept of Church- and Turing-computa-bility can be given and the computational possibilities and limitations of cognitive computing can be investigated. A multilayer theory of complexity can be defined to characterise the problem situations. It can be shown that cognitive processes necessary for the solution of problems of certain complexity will not be cognitive computable, but they will become so by a cognitive computing system with oraculum.

6 AI Based on Cognitive Computing

The proposed cognitive computing theory permits to design systems, which are able to lean on and interact naturally with users to extend the capability of humans and/or machines. So that humans would able to do more of what they could do on their own normally without cognitive computing support.

A cognitive computing system will be able to respond to the environment in an autonomous regime too, without pre-programming. It can sense, learn, infer and interact. Cognitive computing systems can sense or perceive the environment and collect the data on the basis of needs and situations. They understand, interpret and analyse the context based on collected data and information, and they make decision based on reasoning and act accordingly. Various semantics and knowledge-driven cognitive data analysis methods can be represented and realised in a constructive way within the proposed Cognitive computing approach.

Cognitive computing theory provides a possibility for the use of computational approach to realise the understanding processes of natural language. Namely, this theory provides tools to interpret natural language texts in the various levels of cognitive computing.

The development of cognitive computing covers the basics of computing from language design to evaluator implementation with the aim of explaining existing systems at a deep enough level. This will help to adopt and use any of both, the languages and systems that are currently used in artificial intelligence and cognitive system area thus enabling the next generation of cognitive computing designers and implementers to use this as a foundation to build upon which. This is associated/augmented with a methodology that supports the selection of an appropriate specification method together with a constructive language that permits to describe the problem situation so that it prescribes the realization of the cognitive computing processes necessary for the solution of the actual problem situation.

Therefore, the proposed cognitive computing theory provides a constructive foundation of AI, where this abbreviation means Amplifier for Intelligence. This AI will be able to act as genuine problem-solving companion understanding and responding to complex problem situations. This AI system will be able to act either as a partner system for cooperative functioning with a human agent or as an autonomous cognitive system for a well-defined problem area. As to become a cooperative partner for human agents, the system has to function very similarly to humans. E.g., it should be able to communicate and understand natural language, reason in a compatible way, learn from its experience, etc. AI will be able to cognize the environment and itself including the co-operative partner.

7   Appendixes

7.1   Axiomatization of *clFSA*

In order to interpret program execution and different data and control structures, our theory of programming needs appropriate models to be obtained from a relation structure (models) of a given similarity type by building up the corresponding superstructure as we have seen so far. However, to use these superstructures in our theory of programming we have to introduce an appropriate formalism which allows to provide a theory (an axiomatization) the models of which are the structures in question and by the use of which, statements can be formulated and proved about these structures. According to our aim to develop a first order theory of programming the axiomatization of superstructures will be done in an appropriate first order language.

Superstructure construction is followed by a set–theoretic approach so the signature of the language has to contain at least:

- a unary relation symbol *atom* : d

to distinguish the elements of the original relation structure from which the superstructure is built up. These elements may be considered as elementary data;

- the 'element' relation symbol $\in$: d, d
- and the constant symbol $0 :\to d$

which reflects the empty set.

A similarity type σ is called **rich enough** iff it contains the above symbols. We use $\notin$ for the negation of element relation.

The variable symbols of the language correspond to sets and atoms. Therefore, sets and their elements are of the same nature, if the latter ones are not atoms. In other words, we consider hereditary sets the elements of which are either atoms or hereditary sets etc. Though atoms have no elements they are not equivalent to the empty set. Therefore we have to be careful while providing the Axiom of Extensionality and defining some of the set-theoretic operations.

A relation symbol of σ is called <u>non set-theoretical</u> iff it is not equal with either $\in$ or 0 or to *atom*.

The system of axioms FSA_σ axiomatizes the hereditarily finite sets with atoms. Why do we need atoms? As we know the Zermalo-Fraenkel axiomatization is powerful enough to make atoms unnecessary. Set theory, as formalized in ZFC, provides an elegant and powerful way to organize mathematics but it is too strong for the programming theory. The aim to build up an adequate axiom system for this theory dictates to develop a set theory weaker than ZFC, weak in the principles of set existence which they attempt to formalize e.g. by allowing atoms. The latters just have a programming interpretation as elementary data or, if you think about the relation structures as the object modelling computers where the programs run then atoms represent the registers where the data are stored. Atoms also break the finiteness which we intend to axiomatize since they may be infinitely many. We axiomatize the hereditarily finite sets with atoms by modifying the axiom system ZF as follows:

FSA_0: Existential axiom of atoms:
$\quad \exists x\ \underline{atom}(x)$
FSA_1: Extensionality axiom:
$\quad (\neg\underline{atom}(x) \wedge \neg\underline{atom}(y)) \to ((x = y) \leftrightarrow \forall z(z\in x \leftrightarrow z\in y))$
FSA_2: Empty set axiom:
$\quad \forall x(\neg x\in 0)$

FSA_3: Significance axiom of atoms:

$$\forall z(atom(z) \leftrightarrow (z \neq 0 \land \forall x(x \notin z)))$$

This axiom together with FSA_1 declares that though atoms have no elements they differ from the empty set 0.

FSA_4: Foundation axiom:

$$\forall x(\exists y(y \in x) \rightarrow \exists y(y \in x \land \neg \exists z(z \in x \land z \in y)))$$

This axiom says that every non-empty set has a minimal element with respect to $\in$.

$FSA_{5\sigma}$: Comprehension Scheme. For each σ-type formula φ:

$$\forall z \forall w_1 \ldots \forall w_n \exists y \exists x(x \in y \leftrightarrow [x \in z \land \varphi(x, z, w_1, \ldots, w_n)])$$

The y asserted to exist is unique by Extensionality Axiom and it is denoted by

$$\{x | x \in z \land \varphi(x, y, w_1, \ldots, w_n)\} \text{ or } \{x \in z | \varphi\}.$$

Intuitively for a given formula $\varphi(x)$ there need not necessarily exist a set $\{x : \varphi(x)\}$ this collection may be too large to form a set. However, Comprehension Scheme says that if the collection is a subcollection of a given set then it does exist. The following axioms say that certain sets, which should exist, really do exist.

FSA_6: Pairing axiom:

$$\forall x \forall y \exists z(x \in z \land y \in z)$$

FSA_7: Union axiom:

$$\forall F \exists G \forall y((y \in F \land x \in y) \rightarrow x \in G)$$

$FSA_{8\sigma}$: Replacement scheme. For each σ-type formula φ:

$$\forall F \forall w_1 \ldots \forall w_n (\forall x \in F \exists! y \; \varphi(x, y, F, w_1, \ldots, w_n) \rightarrow$$
$$\exists G(\forall x \in F \exists y \in G \; \varphi(x, y, F, w_1, \ldots, w_n))$$

Intuitively (using also $FSA_{5\sigma}$) this axiom says that if $H(x)$ is the unique y satisfying $\varphi(x, y, \ldots)$ then $\{H(x) | x \in F\}$ is a set.

FSA_9: Finiteness axiom:

$$\forall x(set(x) \rightarrow \exists y \exists z(z \text{ is a bijection between } x \text{ and } y) \land$$
$$(y \text{ is finite ordinal}))$$

Definition 23. *The set of axioms of the hereditarily finite sets with atoms is:*

$$FSA_\sigma \leftrightharpoons \{FSA_i | i = 0, 1, 2, 3, 4, 6, 7, 9\} \cup \{FSA_{i\varphi} | i = 5, 8, \; \varphi \in Form_\sigma\}.$$

If $R_1, \ldots, R_k; f_1, \ldots, f_n$ are new relation and function symbols respectively then $FSA_\sigma(R_1, \ldots, R_k; f_1, \ldots, f_n)$ stands for FSA_{σ^*} where $\sigma^* = \sigma \cup (R_1, \ldots, R_k; f_1, \ldots, f_n)$.

The Finiteness Axiom implies the Axiom of Choice, i.e.:

Proposition 4. *In FSA_σ the following statements hold:*

(i) Each set can be well-ordered.
(ii) There exists a choice function on sets.

Moreover, basically from the Finiteness Axiom, it follows that for any set there exists the power set, i.e. the Power Set Axiom is a consequence of FSA_σ.

Proposition 5. *The axioms of FSA_σ ensure that for any set there exists the power set:*

$$FSA_\sigma \models \forall x(\neg \underline{atom}(x) \rightarrow \exists y \forall z(z \in y \leftrightarrow z \subset x)).$$

Therefore, the axiom system FSA_σ is equivalent with the Zermalo-Fraenkel axiom system with the Axiom of Infinity and the Power Set Axiom deleted and Finiteness Axiom added.

Note that all the notions introduced in ZFC can be introduced in FSA_σ as well. E.g. relation, domain, range, function, bijection, surjection, injection are such notions. The expressions that define these notions can also be used as a definition of new relation or function symbols. Adding these new symbols to the similarity type o and their definitions to FSA_σ, we obtain a conservative extention of FSA_σ.

Since in FSA_σ all sets are finite, therefore the following preposition holds for ordinals:

Proposition 6. *Each ordinal is finite in FSA_σ and the usual addition and multiplication on ordinals are commutative.*

Note that in set theory natural numbers are identified with finite ordinals. Namely, an ordinal α is a natural number if for all $\beta \leq \alpha$ if $\beta \neq 0$ then β is a successor of some γ. Again the Finiteness Axiom implies the following:

Proposition 7. *The natural numbers, the ordinals (and the cardinals) are the same in FSA_σ.*

A programming theory needs, among others, tools to handle infinite objects e.g. to represent infinite computation processes. Therefore, beyond finite sets as finite objects, we also have to be able to speak about infinite objects.

Different approaches provide different techniques for this aim, e.g. denotation approach to semantics makes the topological space complete. We introduce the notion of class to handle infinity. This notion is also important in ZFC axiom system, where e.g. the class of all ordinals On is often used. In the axiom system FSA_σ the notion of class has a more important role, since the majority of the usual sets (namely, all infinite sets) cannot be identified with any set in FSA_σ.

Intuitively, a class is but a conglomerate of elements x which satisfy a given formula $\varphi(x)$. Since each σ-type model of FSA_σ has constructive objects (atoms or finite sets) as elements a class is but a defined or specified conglomerate of these objects. Due to the significant role of classes in our further investigations they will frequently appear and we therefore have to precisely define what type of statements can be stated about classes. The definition is based on the followings. Having a given model a class does not consist of arbitrarily collected elements of the universe, but they may be collected only by the use of a given formula. Therefore, we extend the language such that it may contain statements about classes. Let us first fix an arbitrary set cV of the so called <u>class variable</u>. The intended meaning of a class variable in a model of FSA_σ is a conglomerate of objects of the universe.

Let σ be a rich similarity type. In order to handle classes we extend the σ-type classical first order language by adding class terms which provide definable conglomerate of objects of the universe of the models and the class formulas which allow to formulate statements about classes.

Definition 24. (a) *The set of σ-**type class terms** (cTerm$_\sigma$) consists of the terms in the form $\{x|\varphi\}$ where $x\in V$ and $\varphi\in cForm_\sigma$.*

(b) *The set of σ-**type class formulas** (cForm$_\sigma$) is the minimal set satisfying the followings:*
  - *$Atom_\sigma \subset cForm_\sigma$;*
  - *if $x\in Term_\sigma$ and $C\in cV$ then $x\in C$ belongs to $cForm_\sigma$;*
  - *if φ,ψ are of $cForm_\sigma$ then $\neg\varphi$ and $\varphi\wedge\psi$ also belong to $cForm_\sigma$;*
  - *if φ is of $cForm_\sigma$, $x\in V$ then $\exists v\varphi$ also belong to $cForm_\sigma$.*

Now let us see how the semantics of $cForm_\sigma$ can be defined. First of all, we extend the notion of valuation for class variables. A valuation of a class variable is a subset of the universe of the model under consideration.

Definition 25. *Let $\mathbf{A}$ be an arbitrary but fixed σ-type model. A **class valuation** is a function k such that*
  - *$dom(k) = C \cup cV$;*
  - *$k(x)\in A$ for any $x\in V$;*
  - *$k(x)\subset Sb(A)$ for any class variable $x\in cV$.*

As usual let $cVal_\mathbf{A}$ denote the family of all class valuations.

Having the valuation we can define the meaning of class terms and class formulas with respect to a given valuation in an arbitrary but fixed model.

Definition 26. *Let a model $\mathbf{A}\in Mod_\sigma$ be given.*

(a) *The meaning of a class term $t = \{x|\varphi\}$ in the model $\mathbf{A}$ with respect to k is the following family:*

$$t_\mathbf{A} \leftrightharpoons \{a|\mathbf{A} \models \varphi[k + (x,a)]\}.$$

(b) *For any class formula $\varphi\in cForm_\sigma$ and valuation $k\in cVal_\mathbf{A}$ we define the validity φ in $\mathbf{A}$ with respect to k (written as $\mathbf{A} \models \varphi[k]$) by induction on the complexity of φ:*

if $\varphi \in Atom_\sigma$ *then the validity is defined as in (i) and (ii) of 1.2.10;*
if $\varphi \leftrightharpoons \tau \in C$ *then* $\mathbf{A} \models (\tau \in C)[k]$ *iff* $\tau_\mathbf{A}[k]$ *is an element of* $k(C)$ *;*
and (iv) are defined as in (iii) of 1.2.10 (i.e as usual).

In order to make the class valuation more transparent the σ-type models may be extended such that they will contain an entity which refers to classes.

Definition 27. *A pair* $\mathbf{V} = (\mathbf{A}, \underline{Class})$ *is called a class extention of* $\mathbf{A}$ *iff*

- $\mathbf{A}$ *is a* σ*-type model;*
- $\underline{Class} \subset Sb(A);$
- *for any class term* $t \in cTerm_\sigma$ *and valuation* $k \in cVal_\mathbf{A}$ *we have* $k(cV) \subset$ $\underline{Class}$ *implies* $t_\mathbf{A}[k] \in \underline{Class}$.

Let $cMod_\sigma$ denote the family of all class extentions of σ-type models. If $\mathbf{V} \in cMod_\sigma$ then let $Val_\mathbf{V}$ denote those class valuations k for which $k(cV) \subset \underline{Class}$ holds.

Definition 28. *Let* $\mathbf{V} = (\mathbf{A}, \underline{Class})$ *be an arbitrary class extention belonging to* $cMod_\sigma$. *Let* $\varphi \in cForm_\sigma$.

(i) *We say that* φ **is valid in** $\mathbf{V}$ **with respect to a valuation** k *iff* $k \in Val_\mathbf{V}$ *and* $\mathbf{V} \models \varphi[k]$.
(ii) *The class formula* φ *is valid in* $\mathbf{V}$ *iff it is valid with respect to all* $k \in Val_\mathbf{V}$ *i.e.*

$$\mathbf{V} \models \varphi \text{ iff for all } k \in Val_\mathbf{V}, \mathbf{V} \models \varphi[k]$$

(iii) *A class formula* φ *is said to be valid in a* σ*-type model* $\mathbf{A}$ *iff for all class extention* $\mathbf{V} = (\mathbf{A}, \underline{Class})$ *we have* $\mathbf{V} \models \varphi$.

So we have defined the σ-type class language as a triple

$$CL_\sigma \leftrightharpoons (cForm_\sigma, cMod_\sigma, \models)$$

This language is really a two-sorted one. The first sort corresponds to sets and atoms and the second one to classes. However, quantification is allowed only for set variables.

A variable $x \in V \cup cV$ can also be considered as a shorthand for the class term $\{y|y \in x\}$ To have a clearer view of a variable let us see how the "element relation" $\in$ and the equality are defined for class terms.

- $\{x|\varphi\} \in \{y|\psi\} \leftrightharpoons \exists y(\forall x(x \in y \leftrightarrow \varphi) \wedge \psi);$
- $\{x|\varphi\} = \{y|\psi\} \leftrightharpoons \forall x(\varphi \leftrightarrow \psi[x/y]).$

Depending on how we look at x as a variable or a=j a shorthand for $\{y|y \in x\}$ the class formulas $x \in y$ and $x \in C$ have different meanings. However, they are equivalent if we take the Extensionality Axiom (FSA_1).

Proposition 8. *(i)* $FSA_1 \models (x \in y) \leftrightarrow (\{z|z \in x\} \in w|w \in y)$

(ii) $FSA_1 \models (x \in C) \leftrightarrow (\{z | z \in x\} \in \{w | w \in C\})$

Proof. We prove only the statement (i). Working in axiom system $\{FSA_1\}$ *we have the following chain of semantic equivalences:*

$$\{z | z \in x\} \in \{w | w \in y\} \equiv \exists u (\forall z (z \in x \leftrightarrow z \in u) \land u \in y) \equiv u(x = u \land u \in y) \equiv x \in y.$$

$\square$

By using the above proposition we can define the following abbreviations:

$$C = D \leftrightharpoons \forall x (x \in C \leftrightarrow x \in D)$$
$$C = y \leftrightarrow \forall x (x \in C \leftrightarrow x \in y)$$
$$C \in x \leftrightharpoons \exists y (C = y \land y \in x)$$
$$C \in D \leftrightharpoons \exists y (C = y \land y \in D)$$

For the classical first order languages we have defined the simultaneous substitution of terms. This notion can be extended even to the class language. However, we have to make a careful distinction between substitution for variables and for class–terms. The only question is how substitute into a formula $x \in C$?

First let τ be a term belonging $Term_\sigma$. If so then take $(x \in C)[\tau / C] \leftrightharpoons x \in \tau$. Clearly $x \in \tau$ belongs to $cForm_\sigma$. In the case of class terms take $(x \in C)[\tau / C] \leftrightharpoons \varphi[x/y]$ where $\tau = \{y | \varphi\}$. This definition is comform with the fact that $x \in \{y | \varphi\}$ is just a shorthand for $\varphi[x/y]$. In the end if D is a class variable then take $(x \in C)[D/C] \leftrightharpoons x \in D$.

Without spelling out the whole definition we use the notation $\varphi[\tau_i / x_i]_i{}^k$ for the simultaneous substitution of terms τ_i for variables x_i, respectively.

Lemma 1. *Let* $\mathbf{V} \in cMod_\sigma$ *and let* $\varphi \in cForm_\sigma$ *be arbitrary. Let us suppose that* $var(\varphi) \cap cV = \{C_1, \ldots, C_k\}$. *Then for any class terms* $\tau_1, \ldots, \tau_n$ *if* $\mathbf{V} \models \varphi$ *then* $\mathbf{V} \models \varphi[\tau_i / C_i]_i{}^k$.

In order to handle classes axiomatically the axiom system FSA_σ is to be appropriately extended. The extended axiom system denoted by $cFSA_\sigma$ consists of

- axioms which remain the same as they were in FSA_σ dealing with sets only;
- axioms the scope of which is extended to classes;
- the extentions of the axiom schemas by allowing class formulas.

Namely, by extending the axiom system we get the following axiom system $cFSA_\sigma$ where variables $f, g, x, y, z, w, w_1, \ldots, w_n$ are from V and C, D are from cV.

FSA_0 Existential axiom of atoms:
  $\exists x \, \underline{atom}(x)$
FSA_1 Extensionality axiom:
  $(\neg \underline{atom}(x) \land \neg \underline{atom}(y)) \rightarrow ((x = y) \leftrightarrow \forall z (z \in x \leftrightarrow z \in y))$
FSA_2 Empty set axiom:
  $\forall x (\neg x \in 0)$

FSA_3 Significance axiom of atoms:
$$\forall z(atom(z) \leftrightarrow (z \neq 0 \wedge \forall x(x \notin z)))$$

This axiom together with FSA_1 declares that though atoms have no elements they differ from the empty set 0.

FSA_4 Foundation axiom:
$$\forall z(\exists x(x \in z) \rightarrow \exists x(x \in z \wedge \neg \exists y(y \in x \wedge y \in z)))$$
$FSA_{5\sigma}$ Comprehension schema:

$$\forall z \forall w_1 \ldots \forall w_n \exists y \exists x(x \in y \leftrightarrow [x \in z \wedge \varphi(x, z, w_1, \ldots, w_n)])$$

(where $\varphi \in cForm_\sigma$!)
FSA_6 Pairing axiom:
$$\forall x \forall y \exists z(x \in z \wedge y \in z)$$

We remark that since classes have only sets as elements the Pairing Axiom is not extended to classes.

Before reformulating FSA_7 we remark that for any term t one can define its union by taking $\cup t = \{x | \exists y(x \in y \wedge y \in t)\}$. However, our original axiom states that if t is not proper then $\cup t$ is also not proper! Therefore, we have to use FSA_7 without any changes.

FSA_7 Union axiom:
$$\forall x \exists z[\forall y \forall w(y \in x \wedge w \in y) \rightarrow w \in z]$$
$FSA_{8\sigma}$ Replacement scheme. For each σ-type formula φ:

$$\forall f \forall w_1 \ldots \forall w_n(\forall x \in f \exists ! y \ \varphi(x, y, f, w_1, \ldots, w_n) \rightarrow$$
$$\exists g(\forall x \in f \exists y \in g \ \varphi(x, y, f, w_1, \ldots, w_n))$$

(where $\varphi \in cForm_\sigma$)

Similarly to the modification of the Comprehension schema we allow the use of class formulas in the scope of the Replacement schema as well.

FSA_9 Finiteness axiom:
Each set is equivalent with a finite ordinal

Now having the axiom system $cFSA_\sigma$ we clarify some notions. Let $\mathbf{V} = (\mathbf{A}, \underline{Class})$ be an arbitrary class extention of $\mathbf{A}$.

- The elements of A are called **objects**.
- Let $a \in A$ be an object. If $\mathbf{V} \models \underline{atom}(x)[(a, x)]$ then a is said to be an *atom*, otherwise it is a *set*.
- The elements of $\underline{Class}$ are said to be classes.
- An object a and a class U are called equal iff $\mathbf{V} \models \forall y(y \in x \leftrightarrow y \in C)[(x, a) + (C, U)]$.
- A class $U \in \underline{Class}$ is called a **proper** class iff it is not equal to any object of $\mathbf{V}$. Namely U is a proper class if it satisfies the formula $\mathbf{V} \models \neg \exists x(x = C)[(C, U)]$.

We redefine predicate 'set' by taking:

$$\underline{cset}(C) \leftrightharpoons \exists x(x = C \land \neg\underline{atom}(x)).$$

The $\neg\underline{atom}(x)$ part of the conjunction is needed only when one substitutes a variable x for class-variable C:

$$\underline{cset}(C)[x/C] \equiv \exists y(y = x \land \neg\underline{atom}(y) \equiv \neg\underline{atom}(x)).$$

Next we omit 'c' from the name of this redefined predicate because on sets the new and old meanings are the same.

The predicate 'proper' can be defined by taking:

$$\underline{proper}(C) \leftrightharpoons \neg\exists x(x = C).$$

According to the above defined predicates a class term τ is called relational or functional iff $Rel(\tau)$ or $Func(\tau)$ holds respectively.

The followings are two useful proper classes:

- $\underline{Universe} = \{x|x = x\}$;
- $\omega = \{x|Nat(x)\}$.

References

1. A definition of AI: main capabilities and scientific disciplines, Brussels (2018). https://ec.europa.eu/digital-single-market/en/news/definition-artificial-intelligence-main-capabilities-and-scientific-disciplines
2. Akama, S., Murai, T., Kudo, Y.: Reasoning with Rough Sets - Logical Approaches to Granularity-Based Framework. Springer, Switzerland (2018). https://doi.org/10.1007/978-3-319-72691-5
3. Amir, A. et al.: Cognitive computing programming paradigm: a corelet language for composing networks of neurosynaptic cores, In: Proceedings of IEEE International Joint Conference on Neural Networks (IJCNN) (2013)
4. Anshakov, O., Gergely, T.: Cognitive Reasoning - A Formal Approach. Springer, Berlin (2010). https://doi.org/10.1007/978-3-540-68875-4
5. Barwise, J.: The situation in logic. CSLI Lecture Notes Number, vol. 17 (1989)
6. Brasil, L.M., et al.: Hybrid expert system for decision supporting in the medical area: complexity and cognitive computing. Int. J. Med. Inform. **63**(1), 19–30 (2001)
7. Goguen, J.A., Burstall, R.M.: Introducing institutions. In: Clarke, E., Kozen, D. (eds.) Logic of Programs 1983. LNCS, vol. 164, pp. 221–256. Springer, Heidelberg (1984). https://doi.org/10.1007/3-540-12896-4_366
8. Cognitive Catalyst. https://www.ibm.com/downloads/cas/OMZMGNP5
9. Devlin, K.: Logic and Information. Cambridge University Press, Cambridge (1991)
10. Fresco, N.: Physical Computation and Cognitive Science. Springer, Berlin (2014). https://doi.org/10.1007/978-3-642-41375-9
11. Gergely, T., Szőts, M.: Cuttable formulas for logic programming, In: Proceedings of the Symposium on Logic Programming, IEEE Press (1984)
12. Gergely, T., Ury, L.: Programming in topoi. a generalized approach to program semantics, In: Categorical and Algebraic Methods in Computer Science and System Theory, Herdecke, Germany (1980)

13. Gergely, T., Ury, L.: First-Order Programming Theories. EATCS Monographs on Theoretical Computer Science, vol. 24. Springer-Verlag, Berlin (1991). https://doi.org/10.1007/978-3-642-58205-9
14. Grätzer, G.: Universal Algebra, 2nd edn. Springer-Verlag, New York (1979). https://doi.org/10.1007/978-0-387-77487-9
15. Gutierrez-Garcia, J.O., Lopez-Neri, E.: Cognitive computing: a brief survey and open research challenges, In: 3rd International Conference on Applied Computing and Information Technology/2nd International Conference on Computational Science and Intelligence, pp. 328–333 (2015)
16. Hoare, C.A.R., Jifeng, H.: Unifying Theories of Programming. Prentice Hall, New Jersey (1998)
17. Ivancevic, V.G., Ivancevic, T.T.: Computational Mind - A Complex Dynamics Perspective, Studies in Computational Intelligence 60. Springer-Verlag, Berlin (2007). https://doi.org/10.1007/978-3-540-71561-0
18. Kumar, V.S., Dhillipan, J., Shanmugam, D.B.: Survey of recent research in granular computing. Int. J. Emerg. Technol. Comput. Sci. Electron. 24(3), 976–1353 (2017)
19. Maibaum, T.S.E.: Role of abstraction in program development. In: Kugler, H.J. (ed.) Information Processing 1986. Elsevier Science Publisher, Amsterdam (1986)
20. Milkowski, M.: Explaining the Computational Mind. The MIT Press, Cambridge (2013)
21. Piccinini, G.: The computational theory of cognition. In: Müller, V.C. (ed.) Fundamental Issues of Artificial Intelligence, Synthese Library 376, pp. 203–221. Springer, Cham (2016). https://doi.org/10.1007/978-3-319-26485-1_13
22. Schank, R.: The Cognitive Computer: On Language Learning and Artificial Intelligence. Addison Wesley, Reading (1984)
23. Schank, R.: The fraudulent claims made by IBM about Watson and AI (2019). https://www.rogerschank.com/fraudulent-claims-made-by-IBM-about-Watson-and-AI
24. Ury, L., Gergely, T.: A constructive specification theory. In: Declarative Systems Elsevier Science Publishers, pp. 33–83 (1990)
25. Valiant, L.G.: Cognitive computation. In: Proceedings of IEEE 36th Annual Foundations of Computer Science, Milwaukee, WI, USA, pp. 2–3 (1995)
26. Wang, Y., et al.: A layered reference model of the brain (LRMB). IEEE Trans. Syst. Man Cybern. (Part C) 36(2), 124–133 (2006)
27. Wang, Y.: On cognitive computing. Int. J. Softw. Sci. Comput. Intell. 1(3), 1–15 (2009)
28. Wang, Y.: On denotational mathematics foundations for the next generation of computers: cognitive computers for knowledge processing. J. Adv. Math. Appl. 1(1), 121–133 (2012)
29. Wirth, N.: Algorithms + Data Structures = Programs. Prentice Hall, New Jersey (1976)
30. Yao, Y.: Artificial intelligence perspectives on granular computing. In: Pedrycz, W., Chen, S.-M. (eds.) Granular Computing and Intelligent Systems ISRL 13, pp. 17–34. Springer-Verlag, Berlin (2011). https://doi.org/10.1007/978-3-642-19820-5_2
31. https://www.lexico.com/en/definition/artificial-intelligence
32. https://www.britannica.com/technology/artificial-intelligence

A Review of Motivational Systems and Emotions in Cognitive Architectures and Systems

Ricardo R. Gudwin[(✉)]

DCA-FEEC-UNICAMP, Av. Albert Einstein 400, Campinas, SP 13.083-852, Brazil
gudwin@unicamp.br
http://faculty.dca.fee.unicamp.br/gudwin

Abstract. Motivational Systems are specific modules of Cognitive Architectures, responsible for determining the behavior of artificial agents based on cognitive models of human motivations and emotions. In this work we discuss how these ideas coming from psychology can be used in the field of cognitive architectures, explaining how motivational systems differ from other kinds of systems, and how they can be used to build control systems for artificial agents.

Keywords: Motivational systems · Emotions · Cognitive architectures · Intelligent systems

1 Introduction

Cognitive Architectures is a field of research within Artificial Intelligence where computational models of cognitive abilities, like e.g. perception, attention, memory, reasoning, learning, behavior generation, and others, are used to build control systems for artificial agents. Furthermore, cognitive architectures can be theoretical models about how cognitive processes interact and also computational frameworks which can be reused through different applications. Motivational Systems are specific modules of Cognitive Architectures, responsible for determining the behavior of artificial agents based on cognitive models of human motivations. The traditional approach in motivational systems is based on Hull's theory of behavior (Hull 1943, 1952), which identifies the origin of behavior in a set of internal needs, either ontogenetically inherited by the creature, or learned during the course of its life, and providing motivation in the generation of behavior. According to this theory, the level of satisfaction of each of these needs is measured, giving rise to drives. These drives are connected to a set of automatic behaviors, which are supposed to decrease the level of these drives, providing satisfaction to the corresponding need. This mechanism works like a process of homeostasis, regulating drives and satisfying the agent's needs. The generated behavior is said to be a motivated behavior. According to Maslow (1943), needs can be organized in layers, being the lower levels related to

© Springer Nature Switzerland AG 2019
G. S. Osipov et al. (Eds.): Artificial Intelligence, LNAI 11866, pp. 65–84, 2019.
https://doi.org/10.1007/978-3-030-33274-7_4

physiologic needs (food, water, sleep, shelter, sex, etc.), followed by safety needs (maintenance, physical integrity, etc), social needs (social belonging, friendship, intimacy, family) and self-esteem (strength, achievement, adequacy, mastery of competence, reputation, prestige, etc). The higher level needs might be related to self-actualization needs, the need to transcend itself, to evolve and fulfill all its potential. These layers provide a priority among needs in order for them to affect the overall agent behavior, where lower needs are satisfied first, and only after they are satisfied, middle layer needs are considered and only after these, the higher level needs start commanding the agent's overall behavior. The standard approach assumes these needs are all pre-designed and embedded in the motivational system, working since the beginning in the behavior generation process. In this work we discuss how these ideas coming from psychology can be used in the field of cognitive architectures, explaining how motivational systems differ from other kinds of systems, and how they can be used to build control systems for artificial agents. We start introducing the main concepts on what are motivated behaviors and emotions, according to the main theories from psychology and philosophy used within cognitive architectures. Next, we review the main available models for motivations and emotions, focusing in the many differences among the available models. Finally, we propose a new definition for motivations and emotions, which tries do unify the many different approaches and provide a perspective that can conciliate the many different models presented before.

2 What Is a Motivated Behavior?

The study of motivational or emotional capabilities inserts itself under the broader field of behavior systems. Human beings and animals are able to perform many different kinds of behavior, since external behavior, affecting the world, up to internal behavior, affecting internal organs of the body, or even internal behaviors affecting just the mind. There are many possible ways for categorizing behavior. One possible way, inspired on the work of the semiotician Charles Sanders Peirce is to apply his universal categories (firstness, secondness and thirdness)[1] to the possible origin of behaviors, and categorize them on the following classes:

---

[1] According to Peirce, *firstness* is the mode of being of that which is such as it is, positively and without reference to anything else (CP 8.328; 1.295). The idea of First is predominant in the ideas of freshness, life, freedom (CP 1.302), novelty, creation, originality, potentiality, randomness. *Secondness* is the mode of being of that which is such as it is, with respect to a second but regardless of any third (CP 8.328; 1.296). The idea of second is predominant in the ideas of causation and of static force (CP 1.325), comparison, opposition, polarity, differentiation, existence (opposition to everything else). *Thirdness* is the mode of being of that which is such as it is, in bringing a first and second into relation to each other (CP 8.328; 1.297). The idea of third is predominant in the ideas of generality, infinity, continuity, diffusion, growth, intelligence (CP 1.340), meaning, mediation and representation.

- Original Behaviors
- Reactive Behaviors
- Motivated Behaviors

Following the idea of firstness, *original behaviors* are those which do not depend on any sensory input to be generated. In its simplest version, they might be completely random, without influence of anything else. In a more pragmatic account, though, we might have random transformations on previously generated behaviors, making them new behaviors and so, original. What all original behaviors have in common is the fact that, being original, its effect at the environment is previously unknown. Original behaviors are very important for learning. A cognitive architecture might generate original behaviors and test their effect in the world, under many different situations. Depending on the effects they cause in the environment, these original behaviors might be reused in the future. The generation of original behaviors is the source of creativity within a cognitive architecture, allowing the discovery of new means to act in the world. In situations where no other kinds of behaviors are possible, original behaviors also allow the system to move from a problematic state, moving it to a different one, which hopefully, will be treatable. Differently from original behavior, *reactive behaviors* are behaviors that depend on some kind of input, to which the system reacts, following the principles of secondness. Usually, this input is some kind of sensory input, which is transformed internally into an output by the system. The output of a reactive system is basically a deterministic function of its inputs, and possibly some sort of internal variables of the system. Reactive behaviors can be implemented in cognitive architectures in many different ways. They might be generated by rule-based systems, by neural networks or by fuzzy systems. What they all have in common is that reactive behaviors are usually blind to what they cause in the world. They are just mechanically generated and applied, following a recipe, and depending on a situation. Both original behaviors and reactive behaviors are typical in machines and other non-animated objects. Original behaviors are those which do not account on past states to be applied, and reactive behaviors are dependent from the past information in order to be applied. The understanding of the third category is a little bit more trickier. Motivated behaviors are typical in living systems, particularly animals. The idea of a motivated behavior is that this behavior is not just an original behavior or a reaction to something else. The idea of a motivated behavior is that there is a finality in that behavior, a goal that must the reached, a purpose to be accomplished. There is a deep discussion in philosophy regarding this issue. This discussion starts in Aristotle and his notion of final cause, passing through subsequent discussions on teleology, teleonomy and finally reaching cybernetics: the science of control.

There are simple kinds of motivated behaviors. Any closed-loop control system, like a thermostat, performs a sort of motivated behavior. When a thermostat determines the control signals to a cooler system, it is not simply reacting to an input, but they are changing the environment in order for a goal (e.g. a reference temperature) to be reached. And due to the inherent feedback of a closed-loop system, the environment slowly converges to this temperature. It is important to differentiate, though, motivated behaviors from reactive behaviors. A reactive behavior does not have an envisioned future state to achieve. It simply reacts to the inputs, without the requirement of what should come in the future. Motivated systems, on the contrary, have an envisioned future to reach. System outputs are in some sense committed with this expected future.

But motivated systems can be very much more complex than a simple thermostat. The goal to be achieved might require a previous plan, a set of steps which must be performed in order to reach a desired state. The system needs to anticipate the future and select a behavior which will maximize the chance to reach this desired future state. Many things can happen at the environment, and the system needs to find the best behavior to circumvent these extraneous events such that the environment state converges to the desired one. There are many models in the literature trying to explain motivated behavior. The work of (Hull 1943) on the principles of behaviors is one of such models. According to Hull, goal-directed behavior is explained in terms of *needs* intrinsic to living beings, which drive their behavior at the environment. These needs are the motivation for their behavior, and drive the outputs of a living being. Systems which are described in terms of needs, driving their behavior are called then motivational (or motivated) systems.

Motivational systems are being studied in many different works, becoming a field of research in itself (Toates 1986; Baumeister 2016; Reeve 2016). Also, several cognitive architectures provide some sort of implementation of models of motivational systems (Sun 2009; Breazeal et al. 1998; Pezzulo et al. 2014; Bach 2015; McCall 2014). Nevertheless, according to Baumeister (2016), there is still no consolidated theory for explaining all aspects of motivations. According to him, there are at least two important kinds of motivations, which need to be considered, the first one, based on Hull's idea of *drives*, and another one he calls *impulses*. The first kind of motivation (drives) are related to broad dispositional tendencies, recurrent pattterns of desire and frequent behavioral tendencies which are more perennial in its motivational aspect. The second concept of motivation (impulse) refers to a particular desire to perform a particular behavior on a particular occasion. While drives are always being computed, becoming stronger or weaker while affecting behavior, impulses appear in particular instances of time, and disappear as soon as they are satisfied. There is an intrinsic relation between drives and impulses. A motivated creature will always have a hunger drive, causing always the action to eat to reduce it, but the impulse to eat a specific apple you saw in the market store starts at some point (e.g., when you see the apple, or while you remember that there are apples in the market store), and ceases after you eat the apple. In this sense, we might consider that *impulses* are a specific strategy that evolution created for satisfying drives.

Finally, another important remark from Baumeister (2016) is the dichotomy **liking** × **wanting** (Berridge et al. 2009). Both *liking* and *wanting* appear to be related to the motivation mechanism, but in different ways. *Liking* is a phenomenon that is intrinsic to the present. It happens in the present time, without, in principle, any connection to the future. I sense something which I like or dislike. And that's it! *Wanting*, otherwise, occurs in the present but is related to a future, where the wanted thing will consolidate. So, apparently, *wanting* has a direct connection to motivation, providing a goal to be fulfilled. *Wanting* is an important part in the mechanism of *impulse*. I want something, I figure out how to make it happen, I act in the world in order to make my *wanting* to consolidate. But even though they are clearly different things, *liking* and *wanting* are in some form imbricated to each other, because most of the times, I *want* something I *like*, even though it is possible to want something I might not like (Pool et al. 2016). What counts here is the expected reward, not the real reward I receive. According to Pool et al. (2016), the incentive salience hypothesis challenged the drive reduction theory that accounted for motivated behaviors exclusively in terms of the need to reduce drives in order to reestablish homeostasis. In other words, there might be different kinds of reinforcements (rewards/punishments) than simply drive reduction, motivating our behavior. The incentive salience hypothesis postulates that reward processing involves multiple components, including one that is motivational (wanting) and another that is hedonic (liking), which rely on separate neural networks that can be dissociated under particular circumstances.

3 What Are Emotions?

The transposition of ideas from psychology to the construction of artificial systems can be many times misleading, causing a certain discomfort for psychologists and philosophers. This is exactly what happens with the term "emotion". For many researchers, emotions are a unique characteristic of human beings and animals, which should not be used to describe components of a synthetic mind, created by men. In this line of thought, emotions and feelings should be unique to living beings, allowing ourselves to experience the world from a conscious perspective, and should not be attributed to artificial creatures. But is this just human vanity or is really the case? After all, what are emotions? Everyone knows what is to feel fear, happiness, joy, the emotion of our first love, of succeeding in our first job, to be rejected or suffer a punishment for something wrong. But what is the true nature of this phenomenon? Even though everyone has an intuitive idea of what is an emotion, the attempts to formally explain its nature are many and diverse. We can say that we still lack a clear and consensual definition for what are emotions[2]. If we look in the literature, we will discover that emotions are studied in many different fields of knowledge. There are many models, usually incompatible to each other, trying to explain the phenomenon, according to Cabanac (2002) and Izard (2010). Besides that, the term emotion is somewhat linked to many other correlate terms, like affect, feeling, desires, impulses, will, drives, motivations, needs and so on.

---

[2] Izard (2010) compiled 92 different definitions for the term "emotion", collected from books and articles in journals.

If, in a naive move, we look for the term "emotion" at the Wikipedia, for example, we might find the definition of emotion as being "a mental state associated with the nervous system brought on by chemical changes variously associated with thoughts, feelings, behavioural responses, and a degree of pleasure or displeasure. There is currently no scientific consensus on a definition. Emotion is often intertwined with mood, temperament, personality, disposition, and motivation.".

In a search for the etymological origin of the term, emotion comes from Latin *emovere* "to move out, remove, agitate" from assimilated form of *ex* (out) to *movere* (to move), i.e. the etymology is associated to the expression of emotions, but this does not give us a hint on what is the phenomenon from an internal, cognitive perspective.

Even though a great number of models are apparently inconsistent to each other, as Johnson (2009) shows, the use of emotions in intelligent system and particularly in artificial creatures has many interesting contributions (Bates et al. 1994; Blumberg 1997; Koda and Maes 1996; Reilly 1996; El-Nasr 1998; Velásquez 1999; Ventura 2000; Tomlinson and Blumberg 2002; Ortony 2002; Malfaz and Salichs 2004; Sarmento 2004; Cañamero 2005; Meyer 2006; Ziemke and Lowe 2009).

The earlier roots in the study of emotions can be traced back to philosophy, with the distinction between action and passion, the state to be active or passive, as shown by James (1997) and Dixon (2003). In this context, important philosophers as Aristotle, St. Thomas Aquinas, Descartes, Hobbes and Spinoza, just to cite a few, already wrote about the theme. According to Rorty (1982), the concept of passion was gradually refined, in order to achieve the modern concept of emotion, used in psychology. Starting from the idea of passion as a mere passivity to something external to the mind, we evolve to the concepts of feeling, pleasure and displeasure as appraisal reactions to possible courses of actions. From a mere passivity in the beginning, emotions turn into an action of mind, guiding intelligent behavior, assuming an important role in the process of rationality, which was not originally acknowledged[3].

Dixon (2012) points out that the modern concept of "emotion", studied in psychology, appears only at the XIX century, as an abstraction to many different related concepts like appetites, passions, affects and feelings, subjects of philosophical investigation since its beginnings. According to Dixon, the modern concept of emotion was created by the Scottish thinker Thomas Brown (1778–1820), being later used by Darwin and William James. Cornelius (2000) presents the 4 main theoretical perspectives in the modern study of emotions:

The first perspective comes from Darwin (1872), and presents emotions as the result of an evolutionary process. In this process, natural selection gradually shaped a set of behavioral expressions with characteristic functions, important in determining an individual survival while interacting to its environment, in different animal species.

---

[3] See the concept of *emotional intelligence* defended by Goleman (1995), where emotions are pointed out as a foundation in the process of rationality.

The second perspective originates in the work of James (1884), which describes emotions as the perception of affections in the body, causing feelings, perspective also shared by Damasio (1994, 1999, 2003). From his side, Darwin is more concerned with the expression of emotions, documented in his work about the expression of emotions in men and animals. Now James focuses on how the emotional experience modifies the body, before evoking a behavioral disposition, viewed as a tendency on prototypical actions, as a consequence of an evolutionary process (where he agrees with Darwin). So, for James (and also Damásio), emotions are connected to body changes, in a first glance, followed by a feeling, considered as the cognitive effect of the emotion, and further causing a behavioral consequence.

Still, according to Cornelius (2000), the third perspective is a cognitive one. It starts with the work of Arnold (1960) and maybe is one of the most influential in the study of emotions nowadays in psychology. The central idea on this perspective is that thoughts and emotions are inseparable processes. More specifically, emotions are seen as appraisals, i.e. the process by which environmental events are judged good or bad by an individual. Arnold accuses James of too much simplicity in saying that emotions are just the perception of body changes. According to Arnold, James failed in noticing this appraisal aspect of emotions, which will distinguish it from a mere perception. In the same way that James was not able to conceive emotions without body changes, Arnold could not conceive emotions without this appraisal character.

Finally, the fourth perspective about emotions, more recent and more controversial, is the social-constructivist perspective. Opposed to more biological perspectives, which argues for emotions as an adaptation of an evolutionary process, the social-constructivist perspective believes that emotions are a cultural byproduct of learning social rules. According to their defenders, to fully understand the spectrum of complexities around emotions, it is necessary to go beyond the evolutionary aspect and to dig into socio-cultural aspects involving human interaction and their social rules.

These four perspectives implicitly suggest different models to the emotional phenomenon, pointing us to different aspects which might be important in the modeling of emotions. The modeling of emotions is not just related to changes in the body (expression of emotions), or its appraisal aspect, affecting decision-making and behavior. Some authors start to detect other dimensions which seem to be important in the comprehension of the emotional phenomenon. Schlosberg (1954), for example, points out the importance of what he calls the "activation level", or intensity of a given emotion, something which further authors will call the "arousal aspect" of an emotion, pointing out the difference between "strong" emotions and "weak" emotions. Using this dual aspect of appraisal and arousal, different models, as e.g. the PAT (Pleasure-Arousal Theory) from Reisenzein (1994) or the Circumplex Model of affect, developed by Russell (1980) and Posner et al. (2005), besides others, just like e.g. Barrett (1998). After that, other authors start increasing the number of dimensions beyond those. Among them, the dominance-submission axis, according to Russell and Mehrabian (1977) and Mehrabian (1996), or the temporal duration or even a polemic dimension of "quality", according to Cabanac (2002), possibly created due to the fact emotions like fear and hunger have different qualities. The unsolved question of what would be this "quality" started finding a solution when the community decided to substitute a unique hedonic pleasure/displeasure dimension by multiple appraisal dimensions. Then, the term appraisal started being understood as a process evaluating the significance of many different factors for the well being of an individual. This notion of "well being of an individual" started to incorporate the satisfaction or dissatisfaction of potentially multiple needs, values, goals and beliefs of the individual. In other words, anything that should matter for an individual, as pointed out by Moors et al. (2013).

This last evolution in the models of emotions pass through an obvious connection with the model of motivational behavior developed by Hull (1952), which started to be of great importance in the development of new models of emotions in the context of artificial cognition. According to Hull, motivated behavior can be explained due to a set of needs, which drive corresponding actions on the environment. It is implicit in this model that this action should cause a reduction in the corresponding need, or, in other words, that this need should be satisfied by the results of this action. Hull developed then, the concept of *drive*, as a measure evaluating how much a need is not satisfied. A high drive indicates that its corresponding need has a low level of satisfaction, causing more effect in the behavioral decisions. A low drive indicates that the need was properly satisfied. According to Hull, a living organism might have a full set of needs, each of them with a corresponding intensity (or dissatisfaction) level, at each time instant. The role of a motivational system is to evaluate the state of satisfaction of these needs, measured by their corresponding drives, and choose the best action in the sense of satisfying the needs with most intense drives. Drives can be physiological or social. Physiological needs give rise to the so called low level primary drives. Examples of this kind of drives, pointed out in the literature are hunger, thirst, sleep and safety (preservation from physical damages). Social needs give rise to the so called high level primary drives. Examples of such include friendship, social inclusion, reciprocity, curiosity, autonomy, and honor.

Some work in the literature propose a whole hierarchy of needs, as the work from Maslow (1943). In this hierarchy, instead of just two levels (low and high) of priority (low level drives have more priority), different hierarchical levels might be conceived, creating a whole hierarchy of priorities among needs. The literature also points out the existence of secondary drives, which are not only determined by sensory information, as in the case of primary drives. In secondary drives, the need satisfaction is determined by either sensory information and other drives. So, secondary drives are those which are originated from other drives.

It is clear, here, that there is a great connection between theories about emotions and theories about motivations, according to Buck (1988). In fact, in some cases it is either difficult to distinguish where emotions and motivations are different, because both themes are largely imbricated. Needs, drives, motivations and emotions seem to be just components of a more complex motivational system, being an important part in the determination of either human or animal behavior.

Finally, it is important to point out the relevance of emotions for the rational behavior, discussed more recently in works like those from Damasio (1994, 1999, 2003) and Goleman (1995). The authors propose that a rational behavior depends directly from the appraisal aspect of emotions. Without emotions as a criteria, rationality becomes impossible, according to them. In the next sections, we present some of the models developed using these theories about emotions and motivations in building a cognitive architecture.

4   The OCC Model: Ortony, Clore, Collins

One of the pioneer studies of emotions, originated from models in cognitive psychology, but with a great impact in the development of artificial cognitive systems is the model developed by Ortony et al. (1990), regarding the cognitive structure of emotions, called here the OCC Model. It is a typical model originated from the appraisal/arousal dichotomy, called by authors as valency and activation. According to the OCC Model, emotions are internal mental states which can have different intensities, and which are predominantly related to affects. Affects are considered as evaluative reactions to situations considered to be good or bad, being these reactions bounded to:

- Events and their consequences (things which happen and are perceived by an individual);
- Agents and their actions (other people or animated beings actuating in the world - including an estimate of these agent's mental states, giving rise to emotions like proud, admiration, shame and criticism);
- Objects and their properties (emotions aroused from perceptions regarding the object).

The OCC Model specifies 22 emotions implemented in terms of local and global variables. One of the differentials from the OCC Model is the fact of employing artificial intelligence tools in the modeling. These appear in the form of rules, considering the triggering potential of an emotion, the threshold for the triggering of an emotion and the intensity of such emotion. The triggering potential of an emotion can be a desire (of a consequence or of an event), a deserve (of an action onto an agent), or an appeal (of an object). The distinction of the reactions to events, agents and objects, which is a characteristic of the OCC Model, allows us to distinguish between tree different kinds of emotions:

- To be happy or unhappy (with the occurrence of an event - reaction to events)
- Reactions of approval or disapproval (to actions realized by other agents - reaction to agents)
- To like or dislike (a given object or state - reaction to objects)

The OCC Model is a meta-model[4] highly cited in many works involving cognitive architectures for artificial creatures, and the synthesis of artificial emotions (Bates et al. 1994; Reilly 1996; Koda and Maes 1996; El-Nasr 1998; El-Nasr et al. 2000; Velásquez 1998; Wallach et al. 2008).

---

[4] A meta-model is a model of a model, i.e., a kind of abstract model which demands an instance in a concrete model, in order to be used.

5   Damásio and the Somatic Marker

The work of Damasio (1994, 1999, 2003) is another highly cited in many articles involving emotions and intelligent systems, as e.g. the works of Velásquez (1998, 1999), Ventura (2000), Tomlinson and Blumberg (2002), Malfaz and Salichs (2004), Sarmento (2004), Ziemke and Lowe (2009). In "Descartes Error", Damasio (1994) proposes rationality with emotions, and the requirement of a body in the process. The author proposes a distinction between emotions and feelings, proposing that an emotion will be a modification in the body due to external stimuli (following basically the ideas from William James) and feelings would be a cognitive counterpart of emotions, appearing after the conscious acquisition of emotions.

Damásio classifies emotions into primary and secondary. Primary emotions are those we experience since our childhood, those for which there might be a pre-organized inborn mechanism. Secondary emotions are those proper to adult individuals, learned through experience since childhood to adulthood. Primary emotions would be those like fear, joy, sadness, rage, etc. Secondary emotions would be those like jealousy, guilt, pride, etc. Primary emotions are normally triggered due to external or internal stimuli, from sensory organs. Secondary emotions would require cognitive events.

Damásio elaborates then his hypothesis of somatic marker, where emotions are seen as marks of different aspects of situations or the result of possible actions, which might be used as differential aspects in the process of decision-making. When we experience an emotion, the immediate result is a body change, like e.g. an acceleration in our heart beating, or an increase in sweating. To this emotion there would be a related feeling, a cognitive evaluation regarding the convenience or inconvenience of the situation for the individual. This body change marks the situation causing it. In the future, other similar situations will be recognized and classified as good or bad, in the same way. This affects our subsequent decision-making, according to the evoked body changes. More than that, he advocates that the brain systems participating in emotion arousal and decision-making are both involved in the cognitive control and social behavior determination.

Emotions, in this context, work both as an initial criteria in decision-making, where an elaborated reasoning was not yet developed (a kind of unconscious reasoning, instinctive, almost reactive, but clearly motivational), and those more elaborated clearly deliberative reasoning. In the first case, depending on the intensity of the body change, the decision can be really visceral, definitive. In the second case, usually different possible scenarios are analyzed and one of them chosen. In both cases, the judgment criteria comes from an appraisal, originated from an emotional memory.

6 Simon and Sloman: Emotions as Attention Filters and Alarms

A researcher with many contributions in the modeling of emotions and affect in artificial systems is Aaron Sloman, actually at the University of Birmingham - UK, where he directs the project "Cognition and Affect" since 1976 (but in Birmingham since 1991). One of the reasons for us to explicitly mention this line of research (Sloman et al. 2001) is his peculiar model of emotions, which is quite different from the other models presented since so far.

Sloman et al. (2001) developed his model based on a theory of emotions as *interruptions*, previously proposed by Simon (1967). In this theory, Simon also uses the need theory from Hull as a basis, but with different results. According to Simon, there were three different kinds of needs: those from uncertain and non-predictive environmental events (as e.g., the appearance of a predator in the forest); the physiological needs (as e.g. hunger, thirst); and the needs coming from cognitive associations (as, e.g. those associations leading to anxiety). According to Simon, environmental events, memory evocations or motivations might change the current subject's goals, causing its interruption. The unexpected appearance of a predator, for example, might cause the interruption of an animal previous behavior, and the generation of new goals, as the escape from a danger. Simon dedicated to deeply study the process on how goals and targets are interrupted and the consequent change in behavior occasioned by emotions. His theory was that emotions comprise a complex mechanism of interruption, working like a monitor to the many parallel goals managed by the motivational system, causing behavioral changes due to relevant changes in the experienced situation.

Based on the "emotions as interruptions" theory from Simon, Sloman and Croucher (1981), Sloman (1987, 1992) develops then his Attention Filter Penetration Theory (AFP), to explain emotions. Differently from Simon, which terminally aborts the interrupted motivational processes, in Sloman's AFP, the attention filters triggered by emotions just caused a momentary disruption in the course of actions targeting a goal, with the possibility of returning to it later, if the event causing the emotion (and the disruption) was successfully treated. In this new perspective, emotions work as attention filters, or as Sloman (1998) calls it later, *alarms*. The idea of an alarm is that of a process (usually fast and efficient), able to detect specific patterns and trigger a reaction chain determining radical changes in behavior. The justification for these alarms is that behavior generation processes might be slow to generate, and in some particular critic situations, maybe the system might not have time enough to deliberate what to do[5], being a fast action required, even though this action is not necessarily the optimum action. In the animal world, this might happen, e.g., in predatory situations, or other lethal danger. In the human being, this might happen always that dangerous situations are detected or, in an analogous way, while an advantage

---

[5] I.e., in critical situations, there is not enough time for slow decision-making processes, and a fast behavior might be necessary to take the system out of the critical situation.

opportunity (which might cease quickly) requiring a fast move is necessary. So, Sloman (1998) conceives an emotional system as global alarm system, working as an attention filter in either reactive or deliberative processes, aborting certain kinds of behavior and emphasizing others.

7   Cañamero and the Modulation of Motivations

The model developed by Cañamero (1997, 1998, 2001, 2003, 2005) differentiates from the previous ones in many aspects. This researcher proposes an emotional system for autonomous agents where emotions work as motivation modulators, with the definition of synthetic hormones affecting the many homeostatic processes associated to the needs of virtual creatures.

The motivational system developed by Cañamero assumes a set of body variables generating drives for regulatory behavior, with the aim of making the values of such body variables among determined parameters. The body variables are: adrenaline level, blood pressure, blood glucose rate, endorphine level, energy level, heart beat, pain, respiratory rate, temperature and vascular volume. Each of these variables has a reference value and a current value. The difference between the reference value and the current value works as a drive to trigger certain kinds of behavior which, beyond the effect they cause at the environment, actualize the current value of these body variables, in a homeostasis mechanism. So, both the creatures actions and their pragmatic effect in world, affect the regulation of body variables.

At each instant, based on the difference between current and reference values of the many body variables, a landscape of drives is determined (i.e., a set of performance indexes informing how far the body variables are from their reference values). The drive with the highest intensity (i.e., indicating a body variable which is the most far from its reference value) is selected to determine the immediate behavior for the creature, triggering an action over the environment, and at the same time reducing the corresponding drive. This is the basic motivational system, still without emotions.

The emotional mechanism, according to Cañamero, is independent from the motivational mechanism, even though affecting it. Critical situations from the environment trigger the emotion mechanism. The emotions used by Cañamero are: fear, rage, happiness, sadness, boredom and curiosity. Only one of these emotions is active in a given instant. Situations from the environment determine different levels of *arousal* for each of the emotions, and the one with the greatest arousal, since greater than a threshold, is chosen as the current emotion. This emotion causes the release of a hormone, affecting the body variables and causing a change in their values. The same hormone might affect in different ways different variables. Changing the values of body variables, emotions (i.e. the hormones) affect the final behavior, by changing the landscape of drives directing their behavior, modulating it to the criticality of the situation.

In Cañamero's model, emotions are not directly linked to the appraisal aspect of motivations, but work as second order modulators, or amplifiers of motivations, causing a momentary unbalance on the homeostatic process. This turns some drives more intense than others, under special situations, as e.g. those situations of high risk or extremely favourable situations, which do not repeat too often, demanding an opportunistic move in order to bring expressive benefits to the goals of a creature.

8   Picard and Affective Computing

Finally, the last work we want to highlight is the work of Rosalynd Picard, not because it brought a specific model of emotions, but because it brought structure to the study of emotions in artificial systems. Picard (1997) organized the study of what she called Affective Computing, considering different uses of emotions in artificial systems. First, Picard draws our attention that emotions can be used in three different ways in artificial system:

- To recognize Emotions
- To express Emotions
- To have Emotions

In this way, a creature (or system) can simply be able to recognize emotions in human beings or other creatures, without effectively expressing them or having them, indeed. In the same way, it might be capable of expressing a behavior which might be interpreted as being derived from an emotional state (so, just simulating them, without really *having* them, i.e., without using them from a cognitive standpoint). This could be the case, e.g., when the system is interacting with humans, aiming at evoking in them emotions, but without truly using them internally. And finally, we might want the creature or system to truly "have" emotions, i.e., being truly affected in its behavior due to the recognition of perceived situations. Even though these abilities are independent, it might be the case we want the artificial system to hold all of them together, to be able to recognize emotions, to express emotions and to really "have" emotions.

Picard also proposed the possibility of testing the "emotional performance" of a system. In this analysis, she pretend to evaluate the "emotional behavior" of a system, trying to answer the following questions about it: Does the system appears to have emotions? Does it provide a fast response to specific stimuli? Does it interpret the current situation and evaluates it? Does it appear to have different feelings for different emotions? Does these emotions make any influence in its behavior? So, regarding emotions, she asks if these exert any influence on learning and/or on decision-making, or memory recovery.

Also, Picard attempts for the possibility of having many different levels of representation for emotions. In its lower levels, we might have emotional signals (properties), like e.g. emotive response decay, repetitive stimuli, influences in mood and personality, non-linearity, time invariance, saturation, physical and cognitive feedback, background mood. In the medium level, she analyses the subject of emotion expression, in terms of patterns or models. Finally, on the high level, she analyses the cognitive exploitation of emotions, in terms of concepts and ideas, and how these are affected by emotions.

9 Discussion

The many works involving emotions, since from a purely cognitive modeling point of view up to its use in cognitive architectures, for the construction of artificial systems, allows us to state a great number of considerations.

First, it is necessary to acknowledge that there is no unique model, neither a mainstream model in the research regarding emotions and motivations. From one side, we have the studies originated from Darwin on the expression of emotions and the effect they cause in body, something which is recognized by William James, Damásio and others. The idea that emotions affect initially the body, and further leading to its cognitive use leads us to the Appraisal/Arousal dichotomy. The appraisal aspect relates to the evaluative aspect of emotions. The arousal is more related to the dynamic aspect of emotions, the specific reaction to objects, events and situations, as pointed out in the OCC model.

The appraisal aspect of emotions might provide a connection to how motivations work for the human being, influencing a homeostatic process where some internal variables are regulated, just as in a control system, affecting the way we behave and do decision-making. But also here, we have the work of Sloman, which sees emotion only on exception handling behavior, working as alarms, or even the drive modulation scheme, amplifiers of the values affecting judgment, as pointed out by Cañamero. We see then that the notion of emotions is fragmented together with motivations, and each proponent has a good argumentation to background their models. Besides that, these models appear to be radically different among themselves.

Would it be possible to develop a model unifying all these points, such that each of the arguments could be considered, at least in part? It seems to us that the great difficulty in having a unifying model is that there is a unique term: emotion, which is associated to different facets of a behavior generation process, where each author uses as a tag, but focusing in different aspects, mistakenly identifying these parts with emotions as a whole. In other words, maybe this difficulty comes from the non-technical use of the word emotion, as in common language, or even in the use of metaphors in the construction of a definition.

In this sense, trying to consider the many different arguments from multiple authors, and in the attempt of unifying all the proposals, we propose here a new definition for what emotions really are, and what is the relation between emotions and motivations. Even though, this is "one more" definition, in a topic already overloaded of definitions, it is our opinion that this might possibly solve the question of considering all the many different viewpoints.

In the model for motivational/emotional systems we propose in this article, we defend that emotions are a "feature" of advanced motivational systems, particularly used when two or more motivational systems develop some kind of communication among each other, and they need to exchange information regarding their motivations, for the purpose of collaboration and/or competition. The reader should observe that it is a radical move from other definitions of emotions, which propose emotions as foundational elements in their models.

To defend our proposal, we develop an evolutionary analysis regarding emotions in animals, and the evolution of their brains. It is remarkable that motivational behavior appears even in evolutionary older vertebrates, like fishes and reptiles (and either in some kinds of invertebrates like insects). Even though this might be potentially controversial[6], emotional behavior is easily acknowledged only in birds and mammals, where the so called limbic system is more evolved. Now, only on the human being (and possibly some kinds of animals like monkeys, chimpanzees, dolphins and maybe others), the neocortex is more evolved. So, just like Cañamero points out, maybe the motivational systems appeared first in evolutionary older species, still without emotional capacity. Probably, emotional systems only evolved later, since the development of the limbic system, as suggests Panksepp (1982). Then, only after the development of the neocortex, reason was incorporated. Even though appearing later, they don't replace older systems, but enhance them, aggregating new functionalities.

So, our hypothesis is that motivational systems, with a repertoire of needs, with a measure for the satisfaction of these needs (drives), and a homeostatic mechanism generating actions on the environment, causing the reduction of these drives, is an older mechanism, appearing even in animals still without the capacity of emotions. This mechanism is what we call the "Basic Motivational System", maybe found in reptiles and older animals (in the evolutionary scale). These mechanisms might be implemented also in artificial creatures and systems, and should not be confused with emotions.

Even these *basic* motivational systems are already sophisticated, since the homeostasis process leads us to the satisfaction of the creatures assigned needs. Then, creating a suitable repertoire of needs, we might create artificial creatures with a rather sophisticated behavior, becoming apt to perform rather complex purposive behavior. The reader should observe, though, that these systems still do not have emotional capabilities.

A first sophistication we should introduce on basic motivational systems is to give them the ability to substitute *drives* for *impulses*. If we start designing motivational systems, assigning a large number of needs, it will become almost impossible to find actions that are able to reduce all the drives at the same time. Some kind of priority should be established in order to reduce drives. Even though we might think of a system with fixed priorities, in a hierarchy of needs (using ideas like those from Maslow (1943)), maybe a better enhancement would be to treat drive reduction indirectly, with a different strategy, considering *impulses*. Then, instead of having the responsibility of discovering drive reducing actions, able to completely solve the problem (something which could be difficult, depending on the needs we have), we discretize the problem by generating *impulses*, and then creating strategies for solving them. So, while my hunger drive starts to increase, instead of finding an action to reduce this drive, we generate an impulse, which if satisfied, will reduce the drive. Observe that this strategy is just an enhancement of the basic motivational mechanism, but

---

[6] Some people might understand that animals without a limbic system might be able to perform emotional behavior.

which opens great opportunities for newer enhancements. But still, these systems would not be considered emotional, in our proposal, because everything happens still within one creatures "mind", being still inaccessible to others. According to our proposal, emotions will only appear in these systems, when they start sharing and communicating their motivations to each other, with the purpose of collaboration or competition.

And how this should happen? According to our thesis, at some point, evolution discovered that sharing our motivations to others should bring some evolutionary advantage in terms of making collaboration/competition easy. This started with the appearance of the limbic systems in animals. Then, instead of just internalizing drives and using them to generate behavior, the drive determination mechanism was enhanced to include an intermediate step, where some body change was first created, and later internalized in order to generate drives. The result was that now, these body changes could be used to communicate to other creatures, our drives. By observing in other animals the body changes, a creature might estimate their internal drives and design an interaction strategy to foster collaboration or competition with them. This is the expression of emotions, compatible with the ideas of Darwin, James and Damásio.

Observe that the idea of others are not discarded with our proposal. We still might have body changes, as pointed out by Darwin, James and Damásio, we still might have an internalization of this body change in order to measure how specific needs are being (or not) satisfied (the appraisal aspect, pointed out in the OCC model), we still might have alarms, in the generation of particular impulses in order to give preference in critical situations, and we might still have the modulation of motivations, as proposed by Cañamero. We are just not calling them emotions, but reserving this word only in the case the communication of motivations is being exercised among interacting creatures. Observe that this proposal also gives rise to more complex emotional behaviors, where things like moods or personalities are considered.

There is only one final remark which is necessary to approach: the dichotomy *liking* × *wanting*, and how it fits with our proposition for the concept of emotion. Many models consider the hedonic dimension (liking) as being in the roots of what is an emotion. We are not making this connection here. In our proposition, what we might call *feeling* is a composition of two different kinds of information, embedded into internal states: drives and reinforcements. The mechanism exploiting drives, in order to generate impulses and then actions, are in the kernel of our *wanting* mechanism, which is the basis of our model for a motivational system. So, a drive is a measure of insatisfaction of an internal need. A drive is reduced by the generation of an *impulse*, attached to a particular situation where this drive is reduced, creating a goal for the motivational system. The system then must generate a plan for satisfying this goal, and execute it, reaching a future state where this need is satisfied. But this mechanism considers only the *wanting*. What is *liking* good for? Well, in a first glance we are considering that the *liking* first appeared (in an evolutionary point of view) as an instantaneous measure of drive change in time, used with the purpose of learning the actions able to fulfill the purpose of reducing drives and making the motivational machine operational. So, in our hypothesis, maybe the first motivational creatures might not have *liking* at all, only *wanting*. Then, evolution just discovered that there is a cost in measuring drive change in time, and eventually created innate *liking* mechanisms which might accelerate the process of making the motivation machine fully operational faster, providing evolutionary advantage. The main purpose of the *liking* mechanism is to allow learning through reinforcements. Over time, eventually evolution started to provide ontogenetic support for other kinds of reinforcements, not necessarily tied to drive change in time, creating the basis for a full mechanism of reinforcement learning in our cognitive architecture. The result is that today's creatures are equipped with both drives and reinforcements, to provide motivational behavior and learning. And what about emotions? Well, because emotions for us is the process of communication of motivational components among creatures, the messages which are exchanged are exactly these feelings: drives and reinforcements. This is the reason while earlier modelers associated emotions with the hedonic dimension (the *liking* component of feelings). So, feelings are not emotions, but are the messages which are exchanged in an emotional system. So, our proposal seems to be coherent also with these earlier models, just providing a better understanding on how feelings connect with emotions.

10 Final Considerations

As we have seen along this work, there are many available models both for emotions and for motivations, which can be used as a background for the construction of cognitive architectures. Even though they seem to be in conflict, we proposed here a view which unifies all these contributions in a coherent unified model, which describes both a motivational system, based in drive reduction homeostasis, and impulses (as specified by Baumeister (2016)), capable of fulfilling both models for *wanting* and *liking*, where the *wanting* mechanism enables purposive behavior to consolidate and *liking* is used with the purpose to provide reinforcement learning capabilities to our cognitive architecture.

Aligned with an evolutionary perspective on how emotions appeared in animals, we tried not to use the word emotion to designate phenomena which we understand are exclusive to the scope of a motivational system, but reserved this word only to designate a particular strategy, developed by evolution, to communicate motivational information among creatures, with the purpose of collaboration/competition. In this sense, emotions are messages exchanged between creatures, informing their internal motivational components, like e.g. *wanting* and *liking* information, such that with the possession of these information, the motivational system is able to develop more enhanced strategies for dealing with collaboration and competition.

In this work, we presented our ideas in a more conceptual format, sometimes lacking a more precise description of all the involved mechanisms. Even with this constraint, we occupied several pages in order to organize all these ideas.

We are aware that a more precise and mathematical formulation of these ideas is necessary, and we intend to provide such formalization in a future work.

Acknowledgments. The authors thank Ericsson Research Brazil, Ericsson Telecomunicações S.A. Brazil (Proc. FUNCAMP 4881.7) and CEPID/BRAINN (Proc. FAPESP 2013/07559-3) for supporting this research.

References

Arnold, M.B.: Emotion and Personality. Columbia University Press, New York (1960)

Bach, J.: Modeling motivation in MicroPsi 2. In: Bieger, J., Goertzel, B., Potapov, A. (eds.) AGI 2015. LNCS (LNAI), vol. 9205, pp. 3–13. Springer, Cham (2015). https://doi.org/10.1007/978-3-319-21365-1_1

Barrett, L.F.: Discrete emotions or dimensions? The role of valence focus and arousal focus. Cogn. Emot. **12**(4), 579–599 (1998)

Bates, J., et al.: The role of emotion in believable agents. Commun. ACM **37**(7), 122–125 (1994)

Baumeister, R.F.: Toward a general theory of motivation: problems, challenges, opportunities, and the big picture. Motiv. Emot. **40**(1), 1–10 (2016)

Berridge, K.C., Robinson, T.E., Aldridge, J.W.: Dissecting components of reward: 'liking', 'wanting', and learning. Curr. Opin. Pharmacol. **9**(1), 65–73 (2009)

Blumberg, B.M.: Old tricks, new dogs: ethology and interactive creatures. Ph.D. thesis, Massachusetts Institute of Technology (1997)

Breazeal, C., et al.: A motivational system for regulating human-robot interaction. In: AAAI/IAAI, pp. 54–61 (1998)

Buck, R.: Human Motivation and Emotion. Wiley, Chichester (1988)

Cabanac, M.: What is emotion? Behav. Process. **60**(2), 69–83 (2002)

Cañamero, L.: A hormonal model of emotions for behavior control. In: VUB AI-Lab Memo 2006, pp. 1–10 (1997)

Cañamero, L.: Issues in the design of emotional agents. In: Emotional and Intelligent: The Tangled Knot of Cognition. Papers from the 1998 AAAI Fall Symposium, pp. 49–54 (1998)

Cañamero, L.: Emotions and adaptation in autonomous agents: a design perspective. Cybern. Syst. **32**(5), 507–529 (2001)

Cañamero, L.: Designing emotions for activity selection in autonomous agents. Emot. Hum. Artifacts **115**, 148 (2003)

Cañamero, L.: Emotion understanding from the perspective of autonomous robots research. Neural Netw. **18**(4), 445–455 (2005)

Cornelius, R.R.: Theoretical approaches to emotion. In: ISCA Tutorial and Research Workshop (ITRW) on Speech and Emotion (2000)

Damasio, A.R.: Descartes' Error: Emotion, Reason, and the Human Brain. Penguin Books, New York (1994)

Damasio, A.R.: The Feeling of What Happens: Body and Emotion in the Making of Consciousness. Harcourt, New York (1999)

Damasio, A.R.: Looking for Spinoza: Joy, Sorrow, and the Feeling Brain. William Heinemann, London (2003)

Darwin, C.: The Expression of the Emotions in Man and Animals. John Murray, Albermarle St., London (1872)

Dixon, T.: From Passions to Emotions: The Creation of a Secular Psychological Category. Cambridge University Press, Cambridge (2003)

Dixon, T.: "Emotion": the history of a keyword in crisis. Emot. Rev. 4(4), 338–344 (2012)

El-Nasr, M.S.: Modeling emotion dynamics in intelligent agents. Ph.D. thesis, Texas A & M University (1998)

El-Nasr, M.S., Yen, J., Ioerger, T.R.: Flame-fuzzy logic adaptive model of emotions. Auton. Agents Multi-Agent Syst. 3(3), 219–257 (2000)

Goleman, D.: Emotional intelligence. Bantam Books, New York (1995)

Hull, C.L.: Principles of Behavior: An Introduction to Behavior Theory. Appleton-Century, Oxford (1943)

Hull, C.L.: A Behavior System; An Introduction to Behavior Theory Concerning the Individual Organism. Yale University Press, New Haven (1952)

Izard, C.E.: The many meanings/aspects of emotion: definitions, functions, activation, and regulation. Emot. Rev. 2(4), 363–370 (2010)

James, S.: Passion and Action: The Emotions in Seventeenth-Century Philosophy. Oxford University Press, Oxford (1997)

James, W.: What is an emotion? Mind 9, 188–205 (1884)

Johnson, G.: Theories of emotion. In: Internet Encyclopaedia of Philosophy: A Peer-Reviewed Academic Resource (2009)

Koda, T., Maes, P.: Agents with faces: the effect of personification, In: Proceedings 5th IEEE International Workshop on Robot and Human Communication. RO-MAN 1996, Tsukuba, pp. 189–194. IEEE (1996)

Malfaz, M., Salichs, M.A.: A new architecture for autonomous robots based on emotions. In: Fifth IFAC Symposium on Intelligent Autonomous Vehicles. Citeseer (2004)

Maslow, A.H.: A theory of human motivation. Psychol. Rev. 50(4), 370 (1943)

McCall, R.J.: Fundamental motivation and perception for a systems-level cognitive architecture. Ph.D. thesis, University of Memphis (2014)

Mehrabian, A.: Pleasure-arousal-dominance: a general framework for describing and measuring individual differences in temperament. Curr. Psychol. 14(4), 261–292 (1996)

Meyer, J.-J.C.: Reasoning about emotional agents. Int. J. Intell. Syst. 21(6), 601–619 (2006)

Moors, A., Ellsworth, P.C., Scherer, K.R., Frijda, N.H.: Appraisal theories of emotion: state of the art and future development. Emot. Rev. 5(2), 119–124 (2013)

Ortony, A.: On making believable emotional agents believable. In: Trappl, R., Petta, P., Payr, S. (eds.) Emotions in Humans and Artifacts, Chap. 6, pp. 189–212. Bradford Book, MIT Press, Cambridge, London (2002)

Ortony, A., Clore, G.L., Collins, A.: The Cognitive Structure of Emotions. Cambridge University Press, Cambridge (1990)

Panksepp, J.: Toward a general psychobiological theory of emotions. Behav. Brain Sci. 5(3), 407–422 (1982)

Pezzulo, G., Verschure, P.F., Balkenius, C., Pennartz, C.M.: The principles of goal-directed decision-making: from neural mechanisms to computation and robotics. Philos. Trans. R. Soc. B 369(1655), 20130470 (2014)

Picard, R.W.: Affective Computing. MIT Press, Cambridge (1997)

Pool, E., Sennwald, V., Delplanque, S., Brosch, T., Sander, D.: Measuring wanting and liking from animals to humans: a systematic review. Neurosci. Biobehav. Rev. 63, 124–142 (2016)

Posner, J., Russell, J.A., Peterson, B.S.: The circumplex model of affect: an integra-
tive approach to affective neuroscience, cognitive development, and psychopathology.
Dev. Psychopathol. **17**(3), 715–734 (2005)

Reeve, J.: A grand theory of motivation: why not? Motiv. Emot. **40**(1), 31–35 (2016)

Reilly, W.S.: Believable social and emotional agents. Ph.D. thesis, Carnegie Mellon
University, Pittsburgh, PA (1996)

Reisenzein, R.: Pleasure-arousal theory and the intensity of emotions. J. Pers. Soc.
Psychol. **67**(3), 525 (1994)

Rorty, A.O.: From passions to emotions and sentiments. Philosophy **57**(220), 159–172
(1982)

Russell, J.A.: A circumplex model of affect. J. Pers. Soc. Psychol. **39**(6), 1161 (1980)

Russell, J.A., Mehrabian, A.: Evidence for a three-factor theory of emotions. J. Res.
Pers. **11**(3), 273–294 (1977)

Sarmento, L.M.: An emotion-based agent architecture. Master's thesis, FC University
of Porto, Artificial Intelligence and Computer Science (2004)

Schlosberg, H.: Three dimensions of emotion. Psychol. Rev. **61**(2), 81 (1954)

Simon, H.A.: Motivational and emotional controls of cognition. Psychol. Rev. **74**(1),
29 (1967)

Sloman, A.: Motives, mechanisms, and emotions. Cogn. Emot. **1**(3), 217–233 (1987)

Sloman, A.: Prolegomena to a theory of communication and affect. In: Ortony, A.,
Slack, J., Stock, O. (eds.) Communication from an Artificial Intelligence Perspective,
pp. 229–260. Springer, Heidelberg (1992). https://doi.org/10.1007/978-3-642-58146-
5_12

Sloman, A.: Damasio, descartes, alarms and meta-management. In: SMC 1998: Conference Proceedings of 1998 IEEE International Conference on Systems, Man, and
Cybernetics (Cat. No. 98CH36218), vol. 3, pp. 2652–2657. IEEE (1998)

Sloman, A., Croucher, M.: Why robots will have emotions. In: Proceedings of the 7th
International Joint Conference on Artificial Intelligence, vol. 1, pp. 197–202. Morgan
Kaufmann Publishers Inc. (1981)

Sloman, A., et al.: Beyond shallow models of emotion. Cogn. Process. **2**(1), 177–198
(2001)

Sun, R.: Motivational representations within a computational cognitive architecture.
Cogn. Comput. **1**(1), 91–103 (2009)

Toates, F.M.: Motivational Systems. Propblems in the Behavioral Sciences, vol. 4.
Cambridge University Press, Cambridge (1986)

Tomlinson, B., Blumberg, B.: Social synthetic characters. Comput. Graph. **26**(2), 5–7
(2002)

Velásquez, J.: A computational framework for emotion-based control. In: Proceedings
of the Workshop on Grounding Emotions in Adaptive Systems. International Conference on SAB, pp. 62–67 (1998)

Velásquez, J.D.: From affect programs to higher cognitive emotions: An emotion-based
control approach. In: Proceedings of the Emotion-Based Agent Architecture Workshop at the International Conference on Autonomous Agents, pp. 114–120. Citeseer
(1999)

Ventura, R.: Emotion-based agents. Master's thesis, Instituto Superior Técnico, Lisboa,
Portugal (2000)

Wallach, W., Allen, C.: Moral Machines: Teaching Robots Right from Wrong. Oxford
University Press, Oxford (2008)

Ziemke, T., Lowe, R.: On the role of emotion in embodied cognitive architectures: from
organisms to robots. Cogn. Comput. **1**(1), 104–117 (2009)

Selected Challenges in Grammar-Based Text Generation from the Semantic Web

Simon Mille[(✉)] [ID]

Universitat Pompeu Fabra, Barcelona, Spain
simon.mille@upf.edu
http://www.springer.com/gp/computer-science/lncs

Abstract. In this paper, based on the recent outcome of two shared tasks on structured data verbalisation, and examining one system in particular, we present some evidence why grammar-based systems are particularly relevant for the verbalisation of structured data as found in the Semantic Web. We then define possible future lines of research, centered around the FORGe system and the linguistic grounding of Semantic Web datasets.

Keywords: Natural Language Generation · Semantic Web · Grammar-based systems

1 Introduction

Nowadays, thanks to Semantic Web (SW) initiatives such as the W3C Linking Open Data project[1], a tremendous amount of structured knowledge is publicly available in the form of language-independent triples. The Linked Open Data (LOD) cloud[2] currently contains over a thousand interlinked datasets (as, for instance, DBpedia[3] or Wikidata[4]), which cover a large range of domains and amount to billions of different triples. Table 1 shows three DBpedia triples – Subject, Property, Object- related to black rice (arròs negre), representing its origin and two of its ingredients.[5]

The LOD datasets are frequently enriched, manually or automatically, by extracting knowledge from, e.g., multimedia and textual data, and populate already available domain models (i.e., known class and property definitions), as well as acquire new −unknown− ones (ontology learning). Their formal knowledge representation allows for applying powerful algorithms which have proved crucial

---

[1] https://www.w3.org/wiki/SweoIG/TaskForces/CommunityProjects/
LinkingOpenData.
[2] http://lod-cloud.net/.
[3] https://wiki.dbpedia.org/.
[4] https://www.wikidata.org/wiki/Wikidata:Main_Page.
[5] This information appears in the infobox of the corresponding Wikipedia page:
https://en.wikipedia.org/wiki/Arr%C3%B2s_negre.

© Springer Nature Switzerland AG 2019
G. S. Osipov et al. (Eds.): Artificial Intelligence, LNAI 11866, pp. 85–95, 2019.
https://doi.org/10.1007/978-3-030-33274-7_5

Table 1. Sample triples from the food domain (from the English DBpedia).

	Subject	Property	Object
Triple 1	Arròs_negre	Country	Spain
Triple 2	Arròs_negre	Ingredient	White_rice
Triple 3	Arròs_negre	Ingredient	Squid

in fields such as Question Answering [19]. However, there has been relatively little research in applying Natural Language Generation (NLG, or Text Generation) techniques to the multilingual verbalisation from Semantic Web contents, as exemplified in Table 2.

Table 2. Possible verbalisations of the triples from Table 1.

Language	Possible verbalisation
English 1	Arròs negre is a dish from Spain. It contains white rice and squid
English 2	White rice and squid are basic ingredients of the Spanish dish called Arròs negre
Spanish 1	Arròs negre es un plato español basado en arroz blanco y calamar

Existing NLG systems for Semantic Web contents are, on the one hand, not adapted to the richness nor the constant evolution of the LOD cloud and its target users, and, on the other hand, application- and language-specific, and thus have coverage and/or reliability issues. As a result, their usefulness, robustness and portability –some of the most challenging issues in NLG nowadays [8]– are limited. In the remainder of the paper, we argue that grammar-based NLG is efficient for text generation from LOD data; we give a short overview of the most widely used NLG techniques for generating texts from structured data, point out their current limitations, and define a few aspects that would need to be developed in the near future in order to ensure scalability and reusability.

2   Natural Language Generation in the Context of the Semantic Web

2.1   Approaches and Limitations

The Semantic Web and Natural Language Generation communities have for a long time been disconnected: one of the primary applications of the Semantic Web resources is Question Answering, for which the understanding of the questions and the retrieval of the answers is the main focus, rather than the verbalisation of the triples; indeed, returning a simple list of triples as answer to a question may suffice [17]. Very recently, in 2015, the first International Workshop on Natural Language Generation from the Semantic Web was organised in France (WebNLG[6]). As mentioned in the workshop call of papers, on the one hand, Semantic Web applications need to make the contents accessible the potential users, and on the other hand, NLG-based approaches have been used for verbalising structured data coming from, e.g., ontologies [5,13] or time series [3,7]. These two areas are complementary but relatively few attempts have been made to bring them together.

Traditionally, Natural Language Generation is viewed a sequence of three subtasks: (i) content selection, which is responsible for determining the contents to be rendered as text, (ii) text planning, which takes care of packaging the contents into discursively organised units (i.e., sentences) and (iii) linguistic generation, which realises the contents as well-formed text [30]. The advantage of splitting language generation into specific tasks is to allow for a precise and independent modelling of each level of language description (semantics, syntax, topology, morphology).

For the verbalisation of structured data, there are three main approaches to realise each of these subtasks [8,16]: (i) filling slot values in predefined sentence templates (e.g. [1]), (ii) applying grammars (rules) that encode different types of linguistic knowledge (e.g. [35]), and (iii) predicting statistically the most appropriate output (e.g. [4,15]). Template-based systems are very reliable in terms quality, but are the worst in terms of portability since new templates need to be defined for every new domain, style, language, etc. Statistical systems have the widest coverage, but the relevance and the quality of the produced texts cannot be ensured. Furthermore, they are fully dependent on the available –scarce and mostly monolingual– training data [23]. The development of grammar-based systems is time-consuming and usually they have coverage issues, but they are easy to port to a new domain (and also style, language, etc.), do not require training material, allow for a greater control over the outputs (e.g. for mitigating possible errors or tuning the output to a desired style), and the linguistic knowledge used for one domain or language can be reused for other domains and languages. However, due to their complexity, such approaches have undergone few developments within the open-source community in the recent years [16]. In addition, a number of systems actually address the whole sequence as one step, by combining approaches (i) and (iii) and filling the slot values of pre-existing templates using neural network techniques [26].

Last but not least, let us note that another limitation to the Natural Language Generation from Semantic Web data is that until recently, NLG from SW data has been applied to independent datasets only, leaving aside multiple interlinked datasets,[7] and a large part of it has focused on the description of the knowledge model rather than on the verbalisation of the contents [33].

---

[6] http://www.wikicfp.com/cfp/servlet/event.showcfp?eventid=45093.
[7] One of the first papers mentioning multiple datasets was published in 2012 [10].

2.2   FORGe: An Example of a Grammar-Based System

FORGe is an open-source generator developed at the Pompeu Fabra University, implemented as graph-transducers and that covers the last two NLG subtasks (text planning and linguistic generation). FORGe, according to the lines of the Meaning-Text Theory [21], is based on the notion of linguistic dependencies, that is, the semantic, syntactic and morphologic relations between the components of the sentence. Input predicate-argument structures are mapped onto sentences by applying a series of rule-based graph-transducers. The generator handles Semantic Web (SW) inputs by means of introducing abstract predicate-argument (PredArg) templates and micro-planning grammars as previous steps to the core linguistic generation module. A sample PredArg template is shown in Fig. 1: the DBpedia property *floorArea* is mapped to the predicate *floor_area*, which has two arguments, a building and a surface area, which are respectively the subject and the object of the property. Lists of such instantiated (*populated*) PredArg structures are passed on to the generator.

$$
\begin{array}{ccc}
\overset{A1}{\frown} & & \overset{A2}{\frown} \\
subject & floor\_area & object \\
dpos{=}NP & definiteness{=}INDEF & class{=}Literal
\end{array}
$$

Fig. 1. Sample PredArg template for the floor area of a building

For micro planning, on the one hand, generic rules look for shared pairs of predicate and subject argument in the populated templates, and introduce coordinations or quasi-coordinations between the two objects as in: *[Alan Bean]$_S$ [was born]$_P$ [in Wheeler]$_{O1}$ [on March 15, 1932]$_{O2}$*. Other generic rules check if an argument of a predicate appears further down in the ordered list of PredArg structures. If so, the PredArg structures are merged by fusing the common argument; during linguistic generation, this results in the introduction of post-nominal modifiers such as relative and participial clauses or appositions; e.g. *250 Delaware Avenue$_S$, which has a [floor area]$_{P2}$ of [30843.8 square meters]$_{O2}$, [is]$_{P1}$ in Buffalo$_{O1}$*). On the other hand, rules specific to a domain (e.g restaurant domain here) have been implemented so as to aggregate objects that have not been aggregated by the generic rules; between the brackets, detail of the restrictions about co-occurring properties:

- eatType$_{P1}$ + priceRange$_{P2}$: *a cheap$_{O2}$ pub$_{O1}$*.
- eatType$_{P1}$ + familyFriendly$_{P2}$: *a family-friendly$_{O2}$ restaurant$_{O1}$*.
- etc.

For rendering of the aggregated PredArg structures into sentences, the core FORGe grammars [24] perform the following actions: (i) syntacticisation of predicate-argument graphs; (ii) introduction of function words; (iii) linearisation and retrieval of surface forms. First, a deep-syntactic structure is generated: missing parts of speech are assigned, the syntactic root of the sentence is chosen, and from there, a syntactic tree over content words is built node by node. Then, idiosyncratic words (prepositions, auxiliaries, determiners, etc.) are introduced and fine-grained (surface-)syntactic labels are established, using a subcategorisation lexicon. For this purpose, lexical resources are used that can be derived from PropBank [18] or VerbNet [31]; see [25]. Personal and relative pronouns are introduced using the *class* feature, which allows for distinguishing between human and non-human antecedents. Finally, morpho-syntactic agreements are resolved, the syntactic tree is linearised, through the ordering of (i) governor/dependent and (ii) dependents with each other, and the surface forms are retrieved. Post-processing rules are then applied: upper casing, replacement of underscores by spaces, etc.

For illustrating these three steps, consider the *floorArea* property of Fig. 1, from the WebNLG dataset, and selected phenomena: (i) the support verb *be* is established as the root, (ii) the preposition *of* is introduced, and (iii) the *subject* relation between *be* and *floor area* causes the former to be placed after the latter and get morphological agreement features from it (third person singular): *the floor area$_{3sg}$ of building X > is$_{3sg}$ N m^2.*

3 What Grammar-Based Systems Are Good For: Lessons Learnt from the WebNLG and E2E Challenges

3.1 The WebNLG and E2E Challenges

In the past two years, two NLG challenges starting from structured data took place, namely WebNLG [14] and E2E [27], and different types of systems were used to produce outputs: template-based, rule-based, statistical machine translation-based, recurrent neural network-based, etc.; see respective overview papers.

In the framework of the WebNLG challenge, the task consisted in generating texts from up to 7 DBpedia triples from 15 different categories, covering in total 373 different DBpedia properties. 9 categories appeared in the training data (Astronaut, Building, University, Monument, ComicsCharacter, Food, Airport, SportsTeam and WrittenWork), and six categories were "unseen", in that they did not appear in the training data (Athlete, Artist, City, MeanOfTransportation, CelestialBody, and Politician). At the time of the challenge, the WebNLG dataset contained about 25K data-text pairs for about 10K distinct inputs, that is, about 2.5 reference sentences per triple set. The challenge thus focused on verbalising a wide range of inputs.

The input for the E2E challenge is very similar to the WebNLG challenge in the sense that it consisted of a list of up to 8 triples, corresponding to 8 properties from the Restaurant domain (name, location, nearby restaurants, type of food, type of restaurant, price range, customer rating, kid friendliness). The E2E data consisted of about 50K data-text pairs; only 108 different combinations of properties are found in the training set, which gives an average of about 500 reference sentences per triple set. Thus, unlike WebNLG, E2E focuses on the (many) different ways to render a specific set of properties. The evaluation data does not contain unseen combinations of properties. For both challenges, the datasets were released in triple format (*Subject, Property, Object*). In the following, another DBpedia triple and a target reference sentence are shown:

320_South_Boston_Building || architect || George_Winkler
George Winkler designed the 320 South Boston Building.

For both challenges, automatic and human evaluations were carried out; only the common metrics are reported here. BLEU [28] and METEOR [2] are *n*-gram-based metrics that compare word-to-word a candidate with a reference sentence. BLEU matches exact words only, whereas METEOR matches also synonyms; 100 and 1 respectively indicate sameness. For human evaluations, judges are asked to either rank or rate candidate sentences in terms of their adequacy with the input (*Semantics*), their linguistic correctness (*Grammar*), and their *Fluency*. Nine systems were evaluated for WebNLG, and twenty-one for E2E, and most competing systems follow statistical approaches.

3.2 Results and Discussion

Table 3 shows the results obtained by the FORGe system (see Sect. 2.2). The results of the two shared tasks were informative in different aspects. First of all, the best systems (neural systems) score much better than a rule-based system such as FORGe according to basic automatic evaluation metrics: for the BLEU metric, the difference is of about 20 points on seen data (WebNLG: 60.59/40.88, E2E 68.05/42.07), and FORGe obtains core among the lowest. However, when synonymy is taken into account, as in the METEOR metric, the gap is much smaller, and the system ranks can even sometimes be inverted (e.g,. WebNLG *seen*, in which FORGe ranks 3–4 instead of 8 according to BLEU). Second, the results of the human evaluations are rather different, with FORGe ranking much higher than according to the automatic evaluations: at WebNLG, FORGe is consistently in the first half of the ranking, and for E2E, in which the systems end up being clustered in five groups of equivalent ratings, it reaches the second cluster. In other words, even though the outputs produced by a grammar-based system do not reflect faithfully the reference outputs, they tend to be well accepted by human judges, in any case better accepted than suggested by the automatic metrics.

Finally, the evaluation on the unseen properties at WebNLG shows that FORGe was the most adaptable system, attaining the first rank according to both automatic and human metrics. When statistical systems have no training data, they are simply not able to generate correct texts, but a grammar-based system does not rely on the training data, and it is thus possible to tune it to new inputs at a reduced cost.[8] Note however that when enough good quality data is

---

[8] It took about two hours to adapt FORGe to a hundred new DBpedia properties.

Table 3. Scores (and rankings) of FORGe according to BLEU and METEOR, and rankings according to human evaluations (Semantics, Grammar, Fluency).

Dataset	BLEU	METEOR	Semantics	Grammar	Fluency
WebNLG all	38.65 (3–4)	0.39 (1)	1	1	1–2
WebNLG seen	40.88 (8)	0.40 (3–4)	2–4	1–2	4–5
WebNLG uns.	35.70 (1)	0.37 (1)	1	1	1
E2E all (seen)	42.07 (20)	0.37 (20)	10–14 (cluster 2/5)		

provided, the human evaluations of some neural systems can be astounding and even outperform human-written texts, as it was the case for the ADAPT system [11] on the WebNLG seen properties [32].

4 Towards an Efficient Verbalisation of Structured Data

4.1 Challenges for the FORGe Generator

In order to target a multilingual Natural Generation System, a large part of the core resources need to be language-independent and their portability to new languages need to be ensured, as well as their flexibility, so that the tool can be used not only in question/answering systems, but also in applications with more complex input structures that proceed from analysed text, such as text summarisation, text simplification and dialogue interfaces.

With respect to the development of graph-transduction grammars, three critical issues currently need to be highlighted: (i) the packaging of the selected triples into coherent groups (micro-planning), (ii) the definition of a valid sentence structure over each group of triples, and (iii) the creation of grammar-compatible NLG-oriented lexical resources. For the first subtask, micro-planning grammars need to be improved in the sense that they should allow for more types of aggregation than the one described in Sect. 2.2, and be made as domain-independent as possible. This can be done by looking at large amounts of textual data in order to compile the common aggregation patterns in the different languages and domains, and adapting the rules accordingly. For the second subtask, the sentence structuring module needs to be tested on a large scale in order to obtain wide coverage and ensure flexibility and multilinguality. Most of the rules at this level are generic and produce complete syntactic structures, but there is no validation of their correctness so far. As the input structures get more complex (i.e. as the number of triples to verbalize increases), defining a correct sentence structures can get more challenging, and here again the compilation of language-specific preferred syntactic patterns would help controlling the process. For the third subtask, the automatic extraction of NLG- and dependency-suited information from lexica and annotated data (e.g. VerbNet, PropBank) needs to be investigated. In particular, the syntactic information about the participants (e.g. if a preposition is needed *–ingredient of*) is not expressed directly in the existing resources. However, this subcategorisation information can be derived from, e.g., VerbNet, which is neither NLG– nor dependency-friendly. Some steps in this direction have already been done in [20,25].

4.2   Challenges in the Linguistic Grounding of LOD Datasets

As far as input representations are concerned, an NLG pipeline needs to be fed with linguistic structures. These are quite different from the triples found on the LOD cloud, in which the Properties are labeled with an open vocabulary and only two types of relations (Subject and Object) are used. The triples should be mapped onto linguistic concepts and relations, preferably according to standard lexico-semantic resources to ensure reusability (e.g. VerbNet, NomBank [22] and PropBank, which, thanks to the amount of multilingual resources connected to them, can be used as interlingua). For instance, the property *ingredient* as seen in Table 1 would need to be mapped to, e.g., the PropBank predicate contain.01, or the NomBank predicate ingredient.01, and the Subject and Object to be mapped to the corresponding participant slot according to their respective subcategorisation frames. Participant slots can be simple predicate-argument relations –first argument, second argument, etc.– or more "conceptual" relations such as Agent, Patient, Beneficiary. For an informed generation process, basic properties of the participants, e.g. classes such as their type (Country, Ingredient, Person) and gender (Female or Male), found on the LOD cloud in the form of respective class and property assertions, need to be added to the linguistic representation.

To the best of our knowledge, little research has been carried out so far on bringing together SW contents and standard linguistic resources in the context of NLG: on the one hand, standard SW approaches such as *lemon* [34] or word embeddings [29] define their own lexicons to be associated with the properties, and on the other hand linguistic resources such as VerbNet, NomBank and Prop-Bank are generally not connected with SW knowledge bases. One exception is the PreMOn model [9], which specifically aims at linking VerbNet, NomBank, PropBank and FrameNet [12] with an ontology that models semantic classes and their roles; however, PreMon leaves open the mapping to specific LOD datasets such as DBpedia.[9]

The linguistic grounding challenge is thus focused on the mapping of triples onto abstract linguistic structures to serve as input for the NLG pipeline; this includes the mapping of (both *known* and *unknown*) properties, as well as of their arguments (Subject and Object), onto minimal language-independent linguistic structures that contain all the information needed for being verbalised. There is a need to innovate according to the linguistic grounding of database sub-structures based on class and property statements onto sentential semantic structures. Linguistically motivated interface structures based on PropBank and/or VerbNet representations need to be defined, as well as the mappings from both known and unknown LOD triples, to account for the high degree of dynamism of SW databases. The connection of SW lexicons with language-oriented ones need to

---

[9] See also [6] for an overview of models to represent linked data and their issues.

be investigated, together with the use of the semantics of the underlying schema (e.g. taxonomical information) in order to derive basic features (e.g. class, gender, etc.) or generalising the concepts in case some contents are very specific and cannot be mapped onto the exact concept.

5 Conclusions

Statistical text generation systems have been the main focus of the Natural Language Generation community in the past years. However, their low portability to new languages and domains and the lack of control over the final output, as well as the very limited amount of actual linguistic knowledge used during the generation process are currently obstacles to the widespread use of such systems on Semantic Web structured data. In this paper, we show how grammar-based systems are suitable for the verbalisation of structured data and discuss open challenges and future lines of research, centered around (i) the increase of both grammatical and lexical coverage and (ii) the linguistic grounding of Semantic Web datasets.

Acknowledgements. The work reported in this paper has been partly supported by the European Commission in the framework of the H2020 Programme under the contract numbers 700475-IA, 700024-RIA, 779962-RIA, 786731-RIA and 825079-ICT-STARTS.

References

1. Androutsopoulos, I., Lampouras, G., Galanis, D.: Generating natural language descriptions from OWL ontologies: the naturalowl system. J. Artif. Intell. Res. **48**, 671–715 (2013)
2. Banerjee, S., Lavie, A.: METEOR: an automatic metric for MT evaluation with improved correlation with human judgments. In: Proceedings of the ACL Workshop on Intrinsic and Extrinsic Evaluation Measures for Machine Translation and/or Summarization, pp. 65–72 (2005)
3. Belz, A.: Automatic generation of weather forecast texts using comprehensive probabilistic generation-space models. J. Nat. Lang. Eng. **14**(4), 431–455 (2008)
4. Belz, A., White, M., Espinosa, D., Kow, E., Hogan, D., Stent, A.: The first surface realisation shared task: overview and evaluation results. In: Proceedings of the Generation Challenges Session at the 13th European Workshop on Natural Language Generation (ENLG), Nancy, France, pp. 217–226 (2011)
5. Bontcheva, K., Wilks, Y.: Automatic report generation from ontologies: The MIAKT approach. In: Meziane, F., Métais, E. (eds.) NLDB 2004. LNCS, vol. 3136, pp. 324–335. Springer, Heidelberg (2004). https://doi.org/10.1007/978-3-540-27779-8_28
6. Bosque-Gil, J., Gracia, J., Montiel-Ponsoda, E., Gómez-Pérez, A.: Models to represent linguistic linked data. Nat. Lang. Eng. **24**(6), 811–859 (2018)
7. Bouayad-Agha, N., Casamayor, G., Mille, S., Wanner, L.: Perspective-oriented generation of football match summaries: old tasks, new challenges. ACM Trans. Speech Lang. Process. **9**(2), 3:1–3:31 (2012)

8. Bouayad-Agha, N., Casamayor, G., Wanner, L.: Natural language generation in the context of the semantic web. Semant. Web **5**(6), 493–513 (2014)

9. Corcoglioniti, F., Rospocher, M., Aprosio, A.P., Tonelli, S.: PreMON: a lemon extension for exposing predicate models as linked data. In: Proceedings of the 10th International Conference on Language Resources and Evaluation (LREC), pp. 877–884 (2016)

10. Dannélls, D., Damova, M., Enache, R., Chechev, M.: Multilingual online generation from semantic web ontologies. In: Proceedings of the 21st International Conference on World Wide Web, pp. 239–242. ACM (2012)

11. Elder, H., Gehrmann, S., O'Connor, A., Liu, Q.: E2E NLG challenge submission: towards controllable generation of diverse natural language. In: Proceedings of the 11th International Conference on Natural Language Generation, pp. 457–462 (2018)

12. Fillmore, C.J., Baker, C.F., Sato, H.: The FrameNet database and software tools. In: Proceedings of the 3rd International Conference on Language Resources and Evaluation (LREC), Las Palmas, Canary Islands, Spain, pp. 1157–1160 (2002)

13. Galanis, D., Androutsopoulos, I.: Generating multilingual descriptions from linguistically annotated OWL ontologies: the naturalowl system. In: Proceedings of the Eleventh European Workshop on Natural Language Generation, pp. 143–146. Association for Computational Linguistics (2007)

14. Gardent, C., Shimorina, A., Narayan, S., Perez-Beltrachini, L.: Creating training corpora for micro-planners. In: Proceedings of the 55th Annual Meeting of the Association for Computational Linguistics (Volume 1: Long Papers). Association for Computational Linguistics, Vancouver, Canada, August 2017

15. Gardent, C., Shimorina, A., Narayan, S., Perez-Beltrachini, L.: The WebNLG challenge: generating text from RDF data. In: Proceedings of the 10th International Conference on Natural Language Generation, pp. 124–133 (2017)

16. Gatt, A., Krahmer, E.: Survey of the state of the art in natural language generation: core tasks, applications and evaluation. J. Artif. Intell. Res. **61**, 65–170 (2018)

17. Höffner, K., Walter, S., Marx, E., Usbeck, R., Lehmann, J., Ngonga Ngomo, A.C.: Survey on challenges of question answering in the semantic web. Semant. Web **8**(6), 895–920 (2017)

18. Kingsbury, P., Palmer, M.: From TreeBank to PropBank. In: Proceedings of the 3rd International Conference on Language Resources and Evaluation (LREC), Las Palmas, Canary Islands, Spain, pp. 1989–1993 (2002)

19. Kwok, C., Etzioni, O., Weld, D.S.: Scaling question answering to the web. ACM Trans. Inf. Syst. (TOIS) **19**(3), 242–262 (2001)

20. Lareau, F., Lambrey, F., Dubinskaite, I., Galarreta-Piquette, D., Nejat, M.: GenDR: a generic deep realizer with complex lexicalization. In: Proceedings of the 11th International Conference on Language Resources and Evaluation (LREC), Miyazaki, Japan, pp. 3018–3025 (2018)

21. Mel'čuk, I.: Dependency Syntax: Theory and Practice. State University of New York Press, Albany (1988)

22. Meyers, A., et al.: The NomBank project: an interim report. In: Proceedings of the Workshop on Frontiers in Corpus Annotation, Human Language Technology Conference of the North American Chapter of the Association for Computational Linguistics (HLT/NAACL), Boston, MA, USA, pp. 24–31 (2004)

23. Mille, S., Belz, A., Bohnet, B., Graham, Y., Pitler, E., Wanner, L.: The first multi-lingual surface realisation shared task (SR 2018): overview and evaluation results. In: Proceedings of the 1st Workshop on Multilingual Surface Realisation (MSR), 56th Annual Meeting of the Association for Computational Linguistics (ACL), Melbourne, Australia, pp. 1–12 (2018)

24. Mille, S., Carlini, R., Burga, A., Wanner, L.: FORGe at SemEval-2017 task 9: deep sentence generation based on a sequence of graph transducers. In: Proceedings of the 11th International Workshop on Semantic Evaluation (SemEval-2017), Vancouver, Canada, pp. 917–920. Association for Computational Linguistics, August 2017. http://www.aclweb.org/anthology/S17-2158

25. Mille, S., Wanner, L.: Towards large-coverage detailed lexical resources for data-to-text generation. In: Proceedings of the First International Workshop on Data-to-text Generation, Edinburgh, Scotland (2015)

26. Nayak, N., Hakkani-Tür, D., Walker, M.A., Heck, L.P.: To plan or not to plan? discourse planning in slot-value informed sequence to sequence models for language generation. In: Proceedings of INTERSPEECH, Stockholm, Sweden, pp. 3339–3343 (2017)

27. Novikova, J., Dušek, O., Rieser, V.: The E2E dataset: new challenges for end-to-end generation. In: Proceedings of the 18th Annual Meeting of the Special Interest Group on Discourse and Dialogue, Saarbrücken, Germany (2017). https://arxiv.org/abs/1706.09254, arXiv:1706.09254

28. Papineni, K., Roukos, S., Ward, T., Zhu, W.J.: BLEU: a method for automatic evaluation of machine translation. In: Proceedings of the 40th Annual Meeting on Association for Computational Linguistics, pp. 311–318. Association for Computational Linguistics (2002)

29. Perez-Beltrachini, L., Gardent, C.: Learning embeddings to lexicalise RDF properties. In: * SEM 2016, The Fifth Joint Conference on Lexical and Computational Semantics, pp. 219–228 (2016)

30. Rambow, O., Korelsky, T.: Applied text generation. In: Proceedings of the 3rd Conference on Applied Natural Language Processing (ANLP), Trento, Italy, pp. 40–47 (1992)

31. Schuler, K.K.: VerbNet: a broad-coverage, comprehensive verb lexicon. Ph.D. thesis, University of Pennsylvania (2005)

32. Shimorina, A., Gardent, C., Narayan, S., Perez-Beltrachini, L.: The WebNLG challenge: report on human evaluation. Technical report, Université de Lorraine, Nancy, France (2017)

33. Stevens, R., Malone, J., Williams, S., Power, R., Third, A.: Automating generation of textual class definitions from OWL to English. J. Biomed. Semant. **2**, S5 (2011). BioMed Central

34. Walter, S., Unger, C., Cimiano, P.: M-ATOLL: a framework for the lexicalization of ontologies in multiple languages. In: Mika, P., et al. (eds.) ISWC 2014. LNCS, vol. 8796, pp. 472–486. Springer, Cham (2014). https://doi.org/10.1007/978-3-319-11964-9_30

35. Wanner, L., Bohnet, B., Bouayad-Agha, N., Lareau, F., Nicklaß, D.: MARQUIS: generation of user-tailored multilingual air quality bulletins. Appl. Artif. Intell. **24**(10), 914–952 (2010)

Multi-Agent Path Finding – An Overview

Roni Stern[(✉)]

Ben Gurion University of the Negev, Be'er Sheva, Israel
sternron@post.bgu.ac.il

Abstract. Multi-Agent Pathfinding (MAPF) is the problem of finding paths for multiple agents such that every agent reaches its goal and the agents do not collide. In recent years, there has been a growing interest in MAPF in the Artificial Intelligence (AI) research community. This interest is partially because real-world MAPF applications, such as warehouse management, multi-robot teams, and aircraft management, are becoming more prevalent. In this overview, we discuss several possible definitions of the MAPF problem. Then, we survey MAPF algorithms, starting with fast but incomplete algorithms, then fast, complete but not optimal algorithms, and finally optimal algorithms. Then, we describe approximately optimal algorithms and conclude with non-classical MAPF and pointers for future reading and future work.

Keywords: Multi-Agent Pathfinding · Heuristic search

1 Introduction

MAPF is the problem of finding paths for multiple agents such that every agent reaches its desired destination and the agents do not conflict. MAPF has real-world applications in warehouse management [50], airport towing [27], autonomous vehicles, robotics [45], and digital entertainment [26].

Research on MAPF has been developing rapidly in the past decade. In this paper, we provide an overview of MAPF research in the Artificial Intelligence (AI) community. The purpose of this overview is to help researchers and practitioners that are less familiar with MAPF research better understand the problem and current approaches for solving. It is not to intended to serve as a comprehensive survey on MAPF research.

This overview paper is structured as follows. In Sect. 2, we define the problem formally, and discuss several of its notable variants. Then, a simple analysis of the problem is given to illustrate its difficulty. Section 3 starts by describing *prioritized planning* [34], which is still the most common approach in practice to solve MAPF problems. We discuss the limitation of this approach, in particular, the lack of completeness or optimality. Then, we mention several MAPF algorithms that are fast and complete, but may return solutions that are not optimal.

Supported by ISF grant 210/17 to Roni Stern.

© Springer Nature Switzerland AG 2019
G. S. Osipov et al. (Eds.): Artificial Intelligence, LNAI 11866, pp. 96–115, 2019.
https://doi.org/10.1007/978-3-030-33274-7_6

Section 4 surveys several families of MAPF algorithms that are guaranteed to return an optimal solution. Section 5 covers approximately optimal algorithms, i.e., algorithms that guarantee the solution they return is at most a constant factor more costly than an optimal solution. Finally, the paper concludes with a partial list of MAPF extensions (Sect. 6), and pointers to further reading and resources (Sect. 7). In addition, throughout this paper, we point to interesting directions for future work.

2   Problem Definition

The literature includes multiple definitions of the MAPF problem. In this paper, we mostly focus on what is called *classical MAPF* [37]. Section 6 discusses other variants of MAPF. A classical MAPF problem with k agents is defined by a tuple $\langle G, s, t \rangle$ where:

- $G = (V, E)$ is an undirected graph whose vertices are the possible locations agents may occupy and every edge $(n, n') \in E$ represents that an agent can move from n to n' without passing through any other vertex.
- s is a function that maps an agent to its initial location.
- t is a function that maps an agent to its desired destination location.

Time is discretized into time steps. In every time step, each agent can perform a single *action*. There are two types of actions: *wait* and *move*. An agent performing a *wait* action stays in its current location for one time step. A *move* action moves an agent from its location to some other location. Move action takes exactly one time step, and can only move an agent from its current location to one of its adjacent locations. A *valid solution* to a MAPF problem is a joint plan that moves all agents to their goals, in a way that agents do not collide. Next, we define the terms valid solution, joint plan, and collision, in a formal way.

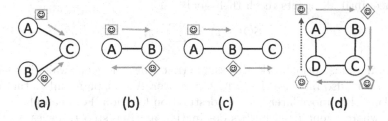

(a)   (b)   (c)   (d)

Fig. 1. Illustration of different types of conflicts, taken from Stern et al. [37]: (a) a vertex conflict, (b) a swapping conflict, (c) a following conflict, and (d) a cycle conflict.

A *single-agent plan* for an agent i is a sequence of actions that if agent i performs these actions in location $s(i)$ it will end up in location $t(i)$. Formally, a single-agent plan for agent i is sequence of actions $\pi = (a_1, \ldots a_n)$ such that

$$a_n(\cdots a_2(a_1(s(i))) \cdots) = t(i) \tag{1}$$

A *joint plan* is a set of single-agent plans, one for each of the k agents. For a joint plan Π, we denote by Π_i its constituent single-agent plan for agent i. A pair of agents i and j have a *vertex conflict* in a joint plan Π if according to their respective single-agent plans Π_i and Π_j both agents are planned to occupy the same vertex at the same time. Similarly, agents have a *swapping conflict* in a joint plan if they are planned to swap locations over the same edge at the same time. A *valid* solution to a MAPF problem is a joint plan that has none of these conflicts.

Some MAPF applications have stricter requirements from a valid solution, prohibiting other types of conflicts. Two notable types of conflicts are *following* conflicts and *cycle* conflicts. A *following conflict* occurs if an agent plans to occupy at time step $t + 1$ a location that was occupied by some other agent at time step t. A *cycle conflict* occurs if a set of agents $i, i + 1, \ldots j$ plan to move in the same time step t in a circular pattern, i.e., agent i plans to move in time step $t + 1$ to agent's $i + 1$ location at time step t, agent $i + 1$ plans to move in time step $t + 1$ to agent's $i + 2$ at time step t, and so on, while agent j plans to move in time step $t + 1$ to agent's i location at time step t. Figure 1 illustrates all these different types of conflicts. See Stern et al. [37] for a comprehensive discussion on different types of conflicts and the relationships between them.

2.1 Optimization

MAPF problems can have more than one valid solution. In many MAPF applications, one would like to find a valid solution that optimizes some objective function. The two most common objective functions used for evaluating a MAPF solution are *makespan* and *sum of costs*. The makespan of a joint plan Π, denoted $M(\Pi)$ is the number of time steps until all agents reach their goal.

$$M(\Pi) = \max_{1 \le i \le k} |\pi_i| \qquad (2)$$

The sum of costs of a joint plan Π, denoted $SOC(\Pi)$ is the sum of actions performed until all agents reach their goal.

$$SOC(\Pi) = \sum_{1 \le i \le k} |\pi_i| \qquad (3)$$

Following most prior work, we assume that when an agent waits in its destination then it also increase the SOC of the overall joint plan, unless that agent is not planned to move later from its destination location. For example, consider the case where agent i reaches its destination at time step t, leaves it at time step t', arrives back to its destination at time step t'', and stays there until all agents reach their destinations. Then this single-agent plan contributes t'' to the SOC of the corresponding joint plan.

2.2 From Single-Agent Pathfinding to MAPF

A single-agent shortest-path problem (SPP) is the problem of finding the shortest path in a graph $G = (V, E)$ from a given source vertex $s \in V$ to a given target vertex $t \in V$. MAPF can be reduced to a shortest-path problem in a graph known as the k-agent search space. This graph, denoted G_k, is different from the single-agent graph G. A vertex in G represents a location that an agent may occupy in a particular time step. A vertex in G_k represents a set of locations, one per agent, that the agents can occupy in a particular time step. Thus, a vertex in G_k is a vector of k vertices in G. An edge in G_k represents a *joint action* of all agents, that is, a set of k actions, one per agent, that the agents can perform *simultaneously* in a particular time step. Joint actions that result in a conflict, will not have a corresponding edge in G_k. The cost of an edge in G_k corresponds to the cost of the corresponding joint action.

Observation 1. *A lowest-cost path in G_k from $\big(s(1), \ldots, s(k)\big)$ to $\big(t(1), \ldots t(k)\big)$ is an optimal solution to the MAPF problem $\langle G, s, t \rangle$ and vice versa.*

Heuristic Search and the A* Algorithm. Heuristic search in general and the A* algorithm in particular [18] are commonly used to solve shortest-path problems. For completeness, we provide a brief background on A*.

A* is a best-first search algorithm. It maintains a list of vertices called OPEN. Initially, OPEN contains the source vertex. In every iteration, a single vertex is removed from OPEN and *expanded*. To expand a vertex means to go over each of its neighbors and *generate it*. To generate a vertex means creating it and adding it to OPEN, unless it has already been generated before. For every generated vertex n, A* maintains several values.

- $g(n)$ is the cost of the lowest-cost path found so far from the source vertex to n.
- *parent*(n) is the vertex before n on that path.
- $h(n)$ is a *heuristic* estimate of the cost of the lowest-cost path from n to the target vertex.

Let $h^*(n)$ be a *perfect* heuristic estimate for n, that is, the cost of the lowest-cost path from n to a goal. If $h^*(n)$ is known for all nodes, then one can find the shortest path from the source vertex to the target by choosing to go to the vertex with the smallest h value. A heuristic function h is called *admissible* iff for every vertex n it holds that $h(n) \leq h^*(n)$. The A* algorithm chooses to expand the vertex n in OPEN that has the smallest $g(n) + h(n)$ value.

Theorem 1 (Optimality of A* [18]). *Given an admissible heuristic, A* is guaranteed to return an optimal solution, i.e., a shortest path from the source vertex to its target.*

Observation 1 and Theorem 1 mean that one can solve a given MAPF problem by running A* on the k-agent search space. A simple way to obtain an admissible heuristic for the k-agent search space is by considering the cost of the shortest path in G from every vertex $v \in V$ to every target vertex $t(1), \ldots t(k)$. This is done as follows. Let $d(v, t(i))$ be the cost of the shortest path from v to $t(i)$.

Computing $d(v, t(i))$ for every $v \in V$ and $i \in \{1, \ldots, k\}$ can be done in time that is polynomial in $|V|$ and k, in the beginning of the search. Then, the following is an admissible heuristic when optimizing for sum of costs

$$h((v_1, \ldots v_k)) = \sum_{i \in \{1, \ldots, k\}} d(v_i, t(i)) \tag{4}$$

and the following is an admissible heuristic when optimizing makespan

$$h((v_1, \ldots v_k)) = \max_{i \in \{1, \ldots, k\}} d(v_i, t(i)) \tag{5}$$

Challenges in Solving MAPF with A*. A very rough way to estimate the hardness of solving a shortest path problem, with A* and other algorithms, is by considering the *size* of the search space and its *branching factor*, which in our case corresponds to the number of vertices in G_k and its average outgoing degree. Thus, in the worst case, the size of the search space is $|V|^k$ and the branching factor is $\left(\frac{|E|}{|V|}\right)^k$. As can be seen, both values are exponential in the number of agents.

To get an estimate of these numbers, consider a MAPF problem with 20 agents on a 4-connected grid with 500×500 cells. In this case, the size of the search space is $25{,}000^{20} \approx 9.09 \cdot 10^{87}$ and the branching factor is $4^{20} \approx 1.1 \cdot 10^{12}$ $|V| \approx 25{,}000$. The exponential branching factor is especially problematic for A*, since A* must at least expand all vertices along an optimal path. The computational cost of expanding a vertex, however, is at least linear in the branching factor. Thus, textbook A* cannot be used to solve a MAPF problem with a large number of agents, even with a perfect heuristic function.

3 Fast MAPF Algorithms

A fundamental approach to address this combinatorial explosion is to try to decouple the MAPF task to k single-agent pathfinding problems with as minimal interaction as possible. Perhaps one of the most popular approaches to do so is *prioritized planning*.

3.1 Prioritized Planning

The first step in prioritized planning is to assign each agent a unique number from $\{1, \ldots k\}$. Then, a single-agent plan is found for each agent in order of their priority. When an agent searches for a plan, it is required to find a plan that avoids creating a conflict with plans already found for agents with higher priority.

A fundamental difference between a textbook shortest-path problem and the problem of finding a plan for the agent with the ith priority is that in the latter an optimal solution may require an agent to wait in its location. Thus, to find a plan for the ith agent, is, in fact, a shortest path problem in a *time-expansion* graph [34]. In a time-expansion graph, every vertex represents a pair (v, t), where v is a vertex in the underlying graph G and t is a time step. There is an edge between vertices (v, t) and (v', t') in the time-expansion graph iff $t' = t+1$ and v' is either equal to v or it is one of its neighbors. The size and branching factor of the corresponding search space is manageable: the number of vertices is $|V| \times T$, where T is an upper bound on the solution makespan, and the branching factor is $\frac{|E|}{|V|} + 1$. For example, in a MAPF problem with 20 agents on a 4-connected grid with 500×500 cells, assuming $T = 1,000$, we have a search space size of 25,000,000 and a branching factor of 5. A* has been successfully applied to much larger search spaces.

The computational efficiency and simplicity of prioritized planning algorithms is the main reason for their widespread adoption by practitioners. Implementing prioritized planning includes many design choices. For example, several methods have been proposed for setting the agents' priorities [1,7]. The Windowed Hierarchical Cooperative A* algorithm (WHCA*) [34] also allowed interleaving planning and execution in a prioritized planning framework. In WHCA*, the agents plans to avoid conflicts only for the next X time steps (the "window"). After performing these X steps, the agents can re-plan the next X steps in the same manner.

Prioritized planning is a *sound* approach for MAPF, in the sense that it returns valid solutions. However, it is neither *complete* nor *optimal*. That is,

- **Not complete.** A prioritized planning algorithm may not find any solution to a solvable MAPF problem.
- **Not optimal.** The solution returned by a prioritized planning algorithm may not be optimal, w.r.t. to a given objective function (e.g., sum of costs or makespan).

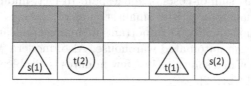

Fig. 2. A MAPF problem in which prioritized planners will not find any solution.

As an example of these prioritized planning limitations, see the MAPF problem depicted in Fig. 2. In this example, any prioritized planning algorithm will fail to find a solution, regardless of which agent has a higher priority. The problem, however, is clearly solvable, by having agent 1 move to the middle grid cell in the upper row, allowing agent 2 to move to its target ($t(2)$), and then moving to its own target ($t(1)$).

3.2   Complete MAPF Solvers

We say that a MAPF algorithm is *fast* if its worst-case time complexity is poly-nomial in the size of the graph G, and not exponential in the number of agents. Surprisingly, there are fast and complete algorithms for solving MAPF problems. The most general of those is Kornhauser's algorithm [20], which is complete and runs in a worst case time complexity of $O(|V|^3)$. This algorithm is regarded as complicated to implement. Thus, a variety of algorithms have been proposed that are also fast and complete, at least for some restricted classes of MAPF prob-lems. Below, we provide a partial list of such algorithms and classes of MAPF problems.

The Push-and-Swap algorithm [24] and its extensions Parallel Push-and-Swap [31] and Push-and-Rotate [11], are fast MAPF algorithms that are com-plete for any MAPF problem in which there are at least two unoccupied vertices in the graph. Very roughly, these algorithms work by executing a set of macro-operators that move an agent towards its goal (push) and swap the location of two agents (swap).

A MAPF problem is *well-formed* if, for any pair of agent i and j, there exists a path from $s(i)$ to $t(i)$ that does not pass through $s(j)$ and $t(j)$. Čáp et al. [9] proved that prioritized planning algorithms that compulsory avoid start locations are complete for well-formed MAPF problems.

A MAPF problem is *slidable* if for any triple of locations v_1, v_2, and v_3, there exists a path from v_1 to v_3 that does not go through v_2.[1] Wang and Botea [49] proposed a fast algorithm called MAPP that is complete for slidable MAPF problems. The BIBOX algorithm is also fast and complete under these conditions [38].

While all the above algorithms are fast and, under certain conditions, com-plete, they do not provide any guarantee regarding the *quality* of the solution they return. In particular, they do not guarantee that the resulting solution is optimal, either w.r.t. sum-of-costs or makespan. In fact, finding a solution that has the smallest makespan or the smallest sum of costs, is NP hard [39,53]. Nevertheless, solution quality is important in many applications, e.g., saving operational costs in an automated warehouse. Also, modern MAPF algorithms can find provably optimal solutions in a few minutes to problems with more than a hundred agents [14,21,32].

In the next section, we present the state-of-the-art in MAPF algorithms that are guaranteed to return a solution that is optimal with respect to a given objective function. Such algorithms are referred to as *optimal MAPF algorithms*.

4   Optimal MAPF Solvers

It is possible to classify optimal MAPF algorithms to four high-level approaches:

---

[1] The exact definition of slidable is slightly more involved. The interested reader can see the exact definition in Wang and Botea's paper [49].

- **Extensions of A*.** These are algorithms that search the k-agent search space using a variant of the A* algorithm.
- **The Increasing Cost Tree Search** [33]. This algorithm splits the MAPF problem into two problems: finding the cost added by each agent, and finding a valid solution with these costs.
- **Conflict-Based Search** [32]. This algorithmic family solves MAPF by solving multiple single-agent pathfinding problems. To achieve coordination, specific constraints are added incrementally to the single-agent pathfinding problems, in a way that verifies soundness, completeness, and optimality.
- **Constraints programming** [6,39]. This approach compiles MAPF to a set of constraints and solves them with a general purpose constraints solver.

4.1   Extensions of A*

Standley [36] proposed two very effective extensions to A* for solving MAPF problems.

Operator Decomposition. The first extension is called *Operator Decomposition* (OD). OD is designed to cope with the exponential branching factor of the k-agent search space. In OD, the agents are sorted according to some arbitrary order. When expanding the source vertex $(s(1), \ldots, s(k))$, only the actions of one agent are considered. This generates a set of vertices that represent a possible location for the first agent in time step 1, and the locations all other agents are occupying at time step 0. These vertices are added to OPEN. When expanding one of these vertices, only the actions of the second agent are considered, generating a new set of vertices. These vertices represent a possible location for the first and second agents in time step 1, and the locations of all other agents are occupying at time step 0. The search continues in this way. Only the kth descendent of the start vertex is a vertex that represents a possible location of all agents at time step 1. Vertices that represent the location of all agents at the same time step are called *full vertices*, while all other vertices are called *intermediate vertices*. The search continues until reaching a full vertex that represents the target $(t(1), \ldots, t(k))$.

The obvious advantage of A* with OD compared to A* without OD is the branching factor. With OD, the branching factor is that of a single agent, while without OD, it is exponential in the number of agents. However, the solution is k times deeper when using OD, since there are k vertices between any pair of full states. In the case of MAPF, this tradeoff is usually beneficial due to the heuristic function. A high heuristic value for an intermediate vertex can help avoid expanding the entire subtree beneath that vertex.

OD can be viewed as a special case of the Enhanced Partial Expansion A* (EPEA*) algorithm [17]. EPEA* is a variant of A* that can avoid generating some of the vertices A* would generate when expanding a vertex. For details on EPEA* and how it relates to OD, see Goldenberg et al. [17].

Independence Detection. The second A* extension proposed by Standley [36] is called *Independence Detection* (ID). ID attempts to decouple a MAPF problem with k agents to smaller MAPF problems with fewer agents. It works as follows. First, each agent finds an optimal single-agent plan for itself while ignoring all other agents. If there is a conflict between the plans of a pair of agents, these agents are *merged* to a single *meta-agent*. Then, A* +OD is used to find an optimal solution for the two agents in this meta-agent, ignoring all other agents. This process continues iteratively: in every iteration a single conflict is detected, the conflicting (meta-)agents are merged, and then solved optimally with A* +OD. The process stops where there are no conflicts between the agents' plans.[2]

In the worst case, ID will end up merging all agents to a single meta-agent and solving the resulting k-agents MAPF problem. However, in other cases, an optimal solution can be returned and guaranteed by only solving smaller MAPF problems with fewer agents. This can have a dramatic impact on runtime. ID is a very general framework for MAPF solvers, as one can replace A* +OD with any other complete and sound MAPF solver.

M*. The M* algorithm [47] also search the k-agent search space like A*. To handle the exponential branching factor, M* dynamically changes the branching factor of the search space, as follows. Initially, whenever a vertex is expanded, it generates only a single vertex that corresponds to all agents moving one step in their own, individual, optimal path. This generates a single path in the k-agent search space. Since the agents are following their individual optimal path, a vertex n may be generated that represents a conflict between a pair of agents i and j. If this occurs, all the vertices along the path from the start vertex to n are re-expanded, this time generating vertices for all combinations of actions agents i and j may perform. In general, a vertex in M* stores a *conflict set*, which is a set of agents for which it will generate all combinations of actions. For agents not in the conflict set, M* only considers a single action – the one on their individual optimal path. Recursive M* (rM*) is a notable improved version of M*. rM* attempts to identify sets of agents in the conflict set that can be solved in a decoupled manner.

M* is similar to OD in that it limits the branching factor of some vertices. rM* also bears some similarity to ID, in that it attempts to identify which sets of agents can be solved separately. Nevertheless, rM*, OD, and ID, can be used together: rM* can be used by ID to find optimal solutions to conflicting meta-agents, and rM* can search the k-agent search space with A* with OD instead of plain A*. The latter is referred to as ODrM* and was shown to be effective in some scenarios [47].

---

[2] This is actually a description of the *simple ID* algorithm. In the full ID algorithm, the conflicting agents attempt to individually avoid the conflict while maintaining their original solution cost.

4.2   The Increasing Cost Tree Search (ICTS)

The Increasing Cost Tree Search (ICTS) [33] algorithm does not search the k-agent search space directly. Instead, it interleaves two search processes. The first, referred to as the *high-level search*, aims to find the sizes of the agents' single-agent plans in an optimal solution for the given MAPF problem. The second, referred to as the *low-level search*, accepts a vector of plan sizes $(c_1, \ldots, c_k)$, and verifies if there exists a valid solution $(\pi_1, \ldots, \pi_k)$ to the given MAPF problem in which the size of every single agent plan π_i is exactly c_i.

The high-level search of ICTS is implemented as a search over the *increasing cost tree* (ICT). The ICT is a tree in which each node is a k-dimensional vector of non-negative values. The root of the ICT is a vector $(c_1, \ldots, c_k)$ where for every agent i, the value c_i is the size of its individual optimal path. The children of a node n in this tree are all vectors that result from adding one to one of the k elements in n. The high-level of ICTS searches the ICT in a breadth-first manner. This is done to verify that the first valid solution found by the low-level search is an optimal solution.

As mentioned above, the low-level search of ICTS accepts an ICT node $(c_1, \ldots c_k)$ from the high-level search, and searches for a valid solution $(\pi_1, \ldots, \pi_k)$ in which $\forall i : |\pi_i| = c_i$. To do so efficiently, ICTS computes for each agent i all single-agent plans of size c_i. Generating these set of plans is done with a simple breadth-first search, and they are stored compactly in a Multi-valued Decision Diagram (MDD) [35]. The cross product of the agents' MDDs is a subgraph of the k-agent search space that contains all joint plans that correspond to the given ICT node. Observe that this cross product is a subgraph of the k-agent search space. ICTS searches this cross product of MDDs for a valid solution. Since this search solves a satisfaction problem and not an optimization problem, a simple depth-first branch-and-bound is commonly used.

An effective way to speedup ICTS is to prune the ICT by quickly identifying subsets of single-agent plan costs for which there is no valid solution [33]. For example, assume an ICT node $(c_1, \ldots c_k)$ given to the low-level search. One can check if there is a pair of single-agent plans for agents 1 and 2 such that their costs is c_1 and c_2, respectively, and they do not conflict. If no such pair of plans exists, then the low-level search can safely return that there is no valid solution for the corresponding ICT node. While this technique for pruning the ICT is highly effective in practice, there is no current theory about how to choose which subsets of costs to check. This is an open question for future research.

4.3   Conflict-Based Search

Conflict-Based Search (CBS) [32] is an optimal MAPF algorithm. It is unique in that it solves a MAPF problem by solving a sequence of single-agent pathfinding problems.

In more detail, CBS, similar to ICTS, runs two interleaving search processes: a *low-level* search and a *high-level* search. The CBS *low-level* search accepts as input an agent i and a set of constraints of the form $\langle i, v, t \rangle$, representing that agent i must not be at vertex v in time step t. The task of the CBS low-level search is to find the lowest-cost single-agent plan for agent i that does not violate the given set of constraints. Existing single-agent pathfinding algorithms, such as A*, can be easily adapted to serve as the CBS low-level search.

The CBS *high-level* searches a set of constraints to impose on the low-level search so that the resulting joint plan is a cost-optimal valid solution. This search is performed over the Constraint Tree (CT). The CT is a binary tree in which each node n is a pair $(n.cont, n.\Pi)$ where $n.cont$ is a set of CBS constraints and $n.\Pi$ is a joint plan consistent with these constraints. A CT node n is generated by first setting its constraints and then using the CBS low-level search to find a single-agent plan for each agent that satisfies its constraints. The root of the CT is a CT node with an empty set of constraints. The objective of the high-level search is to find node n in the CT in which $n.\Pi$ is a cost-optimal valid solution.

The high-level search achieves this objective by searching the CT as follows. First, the root of the CT is generated. If the joint plan for the root has no conflict, meaning it is a valid solution, then the search returns it. Otherwise, one of the conflicts in the joint plan is chosen. Let i, j, x, and t be the pair of agents, location, and time steps for which this conflict has occurred. Two new CT nodes, n_i and n_j, are generated and added as children to the root node. The CT node n_i is generated with the constraint $\langle i, x, t \rangle$ and the CT node n_j is generated with the constraint $\langle j, x, t \rangle$. The *cost* of a CT node is the cost of the joint plan it represents. The high-level search continues to search the CT in a best-first manner, choosing in every iteration to expand a CT node with the lowest cost. Expanding a CT node means choosing one of its conflicts, and resolving them by generating two new CT nodes with an additional constraint as shown above. The search halts when a CT node n is found in which $n.\Pi$ has no conflicts. Then, $n.\Pi$ is returned, and is guaranteed to be optimal.

CBS has many extensions and improvements. Meta-agent CBS [32] is a generalization of CBS in which instead of adding new constraints to resolve a conflict between two agents, the algorithm may choose to merge the conflicting agent to a single meta-agent. Improved CBS [8] attempts to reduce the size of the CT by intelligently choosing which conflict to resolve in every iteration. HCBS [14] adds an admissible heuristic to the high-level search to prune more nodes from the CT. Recent work suggested a different scheme for resolving conflicts. For a conflict in location x at time t between agents i and j, they proposed to generate three CT nodes: one with a constraint that agent i must occupy x at time t, one with a constraint that agent j must occupy x at time t, and one with a constraint that neither agent i nor agent j can occupy x at time t. The benefit of this three-way split is that the sets of solutions that satisfy them is disjoint.

4.4   Constraint Programming

Constraint Programming (CP) is a problem-solving paradigm in which one models a given problem as a *Constraints Satisfaction Problem* (CSP) or a *Constraint Optimization Problems* (COP), and then use a general-purpose *constraints solver* to find a solution. A notable special case of CP is to model a problem as a

Boolean Satisfiability (SAT) problem, which is a special case of CSP, and use a general-purpose SAT solver.

CP is a very general paradigm because many problems, including MAPF, can be modeled as a CSP or a COP. The major benefit of using CP is that current general-purpose constraints solver are very efficient and are constantly getting better. In particular, modern SAT solvers are extremely efficient, solving SAT problems with over a million variables.

A common approach for finding a solution to a given MAPF problem with optimal makespan with CP is by splitting the problem to two problems: (1) finding a valid solution whose makespan is equal to or smaller than a given bound T, and (2) finding a value of T that is equal to the optimal makespan. Next, we provide a brief description of this approach.

Finding a Valid Solution for a Given Makespan Bound. For every triplet of agent a, vertex $v \in V$, and time step t, we define a Boolean variable $\mathcal{X}_{a,v,t}$. Setting $\mathcal{X}_{a,v,t}$ to true means that a is planned to occupy v at time t. The constraints imposed on these variables ensure that:

1. **Agent occupies one vertex in each time step.** For every time step and agent there is exactly one variable $\mathcal{X}_{a,v,t}$ that is assigned true. that is assigned a true value.
2. **No conflicts.** For every time step and location, there is at most one variables $\mathcal{X}_{a,v,t}$ that is assigned true.[3]
3. **Agents start and ends in the desired locations.** For every agent i, $\mathcal{X}_{i,s(i),1}$ and $\mathcal{X}_{i,t(i),C}$.
4. **Agents move along edges.** For every time t before T, agent i, and pair of vertices v and v', if the variables $\mathcal{X}_{i,t,v}$ and $\mathcal{X}_{i,t,v'}$ are both true then there is an edge $(v, v') \in E$.

Any assignment of values to the variables $\mathcal{X}_{a,v,t}$ corresponds to a valid solution for our MAPF problem whose makespan is at most T.

Finding the Optimal Makespan. To find the optimal makespan, we start by setting T to be a lower bound on the optimal makespan. Such a lower bound can be easily obtained by taking the maximum over the agents' individual shortest path to their goal. Then, a constraints solver is used to search for a solution to the CSP defined above. If a solution has been found, we have found an optimal solution. If not, T is incremented by one, and the constraints solver is used again to solve the new CSP. This process continues until an optimal solution is found. Finding a solution with optimal sum-of-costs is also possible with CP, but it requires some additional constraints and changes to the process [6, 42].

---

[3] Actually, this constraint only prevents vertex conflicts. To prevent swapping conflicts, an additional constraint is needed, in which for every time step t before T, pair of agents a and a', and pair of locations v and v', if the variables $\mathcal{X}_{i,t,v}$ and $\mathcal{X}_{i,t',v'}$ are both true then the variables $\mathcal{X}_{j,t,v'}$ and $\mathcal{X}_{j,t',v}$ must not be both true.

It is important to note that the above is not the only way to solve MAPF with CP. Surynek explored five different ways to model MAPF using SAT, showing how different modeling choices impact the SAT solver's runtime [40]. Barták et al. [6] modeled several variants of MAPF using Picat [54], a higher-level CP language. A CP written in Picat can be automatically compiled and solved with either SAT, a CP solver, or a Mixed Integer-Linear Program (MILP) solver [44]. They showed that different modelings and solvers are effective for different MAPF variants and problems. Still, how to choose the best model and solver for a given MAPF problem is, to-date, an open question.

It is worth noting that solving MAPF with CP is, in it self, a special case of a more general approach for solving MAPF in which one compiles MAPF to a different problem, solves it with an algorithm designed for that problem. Prominent examples are MAPF compilation to Answer Set Programming (ASP) [13], to SAT Modulu Theory (SMT) [41], and to multi-commodity network flow [52]. Such MAPF algorithms are sometimes referred to as *reduction-based* MAPF solvers [15].

4.5   Summary of Optimal Solvers

Unfortunately, there are no clear guidelines to predict which of the MAPF algorithms detailed above would work best for a given MAPF problem. Prior work suggested the following rules-of-thumb:

- A*-based and CP approaches are effective for small graphs that are dense with agents.
- CBS and ICTS are effective for large graphs.

However, this rules-of-thumb has not been grounded theoretically and its empirical support is weak. We expect that future work will explore automated methods to select the best solver to use for a given problem. Another appealing direction for future work is to create hybrid algorithms that enjoy the complementary benefits of different MAPF solvers.

5   Approximately Optimal Solvers

While modern optimal MAPF algorithms have pushed the state of the art impressively, there are still many MAPF problems for which current algorithms cannot solve optimally in reasonable time. In such cases, one can always use one of the fast MAPF algorithms described in Sect. 3, but that would mean the solution returned may be very costly.

Approximately optimal MAPF algorithms, also known as *bounded-suboptimal* algorithms, lie in the range between these algorithms and optimal algorithms. An *approximately optimal* algorithm is an algorithm that accepts a parameter $\epsilon > 0$ and returns a solution whose cost is at most $1 + \epsilon$ times the cost of an optimal solution. Ideally, an approximately optimal algorithm would return solutions faster when increasing ϵ, thus providing a controlled trade-off between runtime and solution quality. Approximately optimal MAPF algorithms have been proposed based on each of the optimal MAPF approaches described in the previous section. We describe them briefly below.

5.1   A*-based

Creating an approximately optimal version of an A*-based MAPF algorithm is straightforward, since there are many approximately optimal A*-based algorithm in the heuristic search literature. Perhaps the most well-known approximately optimal A*-based algorithm is *Weighted A** [30], which is a best-first search that uses the $g + (1 + \epsilon)h$ evaluation function to choose which node to expand in every iteration. All A*-based MAPF algorithms can use the same evaluation function and obtain the guarantee: that the solution cost is at most $1 + \epsilon$ times the cost of an optimal solution. Such a variant was mentioned explicitly for M* [47], under the name *inflated M**.

An interesting direction for future work is to use more modern A*-based approximately optimal algorithms to improve the performance of approximately optimal A*-based MAPF algorithms. Explicit Estimation Search (EES) [43] and Dynamic Potential Search (DPS) [16] are some examples of such approximately optimal A*-based algorithms.

5.2   ICTS

To the best of our knowledge, there is no approximately optimal ICTS-based algorithm for classical MAPF. The challenge in creating such an algorithm is that the ICTS high-level search is done in a breadth-first manner. Thus there is no heuristic to inflate, preventing the clear application of Weighted A* and other approximately optimal search algorithms.

However, there is an approximately optimal variant of ICTS for MAPF problems in which moving an agent across different edges can have different costs. This algorithm is based on the Extended ICTS (eICTS) algorithm [48], which is an ICTS-based algorithm designed for this type of MAPF problems. In eICTS, each ICT node is associated with a lower and upper bound. The high-level search in this case becomes a best-first search on the lower bound, and low-level search looks for optimal solutions within these bounds. This allows creating an approximately optimal version of eICTS called wICTS, in which suboptimality is added to both high-level and low-level search.

5.3   CBS

Enhanced CBS [4] is an approximately optimal MAPF algorithm that is based on CBS. It introduces suboptimality in the low-level search and in the high-level search. The low-level search in CBS can be any optimal shortest path algorithm, such as A*. As noted above, there are several approximately optimal algorithms that are based on A*, including Weighted A* [30], EES [43], and DPS [16].

Thus, introducing suboptimality to the low-level search can be done by simply using one of these approximately optimal algorithms.

Introducing suboptimality to the high-level search is slightly more involved. To do so, ECBS uses a *focal search* framework for its high-level search. Focal search is a heuristic search framework introduced by Pearl and Kim [28] in which the node expanded in every iteration is chosen from a subset of nodes called FOCAL. FOCAL contains all nodes in OPEN that may lead to a solution that may be approximately optimal. To choose which node to expand From FOCAL, a secondary heuristic can be used. Importantly, this heuristic can be inadmissible and domain-dependent. ECBS uses the focal search framework, and uses a MAPF-specific secondary heuristic that prioritizes CT node with fewer conflicts. For details, see Barer et al. [4]. Later work proposed an extension to ECBS in which user-defined paths called *highways* are prioritized to further improve runtime [10].

5.4   Constraint Programming

EMDD-SAT is a recently proposed approximately optimal MAPF algorithm from the CP family. This algorithm models MAPF as a SAT problem. It follows the high-level approach we described in Sect. 4.4, except that it is designed for (approximately) optimizing SOC and not makespan.

In a very high-level manner, EMDD-SAT works by creating a SAT model that allows solutions with longer makespan and larger SOC. The suboptimality is controlled by high much larger is the SOC from a computed SOC lower-bound. To the best of our knowledge, there is no approximately optimal MAPF algorithm from this family that is designed for finding solutions with approximately optimal makespan.

In general, significantly less efforts have been dedicated, to date, to develop approximately optimal MAPF algorithms. However, existing approximately optimal MAPF algorithms demonstrate that adding even a very small amount of suboptimality can allow solving much larger problems. For example, ECBS with at most 1% suboptimality is able to solve MAPF problems with 250 agents on large maps [4].

6   Beyond Classical MAPF

The scope of this overview is mostly limited to what is referred to as *classical MAPF* [37]. Classical MAPF assumes that (1) every action takes exactly one time step, (2) time is discretized into time steps, as oppose to continuous, and (3) each agent occupies exactly one vertex. These assumptions do not necessarily hold in real-world MAPF applications. With the maturity of classical MAPF algorithms, recent years have also begun to explore MAPF problems that relax these assumptions. Below, we provide a partial overview of these efforts.

6.1   Beyond One-Time Step Actions

The eICTS algorithm [48] mentioned above is designed for actions that may require more than one time step. Such a setting is sometimes called MAPF with non-unit edge cost. Adapting the CBS algorithm to non-unit edge cost settings is straightforward, as it only requires changing the conflict-detection step.

Barták et al. [5] proposed a CP-based algorithm for MAPF with non-unit edge costs. Their model uses scheduling constraints to support actions with different duration.

6.2   Beyond Discrete Time Steps

Time is continuous, and thus every time step discretization is, by definition an abstraction of the real-world. This abstraction in the context of MAPF may lead to suboptimality and even incompleteness.

As long as the agents do not need to wait, there is no need to directly deal with this problem: the duration of move actions depend on the time required to traverse the corresponding edge. However, when an agent needs to wait and time is not discretized, then each agent has an infinite number of possible wait actions in each vertex.

The key technique used so far to address this problem is to use the Safe Interval Path Planning (SIPP) [29] algorithm. SIPP is a single-agent pathfinding algorithm that is designed to avoid moving obstacles. Since obstacles are moving, the single agent may choose to wait in its location, which raises again the challenge of dealing with continuous time. SIPP addresses this challenge by identifying *safe intervals* in which the agent can occupy each vertex, and runs an A* search on (vertex, safe interval) pairs. Andreychuck et al. showed how to use SIPP to solve MAPF problems with continuous time, in a prioritized planning framework [51] and in a CBS framework [2].

Surynek [41] recently proposed to use a CP-related approach for continuous time. Instead of modeling the problem as a CSP or SAT problem, Surynek proposed to model it as a SAT Modulu Theory (SMT) problem, and then apply an SMT solver.

6.3   Beyond One-Agent per Vertex

The graph G of possible location in classical MAPF is an abstraction of the real world the agents are moving in. Arguably, in most real-world MAPF applications the agents are moving in Euclidean space and have some geometric shape. Thus, an agent may conflict if they stop in different areas, because their geometric shapes overlap. Li et al. [22] referred to this as *MAPF with large agents*. In such settings, an agent may "occupy" multiple vertices and a move action may create a conflict with agents occupying multiple vertices.

Li et al. [22] proposed a CBS-based algorithm for addressing this setting. They showed how to design suitable constraints for large agents and proposed an admissible heuristic to speedup the search. They also described an A*-based algorithm and a SAT-based algorithm for this setting. Atzmon et al. [12] proposed another CBS-based algorithm that can consider agents of arbitrary shape, even without a reference point that is stable to rotations.

Robustness and Kinematic Constraints. Even if an agent only occupies a single vertex, it is still desirable in many scenarios to add a buffer around each agent to further minimize the chance of collisions. Such a buffer can be either spatial or temporal. A prime motivation for having such a buffer is to account for the inherent uncertainty during the executing of the solution. That is, to have the agents' joint plan be valid and executable even if some agents do not fully follow it.

The MAPF-POST [19] algorithm was designed to address such requirements. MAPF-POST accepts as input a solution for a classical MAPF problem and adapts it to consider safety and kinematic constraints. A limitation of MAPF-POST is that it does not retain any guarantee on solution quality. For adding robustness to temporal delays during execution, Atzmon et al. [3] proposed an optimal CBS-based algorithm and CP-based algorithm.

6.4   Beyond One-Shot MAPF

In addition, classical MAPF is a one-shot, offline problem. In some MAPF applications, there is a sequence of related MAPF problems that are being solved sequentially. Some recent work also addresses several types of *online* MAPF settings. This includes settings where there is a fixed set of agents and a stream of pathfinding tasks [25], as well as a setting where new agents appear over time but each agent has a single navigation task [46]. The former setting is referred to as the *MAPF warehouse model* and the latter as the *MAPF intersection model*.

Also, so far we assumed the allocation of agents to goals is given. In the *Multi-Agent Pickup-and-Delivery* (MAPD) problem, this is not the case [23]. In MAPD, there is a fixed set of agents that need to solve a batch of pickup and delivery of tasks. A MAPD algorithm needs to plan paths without conflicts, and also to allocate which agent should go to which destination.

7   Conclusion

This paper provides an overview of the current research on Multi-Agent Path Finding (MAPF). After providing several definitions of MAPF were given, we presented polynomial-time algorithms for solving the problem. Then, a range of algorithms was described that return optimal solutions. These algorithms can be split into four families: A*-based, ICTS, CBS, and CP. Following, we described how to transform several of these optimal algorithms to be approximately optimal algorithms, allowing trading solution quality for runtime. Finally, we presented some extensions of classical MAPF, including non-unit edge costs, continuous time, large agents, and online MAPF. Throughout this paper, we suggested several directions for future work.

It is our hope that this paper will be useful to both researchers and practitioners looking for a brief introduction to MAPF. For formal definitions of MAPF variants and benchmarks, see [37]. For additional MAPF-related resources, including pointers to publications and additional tutorials, see the http://mapf.info web site, created by Sven Koenig's group.

References

1. Andreychuk, A., Yakovlev, K.: Two techniques that enhance the performance of multi-robot prioritized path planning. In: International Conference on Autonomous Agents and MultiAgent Systems (AAMAS), pp. 2177–2179 (2018)
2. Andreychuk, A., Yakovlev, K., Atzmon, D., Stern, R.: Multi-agent pathfinding with continuous time. In: International Joint Conference on Artificial Intelligence (IJCAI), pp. 39–45 (2019)
3. Atzmon, D., Stern, R., Felner, A., Wagner, G., Barták, R., Zhou, N.F.: Robust multi-agent path finding. In: International Conference on Autonomous Agents and Multi Agent Systems (AAMAS), pp. 1862–1864 (2018)
4. Barer, M., Sharon, G., Stern, R., Felner, A.: Suboptimal variants of the conflict-based search algorithm for the multi-agent pathfinding problem. In: Symposium on Combinatorial Search (SoCS) (2014)
5. Barták, R., Švancara, J., Vlk, M., et al.: A scheduling-based approach to multi-agent path finding with weighted and capacitated arcs. In: International Conference on Autonomous Agents and MultiAgent Systems (AAMAS), pp. 748–756. International Foundation for Autonomous Agents and Multiagent Systems (AAMAS) (2018)
6. Barták, R., Zhou, N., Stern, R., Boyarski, E., Surynek, P.: Modeling and solving the multi-agent pathfinding problem in picat. In: IEEE International Conference on Tools with Artificial Intelligence (ICTAI), pp. 959–966 (2017)
7. Bnaya, Z., Felner, A.: Conflict-oriented windowed hierarchical cooperative A. In: IEEE International Conference on Robotics and Automation (ICRA), pp. 3743–3748 (2014)
8. Boyarski, E., et al.: ICBS: improved conflict-based search algorithm for multi-agent pathfinding. In: International Joint Conference on Artificial Intelligence (IJCAI) (2015)
9. Čáp, M., Vokřínek, J., Kleiner, A.: Complete decentralized method for on-line multi-robot trajectory planning in well-formed infrastructures. In: International Conference on Automated Planning and Scheduling (ICAPS) (2015)
10. Cohen, L., Uras, T., Koenig, S.: Feasibility study: using highways for bounded-suboptimal multi-agent path finding. In: Symposium on Combinatorial Search (SoCS) (2015)
11. De Wilde, B., Ter Mors, A.W., Witteveen, C.: Push and rotate: a complete multi-agent pathfinding algorithm. J. Artif. Intell. Res. **51**, 443–492 (2014)
12. Atzmon, D., Diei, A., Rave, D.: Multi-train path finding. In: Symposium on Combinatorial Search (SoCS) (2019)
13. Erdem, E., Kisa, D.G., Oztok, U., Schüller, P.: A general formal framework for pathfinding problems with multiple agents. In: AAAI Conference on Artificial Intelligence (2013)
14. Felner, A., et al.: Adding heuristics to conflict-based search for multi-agent path finding. In: International Conference on Automated Planning and Scheduling (ICAPS) (2018)

15. Felner, A., et al.: Search-based optimal solvers for the multi-agent pathfinding problem: summary and challenges. In: Symposium on Combinatorial Search (SoCS), pp. 29–37 (2017)
16. Gilon, D., Felner, A., Stern, R.: Dynamic potential search-a new bounded suboptimal search. In: Symposium on Combinatorial Search (SoCS) (2016)
17. Goldenberg, M., Felner, A., Sturtevant, N.R., Holte, R.C., Schaeffer, J.: Optimal-generation variants of EPEA. In: SoCS (2013)
18. Hart, P.E., Nilsson, N.J., Raphael, B.: A formal basis for the heuristic determination of minimum cost paths. IEEE Trans. Syst. Sci. Cybern. **SSC-4**(2), 100–107 (1968)
19. Hönig, W., et al.: Summary: multi-agent path finding with kinematic constraints. In: International Joint Conference on Artificial Intelligence (IJCAI), pp. 4869–4873 (2017)
20. Kornhauser, D., Miller, G., Spirakis, P.: Coordinating pebble motion on graphs, the diameter of permutation groups, and applications. In: Symposium on Foundations of Computer Science, pp. 241–250. IEEE (1984)
21. Li, J., Harabor, D., Stuckey, P., Felner, A., Ma, H., Koenig, S.: Disjoint splitting for multi-agent path finding with conflict-based search. In: International Conference on Automated Planning and Scheduling (ICAPS) (2019)
22. Li, J., Surynek, P., Felner, A., Ma., H., Kumar, T.K.S., Koenig, S.: Multi-agent path finding for large agents. In: AAAI Conference on Artificial Intelligence (2019)
23. Liu, M., Ma, H., Li, J., Koenig, S.: Task and path planning for multi-agent pickup and delivery. In: International Conference on Autonomous Agents and MultiAgent Systems (AAMAS), pp. 1152–1160 (2019)
24. Luna, R., Bekris, K.E.: Efficient and complete centralized multi-robot path planning. In: IEEE/RSJ International Conference on Intelligent Robots and Systems, pp. 3268–3275 (2011)
25. Ma, H., Li, J., Kumar, T., Koenig, S.: Lifelong multi-agent path finding for online pickup and delivery tasks. In: Conference on Autonomous Agents and Multiagent Systems (AAMAS), pp. 837–845 (2017)
26. Ma, H., Yang, J., Cohen, L., Kumar, T.K.S., Koenig, S.: Feasibility study: moving non-homogeneous teams in congested video game environments. In: Conference on Artificial Intelligence and Interactive Digital Entertainment (AIIDE), pp. 270–272 (2017)
27. Morris, R., et al.: Planning, scheduling and monitoring for airport surface operations. In: AAAI Workshop: Planning for Hybrid Systems (2016)
28. Pearl, J., Kim, J.H.: Studies in semi-admissible heuristics. IEEE Trans. Pattern Anal. Mach. Intell. **PAMI-4**, 392–399 (1982)
29. Phillips, M., Likhachev, M.: SIPP: safe interval path planning for dynamic environments. In: IEEE International Conference on Robotics and Automation (ICRA), pp. 5628–5635 (2011)
30. Pohl, I.: Heuristic search viewed as path finding in a graph. Artif. Intell. **1**(3–4), 193–204 (1970)
31. Sajid, Q., Luna, R., Bekris, K.E.: Multi-agent pathfinding with simultaneous execution of single-agent primitives. In: SoCS (2012)
32. Sharon, G., Stern, R., Felner, A., Sturtevant, N.R.: Conflict-based search for optimal multi-agent pathfinding. Artif. Intell. **219**, 40–66 (2015)
33. Sharon, G., Stern, R., Goldenberg, M., Felner, A.: The increasing cost tree search for optimal multi-agent pathfinding. Artif. Intell. **195**, 470–495 (2013)
34. Silver, D.: Cooperative pathfinding. In: AIIDE, vol. 1, pp. 117–122 (2005)

35. Srinivasan, A., Ham, T., Malik, S., Brayton, R.K.: Algorithms for discrete function manipulation. In: IEEE International Conference on Computer-Aided Design, pp. 92–95 (1990)
36. Standley, T.S.: Finding optimal solutions to cooperative pathfinding problems. In: AAAI Conference on Artificial Intelligence, pp. 173–178 (2010)
37. Stern, R., et al.: Multi-agent pathfinding: definitions, variants, and benchmarks. In: Symposium on Combinatorial Search (SoCS) (2019)
38. Surynek, P.: A novel approach to path planning for multiple robots in bi-connected graphs. In: IEEE International Conference on Robotics and Automation (ICRA), pp. 3613–3619 (2009)
39. Surynek, P.: An optimization variant of multi-robot path planning is intractable. In: AAAI (2010)
40. Surynek, P.: Makespan optimal solving of cooperative path-finding via reductions to propositional satisfiability. arXiv preprint arXiv:1610.05452 (2016)
41. Surynek, P.: Multi-agent path finding with continuous time viewed through satisfiability modulo theories (SMT). arXiv preprint arXiv:1903.09820 (2019)
42. Surynek, P., Felner, A., Stern, R., Boyarski, E.: Efficient sat approach to multi-agent path finding under the sum of costs objective. In: European Conference on Artificial Intelligence (ECAI), pp. 810–818 (2016)
43. Thayer, J.T., Ruml, W.: Bounded suboptimal search: a direct approach using inadmissible estimates. In: International Joint Conference on Artificial Intelligence (IJCAI) (2011)
44. Van Roy, T.J., Wolsey, L.A.: Solving mixed integer programming problems using automatic reformulation. Oper. Res. 35(1), 45–57 (1987)
45. Veloso, M.M., Biswas, J., Coltin, B., Rosenthal, S.: CoBots: robust symbiotic autonomous mobile service robots. In: IJCAI, p. 4423 (2015)
46. Švancara, J., Vlk, M., Stern, R., Atzmon, D., Barták, R.: Online multi-agent pathfinding. In: AAAI Conference on Artificial Intelligence (2019)
47. Wagner, G., Choset, H.: Subdimensional expansion for multirobot path planning. Artif. Intell. 219, 1–24 (2015)
48. Walker, T.T., Sturtevant, N.R., Felner, A.: Extended increasing cost tree search for non-unit cost domains. In: International Joint Conference on Artificial Intelligence (IJCAI), pp. 534–540 (2018)
49. Wang, K.H.C., Botea, A.: MAPP: a scalable multi-agent path planning algorithm with tractability and completeness guarantees. J. Artif. Intell. Res. 42, 55–90 (2011)
50. Wurman, P.R., D'Andrea, R., Mountz, M.: Coordinating hundreds of cooperative, autonomous vehicles in warehouses. AI Mag. 29(1), 9 (2008)
51. Yakovlev, K., Andreychuk, A.: Any-angle pathfinding for multiple agents based on SIPP algorithm. In: International Conference on Automated Planning and Scheduling (ICAPS), pp. 586–593 (2017)
52. Yu, J., LaValle, S.M.: Multi-agent path planning and network flow. In: Frazzoli, E., Lozano-Perez, T., Roy, N., Rus, D. (eds.) Algorithmic Foundations of Robotics X. STAR, vol. 86, pp. 157–173. Springer, Heidelberg (2013). https://doi.org/10.1007/978-3-642-36279-8_10
53. Yu, J., LaValle, S.M.: Structure and intractability of optimal multi-robot path planning on graphs. In: AAAI (2013)
54. Zhou, N.-F., Kjellerstrand, H., Fruhman, J.: Constraint Solving and Planning with Picat. Springer Briefs in Intelligent Systems. Springer, Cham (2015). https://doi.org/10.1007/978-3-319-25883-6

Young Scientist School Papers

The Use of Reinforcement Learning in the Task of Moving Objects with the Robotic Arm

Ermek E. Aitygulov[✉]

Moscow Institute of Physics and Technology, Moscow, Russia
aytygulov@phystech.edu

Abstract. The article describes the task of controlling a robotic arm to transfer objects in front of it. To select actions, the reinforcement learning algorithm is used. In conclusion, there are presented the results of experiments in the Gazebo simulation environment with two different inputs: either with information about the position of the hand and the object, or with information about the position of the hand and the image with the camera.

Keywords: Robotic arm · Reinforcement learning · Object manipulation

1 Introduction

The purpose of this work is to use reinforcement learning algorithm [6] in the task of forming the rules of object manipulating by the robototechnical system.

Reinforcement learning is a machine learning approach that allows an agent to develop desired behavior through interaction with an environment. This method uses a system of penalties and rewards as response of environment on agent's actions, which allows taking into account the experience of previous interactions. Two variants of input data were considered: either information about the position of the hand and the object, or information about the position of the hand and the image from the camera. To work with the first version of the input data (the position of the hand and the object) was written synthetic environment. The agent studied there, and then the model was transferred to the simulator. To speed up the calculations in the second case (the arm position and the image from the camera) the server was used.

There are two approaches in reinforcement learning: value-based and policy-based. In the first approach, the reward maximizes through value function optimization, in the second, directly through the policy optimization.

An example of the application of the first approach in a similar task on the formation of the rules for moving a manipulator can be found in [1]. In this work, the Q-learning algorithm was used [7], but before that, the action space was reduced. The use of the neural network in [2] made it possible to use Q-learning for a more complex task. As a manipulator, a hand with seven degrees of freedom was used and the agent, using a convolutional neural network, found the value function with image as input. However, in this work, the action space also consisted of a finite number of actions: the agent could change the angle in one of the joints by one degree.

© Springer Nature Switzerland AG 2019
G. S. Osipov et al. (Eds.): Artificial Intelligence, LNAI 11866, pp. 119–126, 2019.
https://doi.org/10.1007/978-3-030-33274-7_7

Various extensions make it possible to use reinforcement learning for tasks with the continual space of actions, as was done in [5]. It is worth noting that the authors experimented with real robots and to speed up the learning process they used several agents that asynchronously updated the strategy. In this paper, the action space is also continual and the policy-based method had been used for learning. In this work TRPO algorithm (Trust Region Policy Optimization) [4] was selected. It is based on the strategy gradient theorem [6], which also allows the work with the continuum action space.

2   Reinforcement Learning

2.1   Agent Interaction Model

As a method for actions synthesizing, the method of reinforcement learning was used - learning, uses the agent interacts with the environment and for each actions that change the state of the system, receives a response from the environment (Fig. 1).

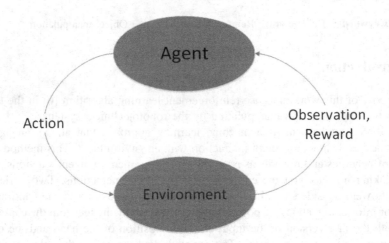

Fig. 1. Agent interaction model.

The agent is a simulation of the CRUMB robotic system, consists of a Turtlebot 2 and a Widow X arm. The task is to learn how to move an object located on the table in front of it (Fig. 2).

To describe the activity of an agent, the probability distribution $\pi(a \mid s)$ is used, which characterizes the probability that an agent chooses an action a in state s. The probability distribution is called a strategy.

$$\pi(a \mid s) = P(a_t = a \mid s_t = s)$$

The agent, following the strategy, applies actions and moves from state to state, receiving reward $r()$, which can be either positive or negative.

Fig. 2. CRUMB in Gazebo

The fundamental equations in reinforcement learning in the presence of information about the environment are the Bellman equations:

1. $V_\pi(s) = E_\pi[r(s_{t+1}) + \gamma V(s_{t+1}) \mid s_t = s]$,
2. $Q_\pi(s, a) = E_\pi[r(s_{t+1}) + \gamma V(s_{t+1}) \mid s_t = s, a_t = a]$,

Where $V_\pi(s)$ denotes the value of the state s with the strategy π, and $Q_\pi(s, a)$ denotes the value of the action a in the state s with the strategy π.

As an evaluation of the strategy, the value $\eta(\pi)$ is considered, which is the mathematical expectation of the discounted reward for the entire session:

$$\eta(\pi) = E_\pi[\sum_{t=0}^{\infty} \gamma^t r(s_t)].$$

The TRPO algorithm described in this paper uses a surrogate function, the maximization of which, with the right choice of step, leads to an optimization of the value $\eta(\pi)$. Combining with the Natural policy gradient [3] algorithm significantly improves the performance of the algorithm.

2.2   TRPO Algorithm

To describe the agent's interaction with the environment, the Markov decision-making process (S, A, P, r, γ) is used, where S-the set of states, A-the set of actions, $P : S \times A \times S \rightarrow [0, 1]$ - the distribution of transition probabilities, the reward function and the discounting factor γ.

In this paper, the action space is continual, therefore, to determine the strategy π, a multidimensional normal distribution $N(\mu, \sum)$ is used, where μ and $\sum$ are defined by a neural network. Thus, the strategy π is parameterized by the weights θ of the neural network, and all functions of π are functions of θ.

The function $\eta(\theta)$, which is the estimation of the strategy π_θ, is replaced by the following surrogate function, which binds two strategies:

$$L_\theta(\tilde{\theta}) = \eta(\theta) + E_{\pi_\theta} \frac{\pi_{\tilde{\theta}}(a\,|\,s)}{\pi_\theta(a\,|\,s)} (Q_\theta(s,a) - V_\theta(s)),$$

where Q_θ and V_θ - value functions defined by following equations:

$$Q_\theta(\tilde{s}_t, \tilde{a}_t) = E_{\pi_\theta}(\sum_{l=0}^{\infty} \gamma^l r(s_{t+l})\,|\,s_t = \tilde{s}_t, a_t = \tilde{a}_t),$$

$$V_\theta(\tilde{s}_t) = E_{\pi_\theta}(\sum_{l=0}^{\infty} \gamma^l r(s_{t+l})|s_t = \tilde{s}_t).$$

Optimization of L_θ with a limit on the average Kullback-Leibler divergence:

$$\overline{D}_{KL}^\theta(\theta_{old}, \theta) = E_\theta[D_{KL}(\pi_\theta(\cdot\,|\,s) \,\|\, \pi_{\theta_{old}}(\cdot\,|\,s))] \leq \delta$$

entails an increase in the original function. The method of natural policy gradient, which uses linear approximation of L and quadratic approximation $\overline{D}_{KL}$, is applied to search in the optimal direction problem:

$$\underset{\theta}{\mathrm{maximaze}}[\nabla_\theta L_{\theta_{old}}(\theta)\,|_{\theta=\theta_{old}} \cdot (\theta - \theta_{old})]$$

with $\frac{1}{2}(\theta_{old} - \theta)^T K(\theta_{old})(\theta_{old} - \theta) \leq \delta$, where $K(\theta_{old}) = \Delta_\theta \overline{D}_{KL}^{\theta_{old}}$.
update rule: $\theta_{new} = \theta_{old} + \alpha K(\theta_{old})^{-1} \nabla_\theta L(\theta)|_{\theta=\theta_{old}}$.

The value of step is found by solving the equation:

$$K(\theta_{old})x = \nabla_\theta L(\theta)|_{\theta=\theta_{old}}$$

the value α is matched by a linear search for the maximum of L with $\overline{D}_{KL}^{\theta_{old}}(\theta_{old}, \theta) \leq \delta$ restrictions.

2.3   Experiments

The work was done in the simulator Gazebo. The written environment used the OpenAI Gym library interface. The interaction between the robot and the written environment occurred through the ROS operating system, which organizes the interaction between the components of the robot and the simulator, allowing to obtain the necessary information and also control the robot. An additional node is created to sent messages to other nodes, which may be responsible for the position of the hand or for the image from the camera, etc. In TRPO, different estimates are used, so a large number of episodes played are needed to reduce the variance. To speed up the work in the first version, the model was trained in a simpler (synthetic) environment, and in the second version, the server was used.

The training took place as follows: the agent, following the current strategy, passed several sessions, no longer n, a total length no more m, then the weights θ of the neural network changed according to TRPO. The training was repeated until the average reward did not exceed the value l.

Experiments with Synthetic Environment

To use the TRPO algorithm, two environments were created: a synthetic learning environment and a environment for applying the algorithm in Gazebo. Two environments have the same state and action spaces. To describe the interaction of the agent with them, an example of the capture of an object on the table by a manipulator is considered.

Figure 3 shows a model of a manipulator in a synthetic environment in the two-dimensional case. Points 1–4 are joints by manipulators. The action is to change the angle in one of them (in three-dimensional rotation is added around the vertical axis). The point B is the target point where the agent must move point 4.

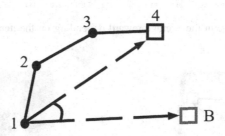

Fig. 3. Model of manipulator in synthetic environment.

The reward system works as follows: if as a result of the action, the length of the vector $\overrightarrow{4B}$ has decreased, then the agent receives a reward in the amount of vector length, if not changed, then he is fined by 5, and if increased, he is penalized by double vector length. If successful, the agent receives a +100 reward.

The state of the agent is a sequence (a_1, a_2, a_3) (a_4 added in 3D), where a_i are angles between the following vectors:

$$a_1 = \angle(\overrightarrow{14}, \overrightarrow{1B}), a_2 = \angle(\overrightarrow{24}, \overrightarrow{2B}), a_3 = \angle(\overrightarrow{34}, \overrightarrow{3B}).$$

In such a state space, the inequality $a_1 \leq 0$ means that the target point B is below the vector and you need to make a turn in junction 1 by the corresponding angle. Such a representation of the position of the manipulator relative to the target point makes the strategy π less dependent on the position B.

A neural network returns a strategy π. Because the space of states and actions for two environments are identical, the neural network trained in a synthetic environment can be used in an environment that interacts with Gazebo. Figure 4 shows the change in the average reward depending on the iteration number with parameters $(n, m, l) = (500, 5000, 530)$. With a random position of the cube at the beginning of the episode, the lack of knowledge about the environment, the algorithm shows a steady improvement in the result.

After learning in a synthetic environment, the model is applied in an environment that interacts with Gazebo (this is possible because the state and action spaces are identical) (Fig. 5).

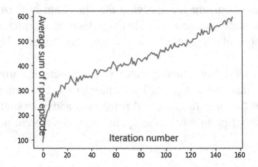

Fig. 4. Change in the average reward depending on the iteration number

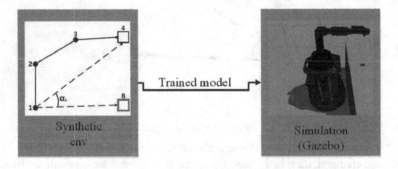

Fig. 5. Synthetic model applying scheme

Experiments with Server

To speed up the simulation worked on the server. It also helped speed up the process of optimizing the approximator using the GPU. When working with the simulation environment, the manipulator can come to such positions from which it cannot escape; therefore, only changes in the angle between −0.6 radians and +0.6 radians are allowed in the environment. Thus the following reward system is used: $-r - \alpha^2$, where r is the distance from the manipulator's hand to the object, and α is the angle change in one of the joints. At a successful capture, the agent receives a +100 reward.

Unlike the first option, the state value function has been added to the gradient of the target functional:

$$\frac{1}{m}\sum_{i=1}^{m}\sum_{t=0}^{H-1}\nabla_\theta \log \pi_\theta(u_t^{(i)}|s_t^{(i)})(\sum_{k=t}^{H-1}R(s_k^{(i)},u_k^{(i)}) - V^\pi(s_t^{(i)}))$$

The sign of the gradient depends not on the sign of the total reward, but on the sign of the following expression:

$$(\sum_{k=t}^{H-1}R(s_k^{(i)},u_k^{(i)}) - V^\pi(s_t^{(i)})).$$

There is the difference between the received award and the expected one, which allows to reduce the variance. For approximation of the state value function, a separate neural network was used. The learning process took place in a similar way, but the additional network approximating of the value function was learned with the image and angles in the joints as input. Also in order to reduce the value function sharp change, there were also episodes from the previous series in the training set. In total, the network was trained in portions of 256 steps from old and new steps (the sample was mixed, because the order is not important) for 20 epochs. An example of a network that calculates a parameter: the image is fed to the input of a convolutional layer, processed by 3 convolutional layers, and then merged with the layers that process the corners (Fig. 6).

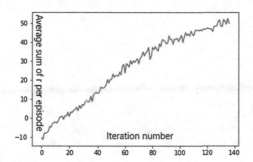

Fig. 6. Change in the average reward depending on the iteration number

3   Conclusion

During the work, one of the reinforcement learning algorithms was implemented. Two options were considered: in the first case, the agent knew the exact location of the cube, in the second case, he received an image at the input and then chose an action. Because of the need for a large number of episodes in both cases, additional funds were used to solve the problem. Work in a synthetic environment does not take into account various factors when learning. For example, the presence of the table, hand constraints, turning error are not taken into account, however, the obtained strategy copes with the first option of the input data. Training in the image in the simulation is closer to reality, however, also does not take into account various problems (such as the charge of the manipulator). In this regard, further it is planned to modify the algorithm that would take into account the model of the environment, in order to improve convergence and application to the manipulator in the laboratory.

References

1. Albers, A., Yan, W., Frietsch, M.: Application of Reinforcement Learning for a 2-DOF Robot Arm Control, November 2009
2. James, S., Johns, E.: 3D Simulation for Robot Arm Control with Deep Q-Learning. 2016
3. Kakade, S.: A natural policy gradient (2002)
4. Schulman, J., Levine, S., Moritz, P., Jordan, M., Abbeel, P.: Trust region policy optimization (2015)
5. Gu, S., Holly, E., Lillicrap, T., Levine, S.: Deep reinforcement learning for robotic manipulation with asynchronous off-policy update (2016)
6. Sutton, R.S., Barto, A.G.: Reinforcement Learning: An Introduction (1998)
7. Watkins, C.J.C.H.: Learning from delayed rewards (1989)

Ontology Models in Intelligent System Engineering: A Case of the Knowledge-Intensive Application Domain

Karina A. Gulyaeva(✉) ⓘD and Irina L. Artemieva

Far Eastern Federal University, Vladivostok, Russia
kgulyayeva@gmail.com, artemeva.il@dvfu.ru

Abstract. The article describes the application of the ontological approach to intelligent system engineering. This approach suggests that the ontology models be presented in the form of interconnected modules of applied logic theories. This approach turns out to be effective in the case of a knowledge-intensive application domain, such as chemistry. Intelligent system that is being developed is supposed to solve the problem of organic compound reaction capacity identification. The problem is solved utilizing the concept systems of several chemistry subdomains. The ontology model is presented. The intelligent system model is provided. The analysis of the intelligent system requirements and interface quality attributes has brought into sharp focus several advantages of the utilized approach, i.e. the extensibility of the system due to the possibility to correct knowledge and metaknowledge during the system lifecycle, the potential to add problem solvers for new classes of tasks, and the increase in user confidence due to the utilization of user-understandable concept systems. These advantages become of paramount importance for the vitality of intelligent systems in the field where the intensification of knowledge-retrieval procedures and constant accumulation of knowledge (associated primarily with organic synthesis) make such knowledge more and more difficult for humans to conceive.

Keywords: Ontology · Intelligent system · Organic chemistry · Applied logic theory

1 Introduction

Today the scientific community is facing diverse knowledge-intensive problems in many domains. Hereinafter "knowledge-intensive" denotes "knowledge-based, or expert" (wrt. system, or information system), "complex-structured" [4] (wrt. application domain), or "requiring complex-structured application domain knowledge base" (wrt. problem, task, or challenge). Problems that arise in the dynamic and fast-paced application areas are of major interest since information systems designed to solve such tasks become obsolete quickly. It can be attributed to the fact that rapid increase in the amount of empirical data leads not only to the alterations in the application area knowledge but also to the changes in the application area metaknowledge, which is contained in the application area ontology models.

© Springer Nature Switzerland AG 2019
G. S. Osipov et al. (Eds.): Artificial Intelligence, LNAI 11866, pp. 127–139, 2019.
https://doi.org/10.1007/978-3-030-33274-7_8

Due to the development of organic synthesis, which has provoked not only the emergence of novel molecular compounds but also the clarification of structure-activity relationships and reaction mechanisms, organic chemistry is one of these knowledge-intensive application domains, where tasks require as accurate, reliable and time-sensitive knowledge bases as possible.

In 2014 the number of compounds in the Chemical Abstracts Service (CAS) registry reached 100 million. Notably, CAS registered more compounds in 2014 alone than during 1965–1990 [6]. For the most part, this increase is due to organics. Ever since, the amount of data and knowledge in this field has been growing. To solve the tasks that require computer assistance, organic chemists frequently utilize (in the multistep procedures) various information resources: software products ranging from scientific calculators to MD/QM systems based on molecular dynamics/quantum mechanics (many of such systems are proprietary: "BIOVIA Discovery Studio" [5], "GAUSSIAN16" [7], etc.); taxonomies (e.g. "Open Biological and Biomedical Ontologies" (OBO) [19]); compound and reaction databases (e.g. Molbase [16], NIST [17], Reaxys [18]); other information systems. Although there is an evident advantage in the fact that the amount of reference data and generated knowledge continues to expand and the number of methods to solve various classes of problems steadily increases, one of the major challenges is that such information volumes are almost human-inconceivable. Here comes the idea of artificial intelligence applications for a variety of knowledge-intensive tasks in organic chemistry. The DENDRAL project has shown that adequate and impeccable knowledge representation can alter the problem status from unsolvable to manageable (e.g. reminisce of a savvy representation of the degree of unsaturation and a "common language of graphs", which helps all Plan-Generate-Test components to communicate) [15].

The article is dedicated to the analysis and application of the ontological approach for intelligent system (IS) engineering in the knowledge-intensive domain of organic chemistry. The major task for the IS centers around the organic compound reaction capacity identification. It has been stated by the Department of Organic Chemistry at Far Eastern Federal University, and it has always been one of the tasks that chemists solve applying not only the laws of chemical kinetics and thermodynamics but also their knowledge and expertise acquired during the years of professional training and experiment trials. Reaction capacity is tightly connected to the electron density distribution in the molecule. It is generally described in the terms of mesomeric and inductive effects (by organic chemists) and applying various approximations related to quantum mechanics (by chemists working in the field of physical, or more specifically, quantum chemistry). In many cases, when the problem itself and the procedures to find a solution are described in the concept systems of various subdomains of the initial domain, the initial domain is called "complex-structured" [4]. Its ontology model development can facilitate IS engineering. It should be noted that ontology models in the form of taxonomies (e.g. OBO) are of minor interest for this research, and the article advocates the development of ontology models in the form of applied logic theories. This methodology, as well as the IS model, and the structure of IS underlying ontology for the organic compound reaction capacity identification are presented in the following sections.

2 Ontology Models in Intelligent System Engineering. The Methodology of Applied Logic Theories

The approach of IS engineering based on application domain ontology models has been developed by Alexander Kleschev and his collaborators at the Institute of Automation and Control Processes (Far Eastern Branch of RAS). Ontology has been defined by the Stanford researcher Thomas Gruber as "an explicit specification of a conceptualization" [8]. Ontology imposes structure on the domain and restrains possible term interpretations. As a rule, ontology is not supposed to alter and represents a uniform understanding of concepts by the domain experts.

A.S. Kleschev and his colleagues have applied the mathematical apparatus of algebraic systems to give a precise definition of "ontology", "knowledge base", and "input and output data". Basic definitions and the examples related to organic chemistry domain are the following.

2.1 Mathematical Abstractions

Ontology

Ontology can be viewed as a signature

$$\sum = \{O, F, P\} \tag{1}$$

Where

O –   object symbol (e.g. "Compound structural formula");
F –   functional symbol (e.g. "Elementary reaction stage", which depends on the time of observation);
P –   predicate symbol (e.g. "To be saturated") [11].

Knowledge Base

The knowledge base can be viewed as a set of axioms A – sentences in the language of the signature $\sum$. Set of axioms A is not a specification of a particular problem. Instead, it is a distinct kind of problem input data.

Given Problem Input Data

Observation Results

$U' \subseteq U$, where U is a carrier set of algebraic system in the signature $\sum$ & $F^1 \subseteq F$ & $P^1 \subseteq P$, for the elements of which partial interpretations are set.

Problem constraints

Problem constraints can be viewed as a set of C – sentences in the language of the signature $\sum$. Set of sentences $A \cup C$ must be consistent taking into account symbol interpretation in the signature $\sum$.

Given Problem Output Data

Given problem output data is a search result among all algebraic systems in the signature $\sum$ that satisfy the following conditions:

1. $U' \subseteq U$, where U is a carrier set of algebraic system in the signature $\sum$;
2. The interpretation of functional symbols of F^1 and predicate symbols of P^1 is the extension of the input datum interpretation up to a complete definition of functions and predicates;
3. All sentences from the set $A \cup C$ are true.

2.2   Semantic Constraints and the Need for Ontology Models Defined as Interconnected Modules of Applied Logic Theories

Evidently, the set of IS input data cannot be defined precisely due to semantic constraints (the set of all theorems of untrivial mathematical theory is undefined). As a rule, it is convenient to define an extended set, which the input data (comprised of a knowledge base, observation results, and problem constraints) belongs to. For this purpose, it is suggested that the application domain ontology model be developed. Afterwards, the knowledge base is developed in the concept system specified by the ontology model. It should be noted that the ontology model is a set of interconnected modules of applied logic theories. Each theory is described with the help of the language of applied logics. The language is declarative. The language includes a modest kernel and the possibility to add extensions. The details of the approach are specified in [9, 10], and the specification of the language (including several extensions, namely "Standard extension" (ST), "Intervals", "Mathematical quantifiers") can be found in the series of articles [12–14]. Special considerations are the following.

Application domain ontology model includes the modules that are related to its subdomains. For instance, the ontology model of the knowledge-intensive domain "Chemistry" is comprised of the modules related to "Analytical chemistry", "Physical chemistry", "Organic chemistry", etc. Ontology models of the mentioned subdomains are, in their turn, modular. These modules encompass the terms that allow to describe various properties of chemical objects (e.g. elements, compounds, reactions) that each of the subdomains focuses on. The terms of each module are thematically connected. They form a distinct concept system. Modularity makes the model more flexible and feasible for the developer (since the representation of a separate subdomain in a singular module can be cumbersome). The major challenge originates in a necessity to describe the relationships among the terms of different modules involving several "Chemistry" subdomains. Moreover, not only the knowledge ontology but also the context ontology, or ontology of situations, should be considered. The former defines the terms that allow to describe the knowledge of the subdomains. The terms of the latter are used to represent the input data and the output data of a problem.

Each applied logic theory is identified by its title. The parameters of applied logic theory demonstrate the extensions needed to define the theory. Propositions of a typical applied logic theory are comprised of supplementary terms, principal terms, and ontology conventions. The following examples clarify some of the mentioned ideas.

Example 1. Applied logic theory. Its Form and Components
Modules "Electron configuration", "Functional groups", and "Carbon skeleton" are needed in the definition of applied logic theory "Chemical compound structural formula" (as well as ontology constants). "Chemical compound structural formula" module utilizes the standard extension of applied logic language, "Intervals" and "Mathematical quantifiers" extensions.

    Chemical compound structural formula(ST, Intervals, Mathe-
matical quantifiers) = < {Electron configuration, Functional
groups, Carbon skeleton, Ontology constants}, SS>
    Where SS = {propositions of the theory "Chemical compound
structural formula"}

Example 2. Supplementary Term
Supplementary terms are introduced to make principal terms and ontology conventions less cumbersome.
    Chemical bond ≡ {single, double, triple}

Example 3. Principal Term
Principal terms denote the concepts. Subject names of a module denote the sets of objects or object characteristics of the subdomain. Functional and predicate names of the module denote the relationships among the objects of the subdomain.

    Sort Stable: the characteristics of a compound that depend on
temperature and pressure(L)

    "Stable" is a predicate (true – if the compound is stable at current temperature and pressure, otherwise - false)

Example 4. Ontology Convention
Each ontology convention defines the relationship among ontology terms. It is comprised of ontology terms and mathematical terms that impose certain constraints.

    (cc: Chemical compound)(t: Temperature tabular values)(p:
Pressure tabular values) Density(cc,t,p) = Molar mass(cc)/
Molar volume(cc,t,p) = Molar mass(cc)/Molar volume(cc,t,p)

2.3   Ontology Model Use in the Intelligent System Development

Intelligent system is supposed to adapt to any alterations in the application domain. The development of IS implies the development and maturation of its information components. In turn, these changes provoke the alterations in the classes of tasks requiring new program components.

Each module of the application domain ontology model is comprised of the structured and the unstructured parts. The structured part can be stored by the means of a database management system (DBMS). Each subdomain is matched with a database, the name of which coincides with the subdomain title. The unstructured part is the text (in the language of applied logics) of ontology conventions and application domain principles. The editor of ontology conventions and application domain principles analyzes the correctness of formulas and generates a parse tree (can be stored by the means of the DBMS as well). The unstructured part of the ontology model and the knowledge is used during the verification of the referential-integrity constraints and the development of task solvers for various classes of tasks. Additionally, it is used by the subsystems of task solver generators.

The process of ontology model (presented as interconnected modules of applied logic theories in the language of applied logics) use in the IS development is depicted in Figs. 1, 2, and 3. Application domain knowledge ontology defines the structure of the information stored in the knowledge base and referential-integrity constraints verified by the editors. Application domain knowledge ontology is used during the development of knowledge editors. Application domain context ontology and task class ontology are utilized in the task class input system development, as well as in the output interpretation system development. Task class solution system, in its turn, uses problem statements and terms from both task class ontology and task solution procedure ontology.

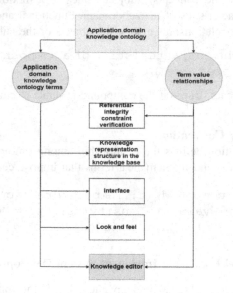

Fig. 1. Application domain knowledge ontology in intelligent system component development

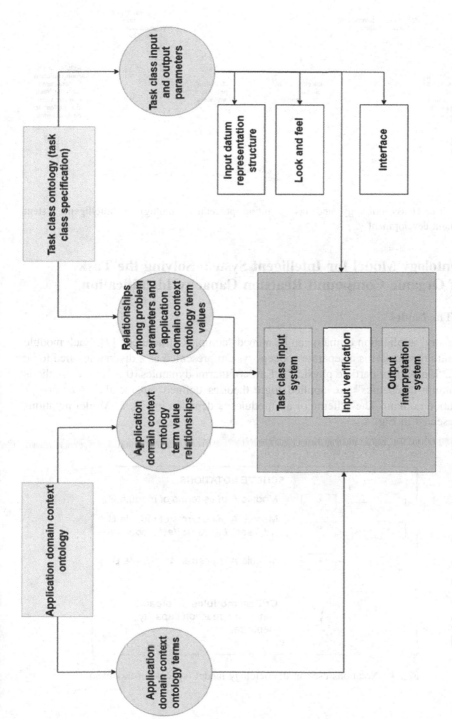

Fig. 2. Application domain context ontology and task class ontology in intelligent system component development

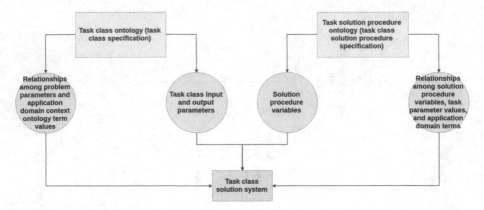

Fig. 3. Task class ontology and task solution procedure ontology in intelligent system component development

3   Ontology Model for Intelligent System Solving the Task of Organic Compound Reaction Capacity Identification

3.1   The Model

"Chemistry" application domain can be named "complex-structured" [4]. Each module of its ontology model is a separate concept system presented as a distinct applied logic theory. "Elementary particle physics", "Laws of thermodynamics (0-3)", and "Methods of quantum mechanics" are applied logic theories defined outside the "Chemistry" application domain. The scheme of all modules is depicted in Fig. 5. Model notations are presented in Fig. 4.

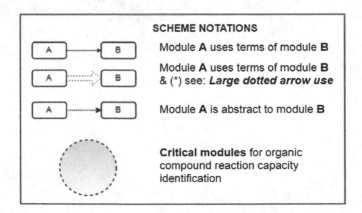

Fig. 4.   Notations used in the ontology model (scheme of modules)

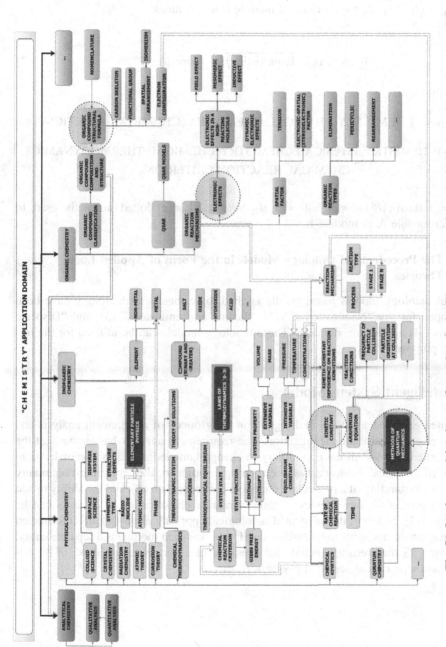

Fig. 5. Ontology model (scheme of modules) for intelligent system solving the task of organic compound reaction capacity identification

3.2   (*) Large Dotted Arrow Use Notation

Large dotted arrow is used in the ontology model if the following condition is true ($lev = 3$ is adequate for the presented model size):

$L_A = \langle l_{1_A}, l_{2_A}, \ldots, l_{|A|_A} \rangle$ - tuple of module A level names;

$L_B = \langle l_{1_B}, l_{2_B}, \ldots, l_{|B|_B} \rangle$ - tuple of module B level names;

$l_{|A|_A} = A$;

$$l_{i_A} \neq l_{i_B} \ \forall i = \overline{1, min(k, \text{lev})}; k = min(|A|, |B|). \tag{2}$$

Example

$$L_A = \langle \text{CHEMISTRY}, \text{PHYSICAL CHEMISTRY}, \text{CHEMICAL KINETICS} \rangle$$

$$L_B = \langle \text{CHEMISTRY}, \text{PHYSICAL CHEMISTRY}, \text{CHEMICAL THERMODYNAMICS},$$
$$\text{CHEMICAL REACTION CRITERION} \rangle$$

$k = min(|A|, |B|) = min(3, 4) = 3;\ l_{3_A} \neq l_{3_B} \Rightarrow$ Large dotted arrow is used to connect module A to module B.

3.3   The Precedents of Ontology Models in the Form of Applied Logic Theories

Several ontology models based on the applied logic theory methodology have been developed for the "Nanomaterials" [2], "Foams and emulsions" [3], and "Disperse systems" [1] application domains. These ontology models can be utilized for the reference purposes.

4 Intelligent System Model

The intelligent system model is designed on the grounds of requirement analysis and interface quality attribute identification. The requirement analysis has shown that the major criteria consist in the opportunity to change knowledge and metaknowledge in the IS (if empirical evidence has been strong enough to alter scientific community shared understanding of a particular concept or concept relations), and the ability to add problem solvers for new classes of tasks. Granular classification of IS tasks can be found in [11]. Notably, the advocated ontological approach allows the IS information and program components to be easily extendible since each module is a separate entity. Additional IS requirements include the presence of a distributed database of experiments and a precedent search subsystem.

Interface quality includes the following attributes: user confidence in the IS (due to the use of a concept system that is universally understood by the users), the ability to customize IS interface for a distinct scientific group, and the presence of knowledge-intensive domain-specific interfaces, such as organic compound structural formula graphic interface, several chemical datum formats (e.g. SMILES, CAS, etc.), and interfaces for several graph types (e.g. histogram, function curve, etc.).

Figure 6 captures the IS model for organic compound reaction capacity identification. The IS model is comprised of information system, support system, and program components. Its information components are based on the ontology model described above. Its architecture considers IS requirements and interface quality attributes.

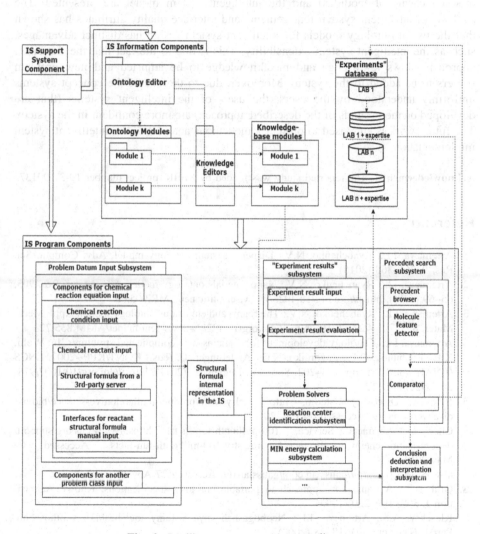

Fig. 6. Intelligent system architecture diagram.

5 Conclusion

The amount of knowledge in the knowledge-intensive application domains, such as organic chemistry, grows rapidly. The adverse effects of this process involve scientific progress impediment due to the human-inconceivable knowledge amounts. Intelligent system engineering is supposed to resolve the issue. Organic compound reaction capacity identification is a knowledge-intensive task. To develop intelligent system that can provide a solution for this task, one should effectively represent the complex-structured application domain. The article utilizes the methodology of ontology model creation in the form of interconnected modules of applied logic theories. The ontology model (scheme of modules) and the intelligent system model are presented. The analysis of intelligent system requirements and interface quality attributes has shown that the use of ontology models for intelligent system design has distinct advantages, such as the intelligent system extensibility. This is due to the fact that the described approach allows knowledge and metaknowledge to be adjusted and new problem solvers to be added to the system. Moreover, due to the use of the concept systems uniformly understood by the users, the users of the intelligent systems (that are developed on the grounds of the described approach) are more confident in the system. The future work is supposed to present a meticulous analysis of the intelligent system implementation.

Acknowledgements. The reported study was funded by RFBR, project number 19-37-90137.

References

1. Artemieva, I.L., Ryabchenko, N.V.: Disperse system ontology model. Adv. Comput. Sci. Res. **9**, 365–368 (2015)
2. Artemieva, I.L., Ryabchenko, N.V.: Nanomaterials ontology model. Adv. Mater. Res. **905**, 65–69 (2014). https://doi.org/10.4028/www.scientific.net/AMR.905.65
3. Artemieva, I.L., Ryabchenko, N.V.: The foams and emulsions ontology model. Appl. Mech. Mater. **835**, 723–727 (2016). https://doi.org/10.4028/www.scientific.net/AMM.835.723
4. Artemieva, I.L.: Ontology development for domains with complicated structures. In: Wolff, K.E., Palchunov, D.E., Zagoruiko, N.G., Andelfinger, U. (eds.) KONT/KPP -2007. LNCS (LNAI), vol. 6581, pp. 184–202. Springer, Heidelberg (2011). https://doi.org/10.1007/978-3-642-22140-8_12
5. BIOVIA Discovery Studio. http://accelrys.com/products/collaborative-science/biovia-discovery-studio/. Accessed 09 July 2018
6. Chemical Abstracts Service. 100-millionth-fun-facts. https://www.cas.org/support/documentation/chemical-substances/cas-registry-100-millionth-fun-facts. Accessed 09 May 2019
7. GAUSSIAN16. http://gaussian.com/gaussian16/. Accessed 27 Apr 2019
8. Gruber, T.: A translation approach to portable ontology specifications. Knowl. Acquisition J. **5**(2), 199–220 (1993)
9. Kleschev, A.S., Artemeva, I.L.: Neobogashchennye sistemy logicheskikh sootnoshenii. Part 1. NTI, ser. **2**(7), 18–28 (2000)

10. Kleschev, A.S., Artemeva, I.L.: Neobogashchennye sistemy logicheskikh sootnoshenii. Part 2. NTI ser. **2**(8), 8–18 (2000)
11. Kleschev, A.S., Shalfeeva, E.A.: An ontology of intellectual activity tasks. Ontol. Designing **5**, 179–205 (2015). https://doi.org/10.18287/2223-9537-2015-5-2-179-205
12. Kleshchev, A.S., Artemjeva, I.L.: A mathematical apparatus for domain ontology simulation. An extendable language of applied logic. Int. J. Inf. Theor. Appl. **12**(2), 149–157 (2005)
13. Kleshchev, A.S., Artemjeva, I.L.: A mathematical apparatus for domain ontology simulation. Logical relationship systems. Int. J. Inf. Theor. Appl. **12**(4), 343–351 (2005)
14. Kleshchev, A.S., Artemjeva, I.L.: A mathematical apparatus for domain ontology simulation. Specialized extensions of the extendable language of applied logic. Int. J. Inf. Theor. Appl. **12**(3), 265–271 (2005)
15. Lindsay, R.K., Buchanan, B.G., Feigenbaum, E.A., Lederberg, J.: Applications of Artificial Intelligence for Organic Chemistry. The DENDRAL Project. McGraw-Hill, New York (1980)
16. MOLBASE. https://www.molbase.com/. Accessed 04 Apr 2019
17. NIST. https://www.nist.gov/data. Accessed 04 Apr 2019
18. Reaxys. https://www.reaxys.com/. Accessed 04 Apr 2019
19. The OBO Foundry. http://www.obofoundry.org/. Accessed 09 July 2018

Automated Acquisition, Representation and Processing of Temporal Knowledge in Dynamic Intelligent Systems

Galina V. Rybina$^{(\boxtimes)}$ ⓘ and Elena S. Fontalina ⓘ

National Research Nuclear University MEPhI, Moscow, Russia
galina@ailab.mephi.ru

Abstract. This paper analyzes the results of automated knowledge base construction for dynamic intelligent systems, in particular dynamic integrated expert systems on the basis of the so-called combined method of knowledge acquisition with temporal extensions. Dynamic intelligent systems are actively in demand in commercial and industrial applications. However, the effect of their application largely depends on the availability of modern software tools that automate the development of intelligent systems. At AI laboratory of NRNU MEPhI we develop dynamic integrated expert systems with AT TECHNOLOGY – software platform that implements problem-oriented methodology.

Keywords: Intelligent systems · Dynamic integrated expert systems ·
Temporal knowledge acquisition · Automated knowledge acquisition ·
Temporal inference

1 Introduction

Dynamic intelligent systems, in particular dynamic integrated expert systems are actively in demand in commercial and industrial applications. However, the effect of their application largely depends on the availability of modern software tools that automate the development of intelligent systems.

At AI laboratory of NRNU MEPhI we develop dynamic integrated expert systems with AT–TECHNOLOGY– software platform that implements problem-oriented methodology [1]. This platform supports and automates processes of prototyping and maintaining integrated expert systems throughout their lifecycle. For a number of criteria (such as knowledge representation models, reasoning tools, object-oriented design support, etc.) AT–TECHNOLOGY is comparable to G2 (Gensym corp., US) – leading software platform for real-time expert systems. Considering the built-in subsystem of outer world simulation, AT–TECHNOLOGY even goes ahead of G2.

While G2 and some other tools lack automated knowledge acquisition, our platform offers original hybrid knowledge acquisition tools enabling fuzzy and temporal knowledge acquisition from various sources. These tools significantly improve the development of knowledge bases in various domains and levels of complexity.

© Springer Nature Switzerland AG 2019
G. S. Osipov et al. (Eds.): Artificial Intelligence, LNAI 11866, pp. 140–145, 2019.
https://doi.org/10.1007/978-3-030-33274-7_9

2 Representation and Processing of Temporal Knowledge

Acquisition, representation, and processing of temporal knowledge (i.e., knowledge considering time as an entity of a problem domain) play important role in the context of the systematic approach to development of dynamic integrated expert systems.

In [1] we have described basic models of knowledge representation and inference tools of AT-TECHNOLOGY – AT–SOLVER. Here we consider temporal aspects of inference performed on knowledge bases containing some unreliable knowledge, i.e., knowledge with such *negative factors* as uncertainty, inaccuracy, fuzziness, and with constraints on variables.

Generalized model of temporal inference with production rules for dynamic integrated expert systems involves processing of knowledge with temporal dependencies together with basic knowledge of the problem domain.

We see the purpose of temporal inference in construction of the event flow model interpretation and in generation of a list of controlling actions for the problem domain. So we applied Allen's logic [2] with some enhancements together with Osipov's logic of control over time [3]. We define global event flow model by a set of temporal objects (events and intervals). Local event flow models in rules are defined by formulas of Allen's logic. Event flow model interpretation may be given as a set of timestamps of events and intervals. We define interval as a pair of timestamps corresponding to the beginning and the ending of an interval.

Formally temporal inference model may be presented in the form of a 5-tuple [4]:

$$I = <V, S, R, W, D>,$$

where

V – process of selection of active rules suitable for problem solving on each inference loop;

S – process of matching of antecedents of active rules with facts, matching temporal and non-temporal parts of rules including construction of *event flow model* interpretation, as well as fuzzification and various evaluations and transformations of negative factors;

R – conflict resolution process that selects a single rule out of the matched ones to be applied to the working memory;

W – rule firing process where truth values of consequents are evaluated considering negative factors;

D – process of defuzzification of fuzzified variables.

The matching stage is complemented by processes that ensure modification of event flow model interpretation and match temporal parts of active rules. Processes are carried out on each inference loop except for D which is executed as the final step of the whole inference. The event flow model interpretation is modified on each loop. When we integrated the basic inference tools and temporal tools [4] we paid special attention to two things: the update operation for the event flow model interpretation and matching of local event flow models in rules with global event flow model interpretation for all types of temporal statements.

To represent temporal knowledge in dynamic integrated expert systems we enhanced knowledge representation language of AT-TECHNOLOGY – AT-KRL [5]. Now it allows representing temporal knowledge together with basic knowledge including knowledge with uncertainty, inaccuracy, and fuzziness. To do so, we introduced new basic types of objects: events and intervals; new type of object properties: condition of event occurrence. We modified the structure of rule antecedents: we added local event flow model requirements. At last, Osipov's control over time concepts lead to adding new rule types into AT–KRL:

- *reactions,* aimed to provide quick response to certain, usually urgent, events in problem domain, and
- *periodic rules,* aimed to track certain duty cycles.

Reaction rules generally correspond to enhanced Allen's logic. Their antecedents are formulas where each operand is a single temporal object (an event or an interval). Antecedents of periodic rules contain extra condition with firing period.

These enhancements of AT-KRL allow us to describe temporal relationships of objects in a problem domain by rules. Decision making is now performed taking into account actual event flow of the problem domain.

As for inference process, the major changes were made in matching procedures: we implemented evaluation of formulas containing temporal arguments in rule antecedents, and construction of event flow interpretation on each inference loop.

When forming event flow interpretation, events and intervals are bound to the time axis by identifying the facts of their occurrence and considering the history of events. Processing of temporal parts of antecedents uses the results of event flow interpretation construction. For active rules AT-SOLVER matches local event flow models with constructed event flow interpretation.

Thus, the synergy of AT-SOLVER and temporal tools addresses both static and dynamic domains. Note that complex discrete systems produce input data for temporal inference in dynamic integrated expert systems. Issues related to models, methods, algorithms, and software for simulation modeling are considered in a number of papers, for example [4, 5].

3   Acquisition of Temporal Knowledge from Various Sources of Knowledge

In expert systems development we can automate experts' work by implementing methods and tools for detecting and extracting temporal knowledge from natural language texts (NL-texts) (Text Mining and Natural Language Processing) and from databases (Data Mining and Knowledge Discovery in Databases). In world practice there is a number of approaches to temporal dependencies acquisition but most of them are focused on processing of English-language texts. Moreover, they do not consider obtaining temporal knowledge for temporal knowledge bases for dynamic intelligent systems and for dynamic integrated expert systems in particular.

Our combined method of knowledge acquisition (CMKA) has proven its efficiency in development of static integrated expert systems with AT-TECHNOLOGY. It automates interviewing of experts using natural sublanguage (business prose style), data mining, and verification of knowledge bases. In [1] we described the client-server architecture and tools for knowledge acquisition from geographically distributed sources of knowledge of various types: experts, natural language texts, databases. In dynamic integrated expert systems methods of automated detection of temporal knowledge remain an unexplored problem. In particular, for extracting information about time from texts in Russian, only the few approaches are proposed that partly help to automate these processes, e.g. [6, 7]. Therefore, we focused on further evolution of combined method of knowledge acquisition and especially its temporal enhancement by developing new methods and tools for automated construction of temporal knowledge bases in dynamic integrated expert systems.

Our approach to knowledge acquisition (directly from experts by automated interviewing) bases on original technique of using patterns for solving typical problems [1]. We have put meta knowledge about strategies of solving into heuristic solving patterns for specific cases: diagnostics, engineering, planning, control, learning, and some other. To support these solving patterns we developed a number of methods and tools for modeling dialog scenarios used in interviewing. These methods address both *thematic structure* of a dialog, i.e. problem solving pattern, and *local structure* of a dialog, i.e. dialog steps – specific actions and reactions between the expert and the system.

As computer-aided interviewing of an expert goes on, the problem solving pattern fills with structured data that can be exported to knowledge base. To derive the "action - reaction" model of dialog we use several techniques, e.g., *simulation of consultation*. Interviewing of experts is carried out automatically by dialog scenario interpreter. The interpreter also generates dialog screens for entering answers and data including such things as uncertainty, imprecision, fuzziness. The specialized linguistic processor and a set of dynamically replenished dictionaries [1] support knowledge acquisition process. Computer-aided interviewing of experts, natural language processing, data mining from databases are tightly coupled in AT-TECHNOLOGY.

In [1] we defined the model of knowledge acquisition method as a 5-tuple:

$$M = <N, S, F, K, Z>,$$

where

N – unstructured descriptions in problem domain (expertise, documents, databases);
S – structured descriptions in problem domain (intermediate representation of knowledge as objects and rules);
F – procedures of mapping N into S;
K – procedures of knowledge formalization using AT-KRL (or another);
Z – knowledge base fragments produced by K.

Each object in S corresponds to one or more answers that an expert gives during an interviewing session. The thematic structure of the dialog and questions themselves are built in such a way that allow to interpret each answer as an object, an attribute, a type, a value, a range of values, or a statement in a rule antecedent or action.

For temporal knowledge, the process of structuring objects and rules involves events and intervals. Antecedents and actions of rules among other things consider relationships between these entities. Accordingly, F-component contains such procedures as obtaining descriptions from distributed sources, matching various structured knowledge fragments (including those with temporal data), combining of structured knowledge fragments.

We developed a technique of detection and interpretation of the simplest *temporal pointers* (i.e., independent individual words and phrases denoting time) within a single sentence. We used generic classification of temporal pointers presented in [8, 9] together with vocabulary of Russian-language lexemes indicating temporal relations. To model dialogs we used business prose linguistic model for medical diagnostics and specialized linguistic processor [1].

We adopted the Random Forest algorithm [8] to work with databases containing temporal data [9]. The ensemble of decision trees is constructed in accordance with the basic Random Forest algorithm. We use multidimensional feature space, one of which is the timestamp. However, the calculation method of the partitioning criterion value has changed to the arithmetic mean of entropy values. Also, the construction of the tree is carried out until all the elements of the subsample are processed without using cut-off procedure.

To convert the ensemble of decision trees to knowledge base format we use some helper tools:

- the main object containing all features of the feature space as attributes;
- the counter to measure time;
- vote counters.

Each leaf is converted to a rule of the following form: if the duration of all intervals corresponding to vertices on the path to the root is greater than zero, then increment the vote counter for the class that corresponds to the current vertex.

When we extract knowledge containing temporal data from various sources of different types (experts, texts, and databases), we get multiple fragments containing objects, types, and rules. To merge all the fragments of knowledge together we use methods, algorithms, and software tools of the combined method of knowledge acquisition from distributed sources taking into account temporal data. Knowledge verification is not considered in this paper but is implemented in AT–TECHOLOGY as well.

4 Conclusion

We implemented temporal extensions for the combined method of knowledge acquisition, including mining of production rules from databases. We studied the distributed knowledge acquisition process where temporal databases in medical domain were used as additional sources of knowledge. We noticed that knowledge base growth ratio lies between 12–25% with 15% in average.

Acknowledgements. This work was partially funded by the RFBR (Russian Foundation for Basic Research), project No. 18-01-00457.

References

1. Rybina, G.V.: Theory and Technology of Integrated Expert System Construction. Nauchtehlitizdat, Moscow (2008). (in Russian)
2. Allen, J.F.: Maintaining knowledge about temporal intervals. Commun. Assoc. Comput. Mach. **22**, 832–843 (1983)
3. Osipov, G.S.: Dynamic intelligent systems (in Russian). Iskusstvennyj intellekt i prinyatie reshenij **1**, 47–54 (2008)
4. Rybina, G.V., Demidov, D.V., Chekalin, D.B.: Collaboration of all-purpose static solver, temporal reasoning and simulation modeling tools in dynamic integrated expert systems. Adv. Intell. Syst. Comput. **449**, 191–196 (2016)
5. Rybina, G.V., Mozgachev, A.V.: The use of temporal inferences in dynamic integrated expert systems. Sci. Tech. Inf. Process. **41**(6), 390–399 (2014)
6. Efimenko, I.V.: Semantic of time: models, methods, and identification algorithms for NLP-systems (in Russian). In: Vestnik Moskovskogo gosudarstvennogo oblastnogo universiteta. Seria "Linguistics", vol. 2, Moscow, MSRU, pp. 179–185 (2007)
7. Arutyunova, N.D., Yanko, T.E.: Logical analysis of language: language and time. Indrik, Moscow (1997). (in Russian)
8. Tzacheva, A.A., Bagavathi, A., Ganesan, P.D.: MR - random forest algorithm for distributed action rules discovery. Int. J. Data Min. Knowl. Manag. Process (IJDKP) **6**(5), 15–30 (2016)
9. Kaufmann, M., et al.: Timeline index: a unified data structure for processing queries on temporal data in SAP HANA. In: Proceedings of the 2013 ACM SIGMOD International Conference on Management of Data, pp. 1173–1184 (2013)

Natural Language Processing with DeepPavlov Library and Additional Semantic Features

Oleg Sattarov[✉]

Moscow Institute of Physics and Technology, Moscow, Russia
oleg.sattarov@phystech.edu

Abstract. In this paper some basic methods of NER task managing in Deep-Pavlov library along with new neural network modifications with additional semantic features are observed. Means of DeepPavlov library were slightly improved and applied to new dataset with unique additional features, which caused feasible improvement of the neural model.

Keywords: Neural networks · Natural language processing · Named entity recognition · DeepPavlov

1 Introduction

Modern society has a great demand to many different automatic natural language processing problems, such as search on demand, classification, knowledge mining, machine translation, named entity recognition and many others. The approaches based on machine learning and on deep learning and neural networks in particular, have now reached the greatest efficiency in solving such problems. A primitive model of neural network has three layers – an input layer in a form of vector, an output layer, which is also a vector and a hidden layer between them. In the hidden layer so-called neurons are situated. Each neuron receives an input vector, makes a linear transformation with coefficients, which can then be altered (or trained), and then imposes nonlinear transformation, which also has trainable coefficients, on this result. The result of many of these independent neurons all sum up to form the final response. For the text processing problem, the input vector of a neural network is usually a vector representation of a word in a multidimensional space that is constructed the way that similar words in it are close and dissimilar are far. Such representation might also be obtained by machine learning methods. Thus, during text processing, the neural network receives only general information about the word based on the statistics of its occurrence in various texts, but the role of this word in this particular case and its syntactic and semantic connection with the rest of the words in this sentence are unknown, and it has to "guess" them during the learning process. The syntactic and semantic structure of the sentence reveals the essence of this sentence and it contains the most important connections between the words it is composed of. Obviously, using this information, it is possible to improve the performance of existing neural networks. For better understanding of what we are talking about, let's focus on the basic ideas of syntactic and semantic description of the text. Syntactic analysis or parsing is the process of

G. S. Osipov et al. (Eds.): Artificial Intelligence, LNAI 11866, pp. 146–159, 2019.
https://doi.org/10.1007/978-3-030-33274-7_10

mapping a sequence of words of a language with its formal grammar. Most models rely either on the dependency grammar [14] or on the phrase grammar structure [15]. Dependency grammar assumes that text sentences are dependency trees in which words are connected by directed graphs denoting syntactic subordination. It is believed that this formalism well reflects the specificity of languages with an arbitrary word order, such as Russian, German or Czech, in which a significant number of intersecting connections can be present between words. In the phrase grammar structure sentences are represented as a hierarchy of components (syntactic groups): all the sentence is divided into disjoint groups, which in turn consist of smaller groups, etc. up to the atomic groups – the words of the sentence, forming a syntactic tree (see Fig. 1). Semantic structure reveals the meaning of the sentence and its words. By semantic analysis of the text we mean the establishment of generalized categorical meaning of syntax and semantic links between them. Syntaxeme represents the minimum syntactic and semantic unit of language that carries a generalized, categorical meaning. For example, among the semantic roles can be such as "agent" - an animated initiator and controller of the action, "tool" of the action, "patient" - a participant undergoing significant changes, and many others.

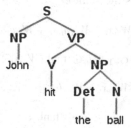

Fig. 1. Syntactic tree.

Using the arsenal of methods of automatic semantic and syntactic analysis of texts, we can apply the results of this analysis to compose new features that can be added to the input of the neural network, with the aim of improving the quality of its work. This idea leads us to the topic of this article.

2 DeepPavlov and Neural Networks

In this paper, a study of the model of natural language processing from the library DeepPavlov, the model of recognition of named entities in particular, was conducted. The architecture of this model was supplemented with the use of semantic features, resulting in an increase in the accuracy of model predictions and the speed of its learning. All models for neural networks for the problem of named entities recognition in this library are based on the approach described in the following article: "Application of a Hybrid Bi-LSTM-CRF model to the task of Russian Named Entity Recognition" [6] (which in turn is based on the results of another article: [7]) However, the parameters can vary from model to model, and it is possible to use other approaches with this library. To understand how this particular model works, it is necessary to focus on some key concepts.

2.1   LSTM

Recurrent neural networks are a family of neural networks that operate with data sequences. The input of such a network receive some sequence of vectors x_t (for example, pre-trained sequences of word embeddings), and the output is a sequence of some other vectors h_t, which contain some information about the part of initial sequence at each step t. At each step such a network receives not only the vector x_t, but also the previous output vector h_t. In theory, such networks can remember information about all elements of the original sequence: the last vector h_t must contain all previous information. In fact, this does not happen, and the last resulting vector mainly reflects information about the last seen input vector. This is due to the gradient descent effect in the update of the output vector during training. LSTM's (Long Short Term Memory networks) are created to deal with this difficulty. The following formulas are used to calculate each of the h_t vectors (there are several slightly different versions of these formulas, but the idea is always the same):

$$i_t = \sigma(W_{xi}x_t + W_{hi}h_{t-1} + W_{ci}c_{t-1} + b_i)$$

$$c_t = (1 - i_t) \odot c_{t-1} + i_t \odot \tanh(W_{xc}x_t + W_{hc}h_{t-1} + b_c)$$

$$o_t = \sigma(W_{xo}x_t + W_{ho}h_{t-1} + W_{co}c_t + b_o)$$

$$h_t = o_t \odot \tanh(c_t)$$

The vector i_t is responsible for how much the current input vector x_t is taken into account by the neural network. If this value is close to one, the network "forgets" previous experience, and relies on the current vector. If it is close to zero, the network does not perceive the current vector and remains almost unchanged comparing to the previous step. The o vector is responsible for what information to use to generate h_t: some elements may not be involved in the current step, but the network will "remember" them to use in the next steps. It is shown empirically that networks with such a configuration are able to detect dependencies between words, even if there is a large number of other words in the text between them. The problem of gradient descent is not so obvious here, and this can be explained by the fact that the network is able to "forget" words if they are not important, and gradients do not have to propagate through the LSTM cells responsible for these words (Fig. 2).

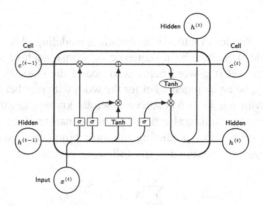

Fig. 2. LSTM scheme.

2.2 Bi-LSTM

Applications to NER use the vector h_t from the chain trained on the sequence of words of the text and corresponding to the vector x_t of the word to decide which class the word belongs to. However, if we recall the method of constructing LSTM, it becomes clear that in this case the vector h_t contains only information about the previous words, but information about the subsequent words, which play an equally important role in the NER problem, is not included in this vector. To solve this problem, the so-called Bi-LSTM is used, that is an architecture that use the union of two vectors obtained from two independent LSTM networks, one of which is trained on the direct sequence of words of the text, and the other – on the reverse sequence. Thus, the resulting vector contains information from neighboring words on both sides (Fig. 3).

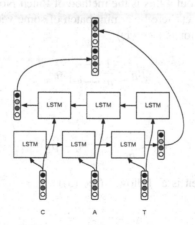

Fig. 3. Bi-LSTM scheme.

2.3   CRF

CRF or Conditional Random Field – is a statistical modeling class which is a type of Markov random field. Let there be a sequence of words, each of which has its own marker from a limited set (the word belongs to one of the classes), and the marker is unknown to us. Let y_i be an assumed label for the word with number i, and probabilities P_{i,y_i} that the word with number i has such a label are known. Let the probability of a word with a marker y_i appearance also depends on the marker of the previous word and is $A_{y_i,y_{i+1}}$. Then the problem of predicting the most probable sequence of markers is reduced to the problem of maximizing the following expression:

$$s(X, y) = \sum_{i=0}^{n} A_{y_i,y_{i+1}} + \sum_{i=1}^{n} P_{i,y_i}$$

Due to the fact that in the NER task there is a relation between neighboring labels (e.g., in IOB naming the I-PER can't follow B-LOC), the use of CRF on top of a deep learning model is a reasonable approach. In this case, the probabilities P_{i,y_i} are calculated by the neural network, for example, Bi-LSTM.

2.4   Batch Normalization

It is known that any machine learning algorithm, including deep learning algorithms, learns faster and better if the input of the model is supplied with data that has good statistics, that is, if the data is normalized. The Batch-Norm technique develops this approach. If a neural network has multiple layers, then after passing through one layer, the data, that used to be normalized before it, is no longer normalized in the output. Between the layers of the neural network artificial normalization of intermediate parameters can be carried out – this is the method of Batch-Norm [8]. In general, it can be described as follows: Let there be a mini-batch of some vectors $x_{1...m}$: $\mathcal{B} = \{x_{1...m}\}$, then the mean of this vector is (see (1))

$$\mu_{\mathcal{B}} = \frac{1}{m} \sum_{i=1}^{m} x_i \tag{1}$$

and variance is (see (2))

$$\sigma_{\mathcal{B}}^2 = \frac{1}{m} \sum_{i=1}^{m} (x_i - \mu_{\mathcal{B}})^2 \tag{2}$$

Normalized vector then is as follows: (see (3))

$$\hat{x}_i = \frac{x_i - \mu_{\mathcal{B}}}{\sqrt{\sigma_{\mathcal{B}}^2 + \epsilon}} \tag{3}$$

and the next layer receive a vector (see (4))

$$y_i = \gamma\hat{x}_i + \beta \equiv BN_{\gamma,\beta}(x_i) \tag{4}$$

where γ and β parameters are trainable. It should be noted that this procedure is not "forced": due to the fact that the normalization parameters are trainable, the neural network can learn to cancel this normalization if it worsens the properties of the model. In the original paper, where this approach was first proposed, it was shown that adding batch-normalization between layers of the neural network can accelerate the convergence of the model by more than ten times.

2.5 CNN

In a conventional perceptron, which is a part of a fully connected neural network, each neuron is connected to all the neurons of the previous layer, and each link has its own personal weighting factor. In convolutional neural network, only a limited matrix of weights of a small size is used in the convolution operation, which is "moved" throughout the processed layer, after each shift forming an activation signal for the neuron of the next layer with a similar position. It means that for different neurons of the output layer, the same weight matrix is used, which is also called the convolution kernel. It is interpreted as a graphical coding of some feature. The result of the convolution with one kernel is called a feature map. With the use of multiple kernels, different feature maps are obtained. After that, the operation of subsampling (or pooling) performs the reduction of dimensionality of the generated feature maps. A typical convolutional neural network consists of a large number of layers. After the initial layer, the signal passes through a series of alternating convolutional and subsampling (pooling) layers. Usually, after passing through several layers, a single feature map degenerates into a vector or even a scalar, but there are hundreds of such feature maps. At the output of the convolutional layers of the network, several layers of a fully connected neural network (perceptron) are added, which receive the terminal feature maps as input. This architecture is well established in the problem of pattern recognition in images (Fig. 4).

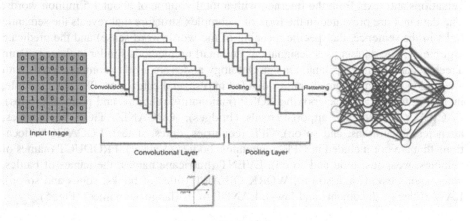

Fig. 4. CNN scheme.

3 Used Datasets

3.1 CoNLL 2003

This dataset [1] was composed of a collection of news articles of the Reuters Corporation "Reuters Corpora". (Reuters is one of the world's largest international news and financial information agencies.) The data itself consists of four columns: in the first column there is a word, in the second - corresponding part of speech (POS-tag), in the third there is a label of belonging to the so-called "syntactic chunk", that is, a certain sequence of words connected semantically (for example, they include noun or verb phrases), and, finally, in the fourth column there is a label of a named entity. In this dataset, words are divided into five categories: persons, geographic locations, organization names, other named entities (miscellaneous) and words that do not belong to named entities. This dataset uses the IOB naming approach (inside, outside, beginning): before the label of each named entity there is the prefix I-, except for the situation when two different named entities of the same type follow each other. In this case, the label of the first word from the second entity is prefixed with B- (Table 1).

Table 1. CoNNL dataset example.

U.N.	NNP	I-NP	I-ORG
official	NN	I-NP	O
Ekeus	NNP	I-NP	I-PER
heads	VBZ	I-NP	O
for	IN	I-NP	O
Baghdad	NNP	I-NP	I-LOC
.	.	O	O

3.2 Ontonotes

This dataset [2] consists of news articles, television news recordings, telephone conversations and texts from the Internet, with a total volume of about 1.5 million words. The data in it are presented in the form of a complex structure that reveals the semantic links in the sentence, the specific meaning of the word (word sense) and the predicate arguments. The dataset uses designations and markup methods similar to those in Penn Treebank and Penn PropBank. Omega Ontology nodes are used to combine words with a common meaning. Named entities divided into several categories: PERSON (people, including fictional characters), the NORP (nationality, religious and political groups), FACILITY (buildings, airports, roads, bridges), ORGANIZATION (companies, agencies, institutions, and so on), GPE (countries, cities, states), LOCATION (locations that are not included in GPE, mountains, bodies of water), PRODUCT (names of vehicles, weapons, food and so on), EVENT (hurricane names, the names of battles, wars, sports events and so on), WORK OF ART (titles of books, songs and so on), LAW (titles of documents and laws), LANGUAGE (language names) (Fig. 5).

```
 1  ---------------------------------------------------------------------------------
 2
 3  Plain sentence:
 4  ---------------
 5      I ground the rye on number 6 click-LRB-out of 8-RRB-in my Champion Juicer grinder.
 6
 7  Treebanked sentence:
 8  --------------------
 9      I ground the rye on number 6 click -LRB- out of 8 -RRB- in my Champion Juicer grinder .
10
11  Tree:
12  -----
13      (TOP (S (NP-SBJ (PRP I))
14              (VP (VBD ground)
15                  (NP (DT the)
16                      (NN rye))
17                  (PP-MNR (IN on)
18                          (NP (NP (NML (NN number)
19                                       (CD 6))
20                                  (NN click))
21                              (-LRB- -LRB-)
22                              (PP (IN out)
23                                  (PP (IN of)
24                                      (NP (CD 8))))
25                              (-RRB- -RRB-)))
26                  (PP-LOC (IN in)
27                          (NP (PRP$ my)
28                              (NML (NNP Champion)
29                                   (NNP Juicer))
30                              (NN grinder))))
31              (. .)))
32
33  Leaves:
34  -------
35      0   I
36      1   ground
37              sense: ground-v.6
38      2   the
39      3   rye
40      4   on
41      5   number
```

Fig. 5. Ontonotes dataset example.

3.3 DSTC

This dataset [3] from the eponymous competition (Dialogue State Tracking Challenge) contains two types of dialogue records: search for tourist information and search for information on restaurants. It was marked up mainly with an emphasis on the task of the dialogue state tracking but from the point of view of named entities recognition, it is only important to note the types of entities placed in it: area, food, pricerange and name.

3.4 Collection3 (Named_Entities_3)

This dataset [4] is an improved version of Persons-1000 [5], and includes the markup of named entities into three types: people names, organization names, and geographical names. The dataset is a set of news reports and includes 1000 documents all in Russian language. Markup and unmodified text are located in different files, separately for each document. The markup file has a following structure: in the first column there is a number of the named entity in this file, in the second - label of this named entity, in the third - number of the first character of this entity and the number of the first character of the word immediately following it, separated by a space. In the fourth column, the unchanged word in Russian is located. Entities marked "O" are skipped in this file (Table 2).

Table 2. Collection3 dataset example.

T1	LOC 0 6	Россия
T2	LOC 50 53	США
T3	LOC 57 63	Грузию
T4	LOC 87 93	МОСКВА

To train the model with DeepPavlov API, a redesigned dataset was used. It is presented in a single text file in a format similar to the CoNLL format (Table 3):

Table 3. Collection3 dataset example for DeepPavlov (with Russian texts).

Барак	B-PER
Обама	I-PER
назначит	O
доктора	O
Томаса	B-PER
Фридена	I-PER

4   DeepPavlov Models Description

Now we are ready to describe the approaches that stand behind DeepPavlov [9] models in named entities recognition task:

4.1   ner_rus

Firstly, the model allocates a sequence of words from the text of the dataset (x_tokens). The words are lowercased and the diacritical marks (x_san) are removed. The dictionary of words of this dataset, as well as the dictionary of named entities is compiled. Source words (x_tokens) are separated by letters, and a dictionary of letters is compiled. Every word (x_san) is mapped to the corresponding pre-trained embedding. Capital letter features for each letter of the word are created. After that the letters of each word in a sentence are being loaded into Bi-LSTM to get word representations at the letter level. In this model, they have a dimension of 100. Further, these representations of words are combined with pre-trained embedding (in the case of ner_rus model it is a 100-dimensional representation trained on news articles dataset based on Lenta.ru [12] portal) and a capital letter feature is added (this information is otherwise would be lost during preprocessing at the stage of lowercasing). These new embeddings are fed to the input of another Bi-LSTM network. On top of this layer two more dense (without dropout) layers of the neural network are trained. All of this is done with batch-normalization between each two layers, as well as dropout mechanism (random disconnection of some neurons during training, which has a regularizing effect). In addition, to speed up the learning process, "Nvidia cuDNN" optimization of calculations on the GPU is used. The result for each word is a probability vector that characterizes belonging of this word to each of the named entities labels. The CRF layer is trained on top of this probability distribution. Hidden layers of Bi-LSTM and dense layers before CRF have a dimension of 128. This model has learning rate of 10^{-2}, and dropout probability of 0.3 (dropout_keep_prob = 0.7) (Fig. 6).

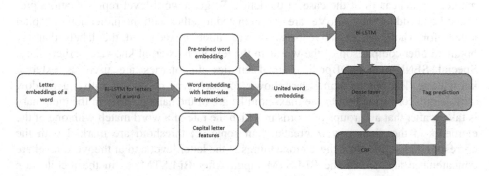

Fig. 6. ner_rus model scheme.

Most of the other models presented here use the same architecture except for a few changes.

4.2   ner_ontonotes

As word embeddings 100-dimentional GloVe [13] vectors are used in this model. Letter embeddings dimensionality is reduced to 32. Hidden layer dimensionality is extended to 256, while amount of layers raised to three. Learning rate is reduced to $3 * 10^{-3}$ and input layer dropout is turned off.

4.3   ner_connl2003

As word embedings it uses 100-dimensional GloVe [13] vector. The dimension of the letter embedding is reduced to 32. The dropout probability increased to 0.5.

4.4   ner_dstc2

Here, due to the simplicity of the dataset, the approach to solving the problem is different: as before, first of all, the sequence of text words (x_tokens) is selected from the dataset and the words are lowercase. A dictionary of these words and named entities tags is compiled, random 100-dimensional embeddings are initialized. These embedding without addition of other additional features are used in a two-layer convolutional neural network with 64 nodes in each layer. The width of a convolutional kernel is set to 7. Further, the network architecture is the same as after the second Bi-LSTM in the models described earlier. Learning rate in this model is 10^{-2}, and dropout probability – 0.5. Input layer dropout is turned off.

4.5 "Chiu and Nichols 2016"

The article "Chiu and Nichols 2016" [10] uses another but very similar approach:

As in DeepPavlov, firstly, word representations at the letter level are constructed, however, this time it is done using CNN. Further, these representations are supplemented by indicators of the case of the letter. To get a word-level representation, pre-trained embedding (also GloVe) are concatenated together with the indication of capital letters for whole words (all caps/starts with upper/mixed) and the labels that are obtained after comparison of the words in the text with external knowledge dictionary. Special SENNA and DBpedia named entities dictionaries are used as external knowledge. The comparison is as follows: for each type of named entity, a window with length corresponding to the maximum length of the named entity in the dictionary is taken, after that all groups of words in which the rate of a word match with one of the elements of the dictionary is greater than some set threshold are marked with the corresponding label. Now these embeddings at the letter level and at the word level are concatenated and fed to the Bi-LSTM input. After Bi-LSTM, as in the architecture from DeepPavlov, there is the CRF layer. In the implementation, which is presented here, there are some differences comparing to the original article, the most important of which is the lack of dictionaries of external knowledge. For this reason, the model was not able to achieve the results indicated in the article (Fig. 7).

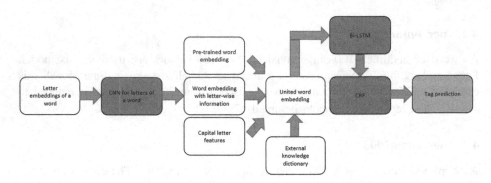

Fig. 7. "Chiu and Nichols 2016" scheme.

5 Experiments Description

5.1 Standard DeepPavlov Models Results

The following are the results of the training of named entity recognition models presented in the DeepPavlov library, as well as the implementation of the model from the article "Chiu and Nichols 2016" and their comparison with the officially announced results. All models were trained on Tesla K80 GPU provided by Google Coollaboratory.

The results for DeepPavlov and "Chiu and Nichols 2016" are presented in the following table (Table 4):

Table 4. Models learning results.

Model	Dataset	F1-mesure (declared)	F1-mesure (reproduced)	Approximate learning time Colab (min)
ner_ontonotes	OntoNotes	87.07	86.97; 86.65	180
ner_rus	Collection3	95.25	95.41; 95.30	45
ner_dstc2	DSTC2	97.17	97.04; 97.37	1
ner_conll2003	CoNLL_2003	89.94	89.98; 89.60	60
"Chiu and Nichols 2016"	CoNLL_2003	91.62	88.54; 89 (80 epochs)	130

It is easy to see that the obtained results are in good agreement with those obtained earlier, and the training time of the models was not too long, which is important for applications.

The implementation of the model from the article "Chiu and Nichols 2016" for the conll_2003 dataset was taken from the repository [11]. This implementation has some differences from the original article, which are presented in the following table (Table 5):

Table 5. Differences in "Chiu and Nichols 2016" realization.

	Original paper	Realization
Epochs	80	30
Dropout	0.68	0.5
LSTM state size	275	200
Optimizer	SGD	Nadam
Lexicons (external knowledge)	Yes	No
Final F1-mesure	91.62	87.09

On Google Collab GPU a model with such parameters was learning for approximately 60 min, and achieved results of 87 units F1-mesure. By increasing the number of epochs to 80 F1-measure increases to 88.54 or 89 points. It was argued that the model with this implementation can reach the F1-mesure exceeding 90 points at the 80th epoch, but this did not happen. If such a model really cannot achieve F1-measure more than 90 points, it might be explained by the fact that this implementation does not use dictionaries of named entities ("lexicons"), which, according to the authors of the article, have made a significant contribution to improving the quality of the model.

5.2 Experiments with New Dataset and Additional Features

For these experiments dataset Collection5 (Named_Entities_5 [4]) was used, which is similar to dataset Collection3, except that it has five marked types of named entities: three from the previous dataset and additional media, and geopolitical names (e.g., States). This dataset was transformed to the format of CoNLL2003, in accordance with DeepPavlov library API. To obtain syntactic and semantic features and part of speech tags, each sentence of the dataset was studied using a special analyzer [16] created by the Institute for System Analysis of the Russian Academy of Sciences. At this moment, there are only the simplest semantic role indicators that are used it this model and in future versions full complexity of semantic and syntactic structure of a sentence will be used. As a result, the resulting dataset has the structure shown in the table (Table 6):

Table 6. New dataset, based on Collection5, structure (with Russian texts).

Word	Part of speech tag	Semantic role	Named entity tag
Глава	N	UNK	O
авиакомпании	N	UNK	O
Виталий	N	UNK	B-PER
Савельев	N	Argument	I-PER
заявлял	V	Predicate	O
журналистам	N	Argument	O

For training the net_rus model described above with some modifications and changes was used. First of all, to concatenated vector representations of the word described in the section "net_rus", one-hot embeddings of labels of the part of speech and semantic role are added. To make use of that change with DeepPavlov API, the "conll2003_reader" class in the DeepPavlov library has been slightly modified. The table below shows the results of experiments on the Collection5 dataset without additional features, with POS tags, semantic roles, and both additional features (Table 7).

Table 7. Experiment results.

Name	F1-mesure	Learning time (min)	Architecture changes
ner_rus_col5	93,88	25	Learning rate = 10^{-3}
ner_rus_col5+POS	94,15	35	Learning rate = 10^{-3}
ner_rus_col5+SEM	93,63	21	Learning rate = 10^{-3}
ner_rus_col5+POS+SEM	94,02	25	Learning rate = 10^{-3}

As we see, the original NER network without any additional features has almost the same result as with additional features, which indicates that these features do not add any new information to the network: it simply figures out these features itself. This leads us to conclusion that simplest semantic and syntactic features that are used in this work are not enough to improve the network. It is not very surprising, because the full potential of all acquired by analyzer [16] information is still not used and further work in using more complex features should be done.

6 Conclusion

The paper describes the main methods of solving the NER problem in the DeepPavlov library, as well as new techniques for modifying neural networks in the application to this problem, using syntactic and semantic features. The library tools have been refined and applied to a new dataset with additional features. It is shown that for modern complex neural networks used for NER task it is ineffective to add POS tagging, because it has no significant effect on F1-measure. Inefficiency of adding simplest semantic features is also shown, however, the effectiveness of adding complex semantic and syntactic features in their full potential is still unclear, and should be validated in future studies.

References

1. CoNLL-2003 shared task page. https://www.clips.uantwerpen.be/conll2003/ner/
2. OntoNotes Release 5.0 page. https://catalog.ldc.upenn.edu/LDC2013T19
3. Dialog State Tracking Challenge 2 & 3 page. http://camdial.org/~mh521/dstc/
4. Named_Entities_5 and 3 collection page. http://labinform.ru/pub/named_entities/descr_ne. htm
5. Persons-1000 collection page. http://ai-center.botik.ru/Airec/index.php/ru/collections/28-persons-1000
6. Anh, L.T., Arkhipov, M.Y., Burtsev, M.S.: Application of a Hybrid Bi-LSTM-CRF model to the task of Russian Named Entity Recognition. ArXiv preprint, arXiv:1709.09686 (2017)
7. Lample, G., Ballesteros, M., Subramanian, S., Kawakami, K., Dyer, C.: Neural Architectures for Named Entity Recognition. ArXiv preprint arXiv:1603.01360 (2016)
8. Ioffe, S., Szegedy, C.: Batch Normalization: Accelerating Deep Network Training by Reducing Internal Covariate Shift. ArXiv preprint, arXiv:1502.03167 (2015)
9. Deeppavlov library documentation. http://docs.deeppavlov.ai/en/latest/components/ner. html#id20
10. Chiu, J.P.C., Nichols, E.: Named Entity Recognition with Bidirectional LSTM-CNNs. ArXiv preprint arXiv:1511.08308 (2016)
11. Bi-LSTM-CNN python implementation on Github. https://github.com/mxhofer/Named-Entity-Recognition-BidirectionalLSTM-CNN-CoNLL
12. Corpus of news articles of Lenta.RU. https://github.com/yutkin/Lenta.Ru-News-Dataset
13. Global Vectors for Word Representation page. https://nlp.stanford.edu/projects/glove/
14. Tesnière L. Elements de syntaxe structurale. Editions Klincksieck (1959)
15. Chomsky, N.: Syntactic Structures, p. 117. Mouton, The Hague (1957)
16. Syntactic-semantic analyzer by Institute for Systems Analysis page. http://nlp.isa.ru/index. php/component/portal/?view=projsintsemanalysis

Toward Faster Reinforcement Learning for Robotics: Using Gaussian Processes

Ali Younes[1] and Aleksandr I. Panov[2,3]([⊠]) [iD]

[1] Bauman Moscow State Technical University, Moscow, Russia
ay20-5-1994@hotmail.com
[2] Artificial Intelligence Research Institute,
Federal Research Center "Computer Science and Control"
of the Russian Academy of Sciences, Moscow, Russia
pan@isa.ru
[3] Moscow Institute of Physics and Technology, Moscow, Russia

Abstract. Standard robotic control works perfectly in case of ordinary conditions, but in the case of a change in the conditions (e.g. damaging of one of the motors), the robot won't achieve its task anymore. We need an algorithm that provide the robot with the ability of adaption to unforeseen situations. Reinforcement learning provide a framework corresponds with that requirements, but it needs big data sets to learn robotic tasks, which is impractical. We discuss using Gaussian processes to improve the efficiency of the Reinforcement learning, where a Gaussian Process will learn a state transition model using data from the robot (interaction) phase, and after that use the learned GP model to simulate trajectories and optimize the robot's controller in a (simulation) phase. PILCO algorithm considered as the most data efficient RL algorithm. It gives promising results in Cart-pole task, where a working controller was learned after seconds of (interaction) on the real robot, but the whole training time, considering the training in the (simulation) was longer. In this work, we will try to leverage the abilities of the computational graphs to produce a ROS friendly python implementation of PILCO, and discuss a case study of a real world robotic task.

Keywords: Robot learning · Reinforcement learning · Gaussian process · Data efficient

1 Introduction

The standard control methods in robotics are based on the dynamical model of the robot, and also on the model of the dynamics of the environment to build the needed closed loop control scheme [1–6]; in the real world to realize such methods for manipulators, we have to follow the following steps: (1) taking an observation of the environment using cameras or sensors (2) estimating the state

This work was supported by the Russian Science Foundation, project no. 18-71-00143.

G. S. Osipov et al. (Eds.): Artificial Intelligence, LNAI 11866, pp. 160–174, 2019.
https://doi.org/10.1007/978-3-030-33274-7_11

of the robot and the task (e.g. position of the end-effector and the goal position) (3) planning the trajectory of motion of the end-effector to achieve the task (4) using low-level controllers (or force controller for harder tasks) to ensure following the planned path by minimizing the errors (5) sending the resulting commands to the joints of the robot. The errors which are occurred in each step, accumulated to produce a cumulative error making the control process hard to realize with desired accuracy.

The essence of the robot learning is to find a way to develop robotic behavior to a human's level behavior. Hence the Reinforcement Learning (RL) [6,7] seems to be the most viable way for robot learning, where the learning process depends on an agent taking actions, noticing the changes in the environment's state and the resulted reward of that action. The goal of RL is to learn the best possible policy to achieve a task by a trial and error hypothesis.

The state of the art deep reinforcement learning algorithms, which has tried to handle robotic tasks can be classified to two major classes: (1) model-free algorithms: (TRPO [9], PPO [10], DDPG [11]) which can learn to achieve the task after sampling training sets from interacting with environment, so we can consider the robot's model as a black-box (2) model-based algorithms ([12–14]): depends on a learned transition model of the environment. The model-free algorithms need days of training to learn basic robotic tasks. On the other hand, ordinary model-based algorithms can learn much faster (less than an hour), but mostly can't adapt to unforeseen situation (the learned model is no longer valid) such in case a damaged motor [15–17].

Model-based algorithms learns a state transition model, that represent how would the next state will be in case of taking an action, without knowing the dynamic model of the robot. When using deterministic models, the results of the RL depend on the accuracy of the model, and mostly it failed with unforeseen states.

In this paper we are interested in the idea of using probabilistic models in RL algorithms [18–21], to handle the uncertainty of model and reduce its training time. The approach uses a Gaussian process (1) its input will be a state x_t (the robot joints' angles and positions) and the control u, (2) the output will be the resulted state x_{t+1} (or the difference $x_{t+1} - x_t$). The reason to use the Gaussian process is its ability to learn from small data sets. After training the model we will use it to simulate the task (generate trajectories), and optimize the controller over that trajectories. We have chosen PILCO algorithm [22], which considered the most data efficient RL algorithm, we are interested in using of computational graphs to implement PILCO, and see how our work could scale to robotic tasks.

The following sections are structured as follows. First we will outline some preliminaries (Sect. 2), which will be a brief introduction to RL, GP, PILCO and computational graphs. Then we describe our work (Sect. 3) and experiments on a robotic task (Sect. 4). Then we discuss out the results (Sect. 5). Finally, we add a discussion (Sect. 6) and future work (Sect. 6).

2   Preliminaries

2.1   Reinforcement Learning

Reinforcement learning is a part of the machine learning, which study how should the agent have to interact in its working space, in order to minimize (maximize) a long-term cost (reward) (see Fig. 1).

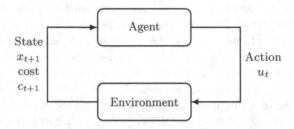

Fig. 1. Reinforcement learning paradigm

We represent the RL problem as a Markov Decision Process (MDP) at Fig. 2.

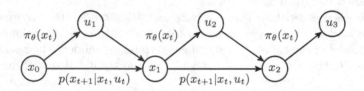

Fig. 2. Markov decision process for RL problem

Where x_t is the state, u_t - control (action), c - cost (reward), the transition function: $x_{t+1} = f(x, u_t) + \omega$, that we aim to learn in model based RL. The policy function, which gives the best action for each state after the training process (could be called as the controller): $u_t = \pi(x_t, \theta)$. The goal is to minimize the expected long-term cost:

$$J(\theta) = \sum_{t=1}^{T} \mathbb{E}[c(x_t)|\theta].$$

2.2   Gaussian Processes

In probability theory and statistics, a Gaussian process is a stochastic process (a collection of random variables indexed by time or space), such that every finite collection of those random variables has a multivariate normal distribution, i.e. every finite linear combination of them is normally distributed.

In other words, a Gaussian process is a probability distribution over possible functions. Gaussian process defined by mean function $m(.)$ and a covariance function (kernel) $k(.,.)$.

We will use an independent Gaussian process for each dimension (variable) of the output. It will describe how would be the next state beginning from the current state and implementing control signal u, $f : x \rightarrow f(x_t, u) = x(t+1)$. The Gaussian process will learn using the data collected from the real robot, the data set consists of transitions x_t, u_t, x_{t+1}, c_t. And the learning process is a regression problem, so if we start from a prior

$$P(f|x) \sim \mathcal{N}(\mu, \Sigma).$$

We get a posterior

$$P(y_*|D, x) \sim \mathcal{N}(\mu_{(y_*|D)}, \Sigma_{(y_*|D)})$$

after a training epoch (the process is called Bayesian inference) (see Fig. 3).

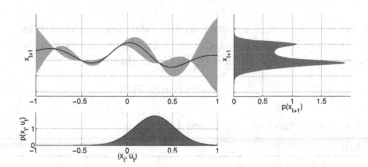

Fig. 3. GP prediction at uncertain input. The input distribution $p(x_t, u_t)$ (the blue curve and term in the equation) propagates though the GP model (the gray model), we obtain the expected distribution of the next state $p(x_{t+1})$ (Color figure online)

And we will use the learned model to make a long term prediction (build trajectories in the simulation steps), so if we make an action u in the state x, we map it through the Gaussian process to get the output as the probability of the next state. Using the formula:

$$p(x_{t+1}|\theta) = \iiint \underbrace{p(x_{t+1}|x_t, u_t)}_{\text{GP prediction}} \underbrace{p(x_t, u_t|\theta)}_{\mathcal{N}(\mu, \Sigma)} \, df \, dx_t \, du_t$$

The output distribution is irregular, so we use the moment matching algorithm to approximate it.

2.3   PILCO Algorithm

PILCO (Probabilistic Inference for Learning COntrol) algorithm [22] is a model-based policy search reinforcement learning algorithm, which achieved unprecedented data-efficiency of several control benchmarks. PILCO is a model based algorithm, which means it consists of two alternating steps:

1. Interaction step in which we run the real robot (using a random policy in the first episode, and the optimized policy afterward), collect the roll-out's data, and train the Gaussian process model on the collected data.
2. Simulation step in which we have to:
   (a) Use the Gaussian process to build long-term predictions over a trajectory from $p(X_0)$ to $p(X_T)$.
   (b) After that compute the long term cost function:

$$J(\theta) = \sum_{t=1}^{T} \mathbb{E}[c(x_t)|\theta]$$

$$J(\theta) = \sum_{t=1}^{T} \int c(x_t) N(x_t|\mu_t, \Sigma_t) dx_t$$

   (c) At the end use the computed cost to optimize the controller's parameters to minimize the cost, by using a line search algorithm based on the gradient of the cost function (L-BFGS-B algorithm):

$$\theta \leftarrow \arg\min_{\theta} J(\theta)$$

PILCO is summarized by Algorithm 1.

Algorithm 1. PILCO

---
1 Define a model and a policy
2 Collect a random roll-out, record data
3 **repeat**
4 | learn the model
5 | Collect trajectories using the model
   | from $p(x_0)$ to $p(x_T)$
6 | evaluate the policy
   | $J(\theta) = \sum_{t=1}^{T} \mathbb{E}[c(x_t)|\theta]$
7 | optimize policy
   | $\theta \leftarrow \arg\min_{\theta} J(\theta)$
8 | run the policy and collect data
   until   *task solved;*

Model bias is a problem that faced model-based algorithms, when selecting only a single dynamic model and assuming that model is the correct model, and hence the prediction errors in the model compound to produce a inaccurate long term predictions. PILCO uses Gaussian processes as a probabilistic models to avoid model bias, by considering all plausible dynamics models in prediction of the next states, i.e. give the model sufficient uncertainty. Which leads to a better results in terms of data efficiency.

2.4   Computational Graphs for Gaussian Process Regression

Computational graphs are directed graphs, in which the nodes are either variables or operations, and the edges define the inputs to each node (see Fig. 4).

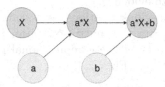

Fig. 4. Simple computation graph; the blue node is the input X, the yellow nodes are constants, and the green nodes are the operations (Color figure online)

There are two key strength of using computational graphs:

- It can be used to form a complex operations from simple operation.
- They enable automatic differentiation, which is needed in optimization.

We propose using computational graphs for Gaussian process regression (Algorithm 1, line 4), where the process of learning the model means fitting a probability model to the collected data, in other words; we start from a (1) prior distribution with zero mean function and an initial covariance function, (2) observe the collected data and compute the posterior distribution, and after that (3) learning the hyper-parameters (length-scales, signal variances and noise variances which define the covariance function) of the GP via evidence maximization.

The bottle-neck in this process, is in (1) the computation of the posterior over the data points, and (2) the differentiation which is needed in the process of evidence maximization.

The formulas to find the mean and the variance of the posterior:

$$m_t(x) = K(x, X_t)[K(X_t, X_t) + \sigma_\epsilon^2 I)]^{-1} y_t$$

$$k_t(x, x) = k(x, x) - K(x, X_t)[K(X_t, X_t) + \sigma_\epsilon^2 I)]^{-1} K(X_t, x)$$

where X_t is the observed inputs, x all possible input points, y_t observed outputs and σ_ϵ noise variance.

We can compute then evidence (log marginal likelihood):

$$\log p(y|X, \phi) = -\frac{1}{2} y^T K_y^{-1} y - \frac{1}{2} \log |K_y| - \frac{n}{2} \log 2\pi$$

where $K_y = K(X, X) + \sigma_\epsilon^2 I$ is the covariance matrix of the noisy outputs y.

The hyper parameters of the GP:

$$\phi = (l, \sigma_f^2, \sigma_\epsilon^2)$$

length-scales l, signal variance σ_f^w, noise variance σ_ϵ^2.

The evidence maximization goal:

$$\hat{\phi} = \arg\max_{\phi} log(p(y|X, \phi))$$

The evidence maximization process, make uses of the partial derivatives of the log marginal likelihood with respect to the hyperparameters to find the combination that maximize evidence.

By representing the previous relations as a computational graph, we can (1) leverage the GPU by run the matrix operations on it, (2) use the automatic differentiation property of the computational graph instead of compute the derivatives analytically (see Fig. 5).

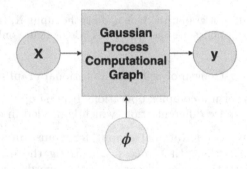

Fig. 5. High level representation of the computational graph used for Gaussian process regression

3   Problem Formulation

We consider using Gaussian process to achieve better data efficiency for reinforcement learning in robotic tasks. We will use PILCO as a base algorithm for our work (as it is the most data efficient RL algorithm). In this work, we start from two observations about PILCO:

– The Robot Operating System (ROS) [25] is an open source, flexible framework for writing robot software. It is a collection of tools, libraries, and conventions that aim to simplify the task of creating complex and robust robot behavior across a wide variety of robotic platforms. Most of the robotics laboratories are using ROS in research experiments and projects, and it has been used widely in the industry, making it as the most powerful tool in the robotics community. ROS support C++ and Python only, but the official code release of PILCO [26] was written in Matlab, which makes it not compatible with ROS, So we decided to reproduce PILCO in Python to make it compatible with ROS.

– The recent revolution of the deep learning relies on exploiting the computing power of the GPU, the father of the RL Richard Sutton has mentioned it in his "bitter lesson" [27]. PILCO reduces the amount of interaction time on the real robot, but it takes a relatively long time after that for inference and controller optimization. Reducing this time may give the algorithm the ability to learn in real time (or with a little latency), for robotics, it means the ability to adapt to unforeseen cases, which is a step toward the intelligent robot. We used GPflow library [23], which is a Gaussian process library that uses TensorFlow for its core computations and Python for its front. GPflow follows the computation graphs of the TensorFlow, which make the best use of the GPU power. That facts reduce the training time (especially when working with large scales).

We evaluated our implementation on a 7-DoF robotic arm task, in the OpenAI gym [24] to robotic environment. In the following, we will discuss the Experimental setup of this experiment, with an explanation that is needed to understand the points of interest, and sample of results with discussion.

4 Experimental Setup

We applied our implementation on a 7-DoF robotic arm (Fig. 6). We assume that we don't know any thing about the model of the robotic arm or the environment, we can just observe the coordinates of the end effector and joints' angles, and receive a reward (cost) after each movement. We can control the robotic arm by sending 7 control signals to each of its joints. For the algorithm, it is not needed to know what the state or the control signal represents, but to make our experiment more applicable to real world robots, we will constrain the control signal, and we will also constrain the length of the interaction phase.

Firstly we will define the following:

– **State:** the coordinates of the end effector and the joints' angles

$$X_e = [x_e, y_e, z_e, j_0, ..., j_7] \in \mathbb{R}^{10}$$

– **Target:** the coordinates of the target

$$X* = [x*, y*, z*] \in \mathbb{R}^3$$

– **Actions:** the control signal for each joint

$$U_j = [u_0, u_1, ..., u_7] \in \mathbb{R}^7$$

– **The cost function:**

$$c(x) = 1 - exp(-\frac{1}{2\sigma_c^2}d(X_e, X*)^2) \in [0, 1]$$

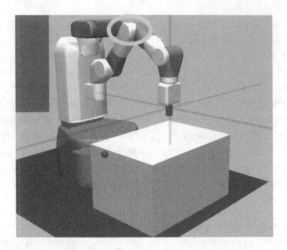

Fig. 6. A 7-Dof robotic arm's task in simulation, the control signal u is just a relative rotation angle for each joint, the state is the position of the end effector and joints' angles, the goal is to reach the red point. The joint which is surrounded by an ellipse, is the broken (unresponsive) joint in the second part in results (Color figure online)

- **The transition model** the model consists of an independent stochastic GP regression model for each variable of the output. In our test case, we have 10 GPs, each one takes the state and the control command as an input, and the output is resulted difference of one of the state variables (Fig. 7a).
- **Controller** we have used RBF (Radial Basis Function) as a controller. We can use the RBF controller as a deterministic GP regression model, by considering it like that, we exploit the multi output GP class that we have already used for the transition model (Fig. 7b).

5   Experimental Results

5.1   Classic Reaching Task

As we are interested in an implementation that could be applicable in the real world robotics applications, we have tested our work on the task of reaching a goal in the workspace of the robotic arm, that task is a sub task of any industrial task for manipulators, in the following we will give the results of the experiment with an analysis and comments.

For the following hyperparameters:

- Number of the basis function of the controller = 50.
- Number of the iterations in each episode on the real robot (horizon) = 50.
- The control function is constrained to 0.1.

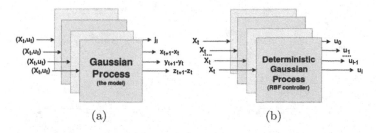

Fig. 7. (a) The transition model: multi-output Gaussian process regression model, the input is a for each sub GP is the state X_t and the control U_t, the output is the resulted difference of an output variable. (b) The controller: multi-output Gaussian process regression model, the input a for each sub GP is the state X_t, the output is a control variable u_i.

The average time results was:

- The time of interaction (running the robot) = 21.22 s.
- The time of training the transition model = 37.53 s.
- The time of optimizing the controller = 1380.95 s.
- The program running time = 1598 s

The corresponding plots for this case are presented on Fig. 8.

The algorithm can learn the inverse kinematics of the robot and achieved the task in a considerable time, and improved the trajectory also. Here we have to mention that, the performance of the algorithm was impressing because of the formulation of the experimental setup in a way exploiting the best of the PILCO algorithm, and matching the needs of such algorithm.

One of the interesting experimental results, is to monitor the confidence of our learned model, and how it match the real transition model. In the following we will list samples form one step prediction for the three coordinates of the end effector (Fig. 9).

5.2   Damaged Robot

To asses our implementation on one of the most interesting features of reinforcement learning algorithm, we have use a test case that could be happen for any robot. The damage of any joint's motor could lead the ordinary control algorithms to a complete fail in achieving the task. In our test case, we are considering the damage of a joint's motor (the joint which is surrounded by a red ellipse in Fig. 4), so the joint will be unresponsive.

We have used the same implementation with similar hyperparameters from the last experiment, the robot could adapt to the damage, and learned to achieve the task. The plots for that case in the right (Figs. 10 and 11). The speed of the learning process hasn't been affected by the damaging of the motor, because the algorithm doesn't depend on the dynamical model of the robot.

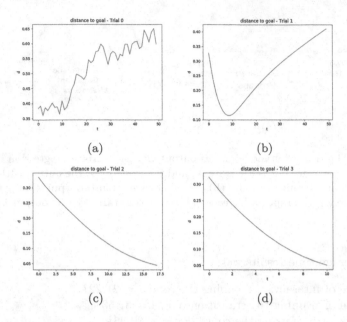

Fig. 8. The distance between the end effector and the target position, (a) is the random roll-out, (b) is the first roll-out after optimizing the controller in the simulation, we can see the robot approaches the target point here, but after that go away from it, but in (c) it learns to reach the goal after just 20 time steps, and improve that time by reach it in 10 time steps only in (d)

5.3   Comparison with the Matlab Implementation

We were interested in comparing how much using the computational graph could help us speed up the learning process for PILCO algorithm. We have tested our implementation in the Cartpole environment, with a similar hyperparameters to ones in the Matlab implementation, and same conditions.

The average time for running both implementations for 8 epochs:

- PILCO in python with computational graphs = 671 s.
- PILCO original implementation = 1265 s.

The using of the computational graphs, leverage the GPU power, and give as a speed up by a factor

$$S = \frac{T_{Matalb}}{T_{python}} = \frac{1265}{671} = 1.885.$$

Which is considered as a satisfying result.

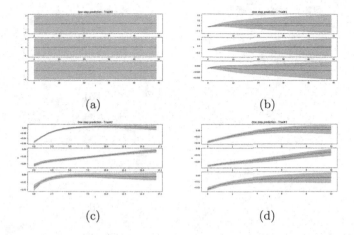

(a)   (b)

(c)   (d)

Fig. 9. The one step prediction of the transition model: the plot shows the difference between the states and the confidence level for each prediction; in (a) we can see the model is not confident in the first iteration. After the first learning epoch (b) it reduce the margin of uncertainty, but it failed to follow the real transition (orange line in the plot), the model has reduce the uncertainty about transition over the next iterations (c) and (d), reaching a small margin (d is better than c-check the scale of y-axis) (Color figure online)

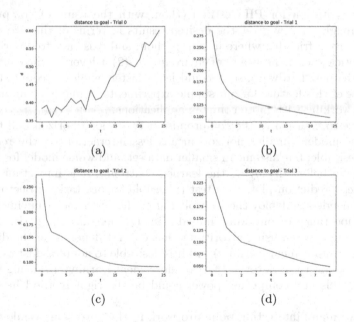

(a)   (b)

(c)   (d)

Fig. 10. The distance between the end effector and the target position - the case of an unresponsive joint, similar results to the previous case, the robot approaches the target in the second iteration (b) and third (c), reaches it in the in the fourth (d) after just 8 time steps.

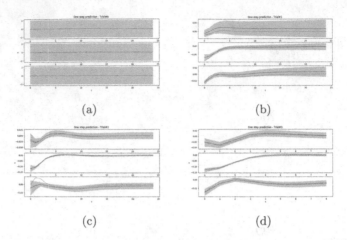

(a)   (b)

(c)   (d)

Fig. 11. The one step prediction of the transition model- the case of an unresponsive joint; confidence over the x axis was bigger than other two coordinates in (b), but the robot could learn to solve the task and reduce the margin of the uncertainty in (c) and (d).

6   Discussion and Future Work

Our implementation for PILCO in Python, with the using of computational graphs through GPflow gives the desired results in terms of the two goal proprieties (1) ROS friendly, where it is in python, and it is easy to describe a real world robotic experiment as a gym environment. (2) it leverage the computation power of the new hardware, so it could learn faster; while we couldn't feel the importance of this feature for our simple experiments, it may play an important role when working with more complex applications.

We have to mention to the compromise between long horizon and the accuracy of the model. Smaller horizon means less interaction on the real robot, which is desirable; but also mean smaller data set, and worse model for the state transition. So before deploying the learned controller, it is important to check the one step prediction plots over test (plausible for our task) trajectories. It is not recommended to deploy the controller after the first time achieving the task.

The importance of our work impedes in: (1) demonstrating the ability of adapt for robots when using algorithms that doesn't depends on the dynamical model (e.g reinforcement learning), (2) it is desirable to adapt as fast as possible, so it is important to work toward fast reinforcement learning, (3) using the probabilistic models and computing power could be the right method in achieving that goals.

We have many interesting points to work in this direction. While GP gives a good results, but it has some down points, like it can't handle discontinuities in the state, so using our implementation we can easily try to use Deep GPs instead of shallow GPs and compare the results. The computation complexity of the GP equals $O(n^3)$ which cause problem when working on a scale, in our work we used computational graphs to speed up the inference process of GPs, but we can work also on using GPU in other parts of the algorithm. In robotics, sometimes we are working with sparse rewards, so we can study how to solve such problems efficiently, and how we could make use of GPs.

References

1. McFarlane, D.C., Glover, K.: Robust Controller Design Procedure Using Normalized Coprime Factor Plant Descriptions. Lecture Notes in Control and Information Sciences, vol. 138. Springer, Heidelberg (1990). https://doi.org/10.1007/BFb0043199
2. Rocco, P.: Stability of PID control for industrial robot arms. IEEE Trans. Robot. Autom. **12**(4), 606–614 (1996)
3. Åström, K.J., Wittenmark, B.: Adaptive Control. Courier Corporation, Mineola (2013)
4. Wen, J.T., Murphy, S.H.: PID control for robot manipulators. Rensselaer Polytechnic Institute (1990)
5. Teixeira, R.A., Braga, A.D.P., De Menezes, B.R.: Control of a robotic manipulator using artificial neural networks with on-line adaptation. Neural Process. Lett. **12**(1), 19–31 (2000)
6. Nesnas, I.A., et al.: CLARAty: challenges and steps toward reusable robotic software. Int. J. Adv. Robot. Syst. **3**(1), 5 (2006)
7. Sutton, R.S., Barto, A.G.: Introduction to Reinforcement Learning, vol. 135. MIT Press, Cambridge (1998)
8. Kaelbling, L.P., Littman, M.L., Moore, A.W.: Reinforcement learning: a survey. J. Artif. Intell. Res. **4**, 237–285 (1996)
9. Schulman, J., Levine, S., Abbeel, P., Jordan, M., Moritz, P.: Trust region policy optimization. In: International Conference on Machine Learning, pp. 1889–1897, June 2015
10. Schulman, J., Wolski, F., Dhariwal, P., Radford, A., Klimov, O.: Proximal policy optimization algorithms. arXiv preprint arXiv:1707.06347 (2017)
11. Lillicrap, T.P., et al.: Continuous control with deep reinforcement learning. arXiv preprint arXiv:1509.02971 (2015)
12. Mnih, V., et al.: Human-level control through deep reinforcement learning. Nature **518**(7540), 529 (2015)
13. LeCun, Y., Bengio, Y., Hinton, G.: Deep learning. Nature **521**(7553), 436 (2015)
14. Deisenroth, M.P., Neumann, G., Peters, J.: A survey on policy search for robotics. Found. Trends® Robot. **2**(1–2), 1–142 (2013)
15. Carlson, J., Murphy, R.R.: How UGVs physically fail in the field. IEEE Trans. Robot. **21**(3), 423–437 (2005)
16. Cully, A., Clune, J., Tarapore, D., Mouret, J.B.: Robots that can adapt like animals. Nature **521**(7553), 503 (2015)
17. Nagatani, K., et al.: Emergency response to the nuclear accident at the Fukushima Daiichi Nuclear Power Plants using mobile rescue robots. J. Field Robot. **30**(1), 44–63 (2013)
18. Rasmussen, C.E., Williams, C.K.I.: Gaussian Processes for Machine Learning. The MIT Press, Cambridge (2006)

19. Ko, J., Klein, D.J., Fox, D., Haehnel, D.: Gaussian processes and reinforcement learning for identification and control of an autonomous blimp. In: Proceedings 2007 IEEE International Conference on Robotics and Automation, pp. 742–747. IEEE, April 2007
20. Wilson, A., Fern, A., Tadepalli, P.: Incorporating domain models into Bayesian optimization for RL. In: Balcázar, J.L., Bonchi, F., Gionis, A., Sebag, M. (eds.) ECML PKDD 2010. LNCS (LNAI), vol. 6323, pp. 467–482. Springer, Heidelberg (2010). https://doi.org/10.1007/978-3-642-15939-8_30
21. Engel, Y., Mannor, S., Meir, R.: Bayes meets Bellman: The Gaussian process approach to temporal difference learning. In: Proceedings of the 20th International Conference on Machine Learning, ICML 2003, pp. 154–161 (2003)
22. Deisenroth, M.P., Fox, D., Rasmussen, C.E.: Gaussian processes for data-efficient learning in robotics and control. IEEE Trans. Pattern Anal. Mach. Intell. **37**(2), 408–423 (2015)
23. Matthews, D.G., et al.: GPflow: a Gaussian process library using TensorFlow. J. Mach. Learn. Res. **18**(1), 1299–1304 (2017)
24. Brockman, G., et al.: Openai gym. arXiv preprint arXiv:1606.01540 (2016)
25. http://www.ros.org
26. http://mlg.eng.cam.ac.uk/pilco/
27. http://www.incompleteideas.net/IncIdeas/BitterLesson.html

Author Index

Printed in the United States
By Bookmasters